POTOMAC TRAILS

POTOMAC TRAILS

D.C., Virginia, Maryland, and West Virginia

Allan Sutton

Fulcrum Publishing
Golden, Colorado

Library of Congress Cataloging-in-Publication Data

Sutton, Allan
    Potomac trails : D.C., Virginia, Maryland, and West Virginia /
Allan Sutton.
        p. cm.
    Includes bibliographical references and index.
    ISBN 1-55591-229-X (pbk.)
        1. Hiking—Potomac River Valley—Guidebooks. 2. Trails—Potomac
River Valley—Guidebooks. 3. Potomac River Valley—Guidebooks.
    I. Title.   96-47640
GV199.42.P68S88 1997   CIP

Printed in the United States of America
0 9 8 7 6 5 4 3 2 1

Fulcrum Publishing
350 Indiana Street, Suite 350
Golden, Colorado 80401-5093
(800) 992-2908 • (303) 277-1623

CONTENTS

PREFACE

Within a few hours' driving time of the nation's capital lies some of the last wilderness remaining in the middle-Atlantic states. Thanks to the vision of conservation-minded men and women, a large section of the Appalachians has been preserved and nursed back to health after having been raped and abandoned early in this century.

The battle isn't won, of course; these areas face increasing pressures from pro-development forces, special interests, and a burgeoning population. But as more people discover the rugged beauty of the Potomac region, I believe that we'll see an even stronger resolve to preserve what remains.

Potomac Trails is an introduction to many of the best natural areas in the Potomac River drainage. The nearest to Washington, D.C., along the historic Chesapeake & Ohio Canal, is an easy walk from downtown; the farthest, along the Allegheny Front in West Virginia, is a scenic four-hour drive away.

Although I began this book as a basic hiker's guide, I soon realized that simple trail descriptions don't do justice to the area's rich history, both human and natural. I hope that the background information included with each section will enrich your travels in the Potomac region.

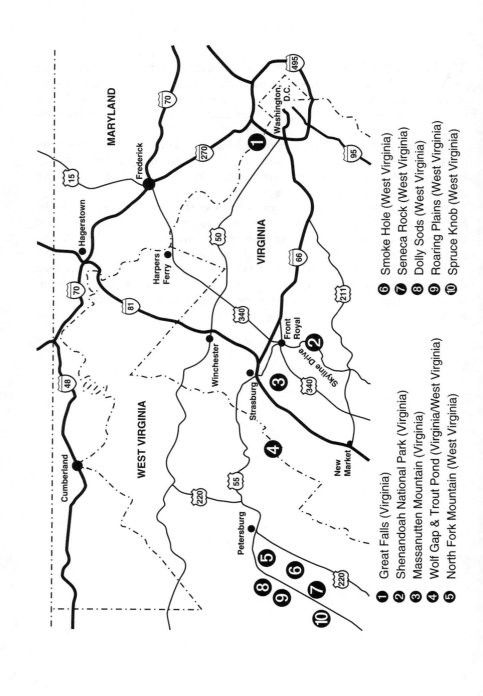

① Great Falls (Virginia)
② Shenandoah National Park (Virginia)
③ Massanutten Mountain (Virginia)
④ Wolf Gap & Trout Pond (Virginia/West Virginia)
⑤ North Fork Mountain (West Virginia)
⑥ Smoke Hole (West Virginia)
⑦ Seneca Rock (West Virginia)
⑧ Dolly Sods (West Virginia)
⑨ Roaring Plains (West Virginia)
⑩ Spruce Knob (West Virginia)

INTRODUCTION

*P*otomac Trails is a hikers' guide to outstanding natural areas in the upper Potomac and Shenandoah watersheds. All of the areas in this book are within a 150-mile radius of Washington, D.C. Most are on federal lands, and all were selected based on above-average scenic, natural, or historic value.

The Trail Guides

The trail guides were compiled from firsthand observation and were double-checked against current U.S. Geological Survey, Forest Service, and Park Service topographic maps. To the best of my knowledge, all trail data is correct at the time of writing, but changes can occur from time to time. Natural disasters, government policy shifts, and private land closures have brought changes in many trails recently. For each trail, the guide lists:

- Length—All trail lengths are approximate, based on the latest USGS maps or other reliable sources. Unless noted otherwise, distances cited are for a one-way hike, from one trailhead to the other. For out-and-back hikes, double the distances shown. Figures cited for circuit hikes, which usually combine several trails into a loop, are for the entire hike.

- Elevation change—This figure shows the approximate difference between the trail's highest and lowest points. You may actually do considerably more climbing if a trail has many ups and downs throughout its course. Expect to make a fairly strenuous effort on any trail that climbs more than 800 feet.

- Level of difficulty—Trails are rated by the level of difficulty they present to the average adult in moderately good physical condition. Few of the trails presented in this guide will pose any great challenge to an experienced, well-conditioned hiker; however, many may prove impossible for the chronically sedentary. Trails are classified as:

  Easy—Level or gently sloping. Well-graded, marked, and maintained, presenting no significant obstacles. All are suitable for small children, and a few are wheelchair-accessible.

  Moderate—Applies to most of the trails in this guide. Trails may vary from smooth to fairly rough and may present such obstacles as shallow stream crossings or easy rock scrambles. Trails that present minor obstacles but require sustained climbing are designated "moderate (strenuous)." Some trails may be too challenging for small children.

Moderately difficult—As above, but these trails are generally more hazardous and require more sustained effort. Trails may be rough, and stream crossings may be difficult or even impossible in high water. Some trails are unmarked and hard to follow. A compass and USGS quad map are recommended. These trails generally pose an above-average risk for injury and are not suitable for young children or poorly conditioned adults. They are recommended for experienced and properly equipped hikers only.

Difficult—Few of the trails in this region are truly difficult. On those that are, expect hazardous conditions, major obstacles, and rough terrain throughout. These trails are for experienced and properly equipped hikers only.

USGS Quad Maps

Throughout this guide I refer to USGS quad maps, the 7.5-minute topographic maps produced by the U.S. Geological Survey (USGS). Although minutely detailed, many are outdated and don't always shows trails accurately. Regardless, they are essential if you plan to explore off the main trails. The maps included in this guidebook are intended only for general orientation and necessarily eliminate many topographic details.

Trail Gear

What you take on the trail is largely a matter of personal preference, but there are several points to keep in mind when hiking the Potomac region, based on my experience here.

Choose a sturdy, waterproof leather boot with a good non-slip sole. Lightweight fabric boots may be fashionable, but they simply aren't rugged enough to stand up to rocky trails for any length of time. Athletic shoes are too flimsy for use on most trails and provide little protection.

Avoid down-filled clothing or sleeping bags. Rain, fog, and high humidity are common in the eastern mountains, and down loses its insulating ability once it is wet. The new lightweight synthetic fills insulate when wet, dry quickly, and are better suited to the changeable Appalachian climate.

Carry a canteen and water purification tablets. Springs and streams are abundant, but few are protected.

Finally, if you plan to hike any distance from the road, carry a compass and detailed topographic maps, and know how to use them. The trail guides list the appropriate USGS topographic maps for each hike.

The Weather

Weather at lower altitudes (up to about 2,500 feet) generally reflects that of the neighboring valleys and lowlands. But above 2,500 feet, conditions can change very quickly. The Blue Ridge and Allegheny Front areas are especially susceptible to sudden violent storms at any time of the year.

Winters in the higher elevations tend to be cold and moist, with frequent flurries and occasional major snowfalls. Sleet and freezing rain can pose a particular threat, snapping large limbs and glazing roads and trails with ice. Big Meadows, in Shenandoah National Park, receives 13 inches of snow and 3 inches of rain in a typical January. Above 3,500 feet, sudden and unexpected snowfall, often accompanied by high winds and deep drifting, is common from late November through early April.

Winter lingers on the highest peaks long after the first signs of spring have appeared in the valleys. Springtime green glides up the slopes slowly, gaining about 100 feet of altitude daily. Using that handy figure, you can quickly calculate spring's arrival on a given peak. For example, if oaks first bud in Shenandoah Valley on April 1, it will be another 34 days—or early May—before they bud on Hawksbill summit, 3,400 feet above the valley.

Summer brings hot, humid days and cool, humid nights at the higher elevations. The high humidity can be especially troubling to hikers, since it prevents evaporation of perspiration and can lead to heat stroke. Summertime views are often obscured by natural haze, now supplemented by human-produced smog. Afternoon thunderstorms present a real hazard to hikers on high, exposed ridges and may result in local flash flooding in the steeper canyons. Despite these drawbacks, tourists flock to the mountains throughout the summer months.

Shenandoah N.P., VA — Icicles at Rose River

But autumn is undoubtedly the best time to see the Potomac region. Most of the crowds and insects are gone, humidity and temperatures are down, and the air is often crystalline. Early-morning fog settling in the valleys leaves the high peaks appearing to float above an ocean of clouds. Days are generally mild from mid-September through early November, although nighttime temperatures often fall below freezing and you may see a snow flurry or two. The fall colors, which reach their peak in the second or third week of October, bring another brief tourist crunch, but these folks tend not to stray very far from their cars and campers.

Camping

This guide lists non-commercial car campgrounds and suggests suitable backcountry (hike-in) sites. Camping regulations vary widely, depending on the area. In heavily regulated Shenandoah National Park, car-camping is restricted to several sprawling developments, and permits are required for backcountry camping.

In contrast, you are welcome to set up camp virtually anywhere, without a permit, in vast stretches of the George Washington and Monongahela National Forests. Expend a little time and effort, and you should have no trouble finding a spot that suits you. In Virginia, you will need to carry a campstove in the spring. Virginia law allows open fires only between 4 P.M. and midnight from March 1 to May 15.

These are the regulations for camping in the George Washington and Monongahela National Forests:

1. Camping is permitted in developed recreation areas and other reasonable places where traffic is not impeded. It is prohibited in designated watershed areas. Observe posted regulations.

2. Make small campfires in designated fireplaces or other safe locations.

3. Clear the ground of flammable material within 4 feet of the fire.

4. Use charcoal or campstoves when possible. Fire permits are not required. The Virginia brush-burning law allows open-air fires from March 1 to May 15 only between 4 P.M. and midnight.

5. Campfires must be dead before campers leave.

6. Report forest fires to the appropriate ranger district.

7. Protect natural scenery from defacement. To preserve ground cover and prevent erosion, please refrain from cutting across trail switchbacks.

8. Fishing and hunting are permitted. State regulations apply. State licenses and a National Forest stamp are required.

9. Carry out all unburnable trash.

10. Cover all body waste with 6 inches of soil.

Roads

Road conditions also vary widely. Many of the sites covered here can be reached via interstate, federal, or paved state roads. But a few, like Dolly Sods or Spruce Knob, are accessible only on rough, unpaved Forest Service routes.

Most of the Forest Service roads listed in this guide are passable in good weather to ordinary passenger cars with good ground clearance. A four-wheel-drive vehicle is recommended when the roads are wet and is essential when they are muddy, icy, or snow-covered.

Off-road vehicle use is prohibited in all of the areas covered by this book. ATVs and mountain bikes are allowed on some trails in the national forests, but abuses have left trails in such poor condition that this activity is now being restricted in some areas. Vehicles of any kind, including mountain bikes, are prohibited on trails and fire roads in Shenandoah National Park and the Dolly Sods Wilderness Area.

Wildlife

Wildlife is abundant in the eastern mountains. However, most of it is shy and reclusive, and you can count yourself lucky if you see much of it by day. Of the many species that inhabit the mountains, only black bears and two species of snake pose any threat to the hiker.

Black bears are not naturally aggressive, but any encounter calls for caution. Keep all food and food odors out of your tent or vehicle, and never feed a bear under any circumstances. If a bear pursues you, it is probably interested in your food; set it down and walk (don't run) away. If you see a bear on the trail, make plenty of noise to let it know you're there; bears are near-sighted and are more likely to attack when startled. Keep your distance from a mother with cubs.

The central Appalachians are home to two poisonous snakes, the copperhead and the eastern timber rattler. Both inhabit rocky areas; copperheads prefer stream banks and damp areas, whereas rattlers are more common in drier areas. Neither is aggressive, but they will bite if startled or threatened.

Precautions

Statistically, the areas covered in this guide are probably safer than your own neighborhood. That doesn't mean they are trouble free. Although violent crime in these areas is still rare, theft and vandalism have increased. Take the same precautions that you would in any unfamiliar area. Fill your gas tank before venturing into undeveloped areas, and always use a locking gas cap Park at an established trailhead if possible, and don't leave valuables in your car. Despite what some guides tell you, never leave a note with your vehicle giving your destination or return time. Car alarms are basically useless in these areas and actually may be counterproductive. Your alarm is more likely to be triggered by a curious bear or raccoon than by a thief, and campers by a blaring siren have been known to take extreme measures to silence the offending vehicle. Instead, secure your steering wheel with a "club"-type device, but leave the alarm disabled.

On the trail, be pleasant but remain cautious, and don't reveal your plans. Establish backcountry camps out of sight of roads and trails (for aesthetic and legal as much as safety reasons), and avoid areas that show evidence of being frequented by partiers. Most of these areas are near roads or private land; problems tend to escalate during hunting season.

Personal protection is a thorny issue, but if your outlook is so poor that you feel you must carry a gun on the trail, you may be better off staying home. In fifteen years of hiking this region, I've never encountered a situation in which I felt the need for a weapon. Keep in mind that hunting is allowed in many of the areas covered here, which are best avoided during hunting season (see Appendix I for addresses of state departments of natural resources). Hunting is prohibited in Shenandoah National Park and many of the Forest Service recreation areas.

Be courteous but cautious, rely on common sense and gut instinct, and you'll have a safe journey.

North Fork Mountain, WV —
View south from Chimney Top

Part One

THE
POTOMAC RIVER

Harpers Ferry, WV — Potomac at Shenandoah confluence

The Potomac River

The Potomac River is the thread that ties this guide together. From its beginnings high in the Appalachians, the Potomac gathers force as it winds through narrow valleys to finally break free of the mountains in a spectacular water gap at Harpers Ferry, on the borders of Maryland, Virginia, and West Virginia.

Below Harpers Ferry the river becomes more placid, disrupted by only occasional riffles, until it makes one final plunge at Great Falls on the outskirts of Washington, D.C. Below the falls, the river widens and comes under the influence of Chesapeake Bay: This is the beginning of the tidewater Potomac, and the lower limit of this guide's range.

Captain John Smith would be astounded by the changes that have taken place on the Potomac since he first explored it in 1608. Venturing upstream as far as Little Falls, Smith found a wilderness sparsely populated by native tribes and reported that fish were "lying so thicke with their heads above the water ... we attempted to catch them with a frying pan: but we found it a very bad instrument to catch fish with."

Great Falls, VA — Main Falls, Virginia side

For nearly two centuries after Smith's expedition, the Potomac Valley above Great Falls remained largely wilderness, broken only by occasional farms and small settlements. But in 1791, Charles L'Enfant began to lay out a new national capital at a site selected by George Washington near the confluence of the Potomac and Anacostia Rivers. Washington's choice wasn't an arbitrary one. As a teenager, he had surveyed the Potomac's upper reaches and realized the river's potential as a route to the Allegheny Mountains and the rich Ohio River Valley that lay beyond. By 1795, Washington's Patowmack Canal Company had begun construction of a canal skirting Great Falls, and similar projects farther upstream soon opened navigation to the foot of the Allegheny Mountains in western Maryland. In 1811, Congress approved construction of the National Road, a primitive turnpike that in part followed the Potomac Valley to Cumberland, MD. In 1828, ground was broken for both the Chesapeake & Ohio (C&O) Canal and the Baltimore & Ohio Railroad, which would vie bitterly for rights-of-way through the narrow valley. River towns like Harpers Ferry, Hancock, Williamsport, and Cumberland emerged as important transportation and industrial centers.

C&O Canal, MD —
Lock 33, Harpers Ferry

But in the end, the upper Potomac Valley failed to thrive. The ravages of the Civil War, a series of disastrous floods, the failure of the C&O Canal, the decline of the coal industry, and a loss of manufacturing to larger urban centers all limited development along the Potomac.

C&O Canal, MD —
Marsh near Great Falls

In time, Congress turned its attention to the sorry plight of the river's historic artifacts. In 1938, the Park Service purchased the entire C&O Canal right-of-way, and in 1944 funds were appropriated to purchase

4

deteriorated property at Harpers Ferry. Chief Justice William O. Douglas and a dedicated band of canal enthusiasts defeated a plan that would have paved over the C&O Canal towpath way for a highway.

Water quality, abysmal in 1960, improved slowly as new regulations brought an end to dumping of raw sewage and industrial wastes. Today, Potomac water is still far from perfect—the Park Service at Harpers Ferry advises that it "does not monitor the water for pollutants; therefore, swimming is not advised"—but the improvement over the past two decades has been encouraging. Whether that improvement will continue, given the current anti-environmental sentiment in Congress, is anyone's guess.

This section covers two major natural areas on the Potomac near Washington. Great Falls has been a favorite D.C. playground for over a century, and the hiker who is willing to venture away from the inevitable crowds may be amazed by the rugged quality of this little slice of wilderness just north of the Capital Beltway (I-495). The C&O Canal towpath, as it winds along the Potomac for 185 miles from tidewater to mountain, is truly a walk back in time and offers an unforgettable introduction to this historic American river.

C&O Canal, MD — Lock 33 and Salty Dog Tavern ruins near Harpers Ferry

Chapter 1

CHESAPEAKE & OHIO CANAL NATIONAL HISTORICAL PARK

The Chesapeake & Ohio Canal is America's longest and narrowest national park, stretching for 185 miles but averaging only a thousand feet in width. The park follows the twisting course of the C&O Canal, a nineteenth-century waterway that was already obsolete before its final section opened in 1850. Following the Potomac from the coastal plain at Washington, D.C., to the foot of the Allegheny Mountains at Cumberland, MD, the towpath offers sweeping river vistas as it passes through areas rich in history and natural diversity.

At a time when the eastern mountains presented a formidable barrier to transportation, early settlers saw the Potomac Valley as a promising westward route. Long stretches of the river were navigable upstream from Washington, but falls and rapids blocked passage at many points. In 1795, George Washington's Patowmack Company built the first of several short canals skirting the worst obstacles. The Patowmack Company structures opened the river to downstream travel, but boatmen scuttled their barges and rafts at journey's end rather than battle the strong river currents on a return trip.

Inspired by the success of New York's Erie Canal, a group of investors formed the Chesapeake & Ohio Canal Company in the 1820s and mapped a bold project intended to link the Chesapeake Bay to the Ohio River. The canal company broke ground on July 4, 1828, the same day that the Baltimore & Ohio Railroad did the same in nearby Baltimore. For the next several decades, canal and railroad would battle over access and rights-of-way. In the end, the railroad won.

The C&O Canal was opened to Seneca Creek in 1831, to Harpers Ferry in 1833, and to a point near Hancock in 1838. But the canal company underestimated the ruggedness of the mountain terrain in western Maryland, and the canal's upper portion didn't open until 1850, after one bankruptcy, tremendous cost overruns, several disease epidemics, and a period of open warfare among canal workers. In the meantime, the railroad had already reached western Maryland and was preparing to extend its right-of-way to Pittsburgh just as the canal company was dropping its plans to do so.

Although the railroad had won the westward race, the canal survived as an inexpensive, if leisurely, means of transporting coal and other bulky cargo.

Mule-drawn barges on the C&O Canal averaged 14.5 feet in width and 92 feet in length, and operation was often a family affair. Crews lived with their mules aboard the barges during the five-day downstream trip from Cumberland to Georgetown. If you're interested in life on the canal, I recommend Thomas Hahn's fascinating compilation of historic photos and first-hand accounts, *The C&O Canal Boatmen,* available from the American Canal and Transportation Center (see Appendix I).

The C&O Canal was plagued by floods throughout its history, but those in 1877 and 1889 crippled operations for many months and undermined the company's already shaky finances. After decades of operating at a loss, the company suspended operations in 1924, following yet another major flood on the Potomac that destroyed parts of the aging structure.

In 1938, C&O Canal property was transferred to the National Park Service, and from 1939 through 1942 the Park Service restored and rewatered 22 miles of canal near Washington, D.C. A postwar plan to pave the canal right-of-way for a scenic highway was defeated through the persistent efforts of Chief Justice William O. Douglas, and President Eisenhower proclaimed the entire canal a National Monument during the last moments of his presidency in 1961. On January 8, 1972, the C&O Canal was declared a National Historical Park.

Hiking

The entire 185-mile canal towpath is open to hikers, horseback riders, and bicyclists. Motorized vehicles of any kind are prohibited. Allow approximately 3–4 days by bike or 8–10 days on foot to cover the canal's entire length. The towpath is essentially level, rising only 609 feet between Washington and Cumberland; it is in generally good condition, although you'll find it muddy or rocky in spots. Expect weekend and holiday crowds around Georgetown, Great Falls, Harpers Ferry, the Paw Paw Tunnel, and scattered recreational areas. Lesser-known sections are often virtually deserted.

Camping

Several canal-side recreation areas provide semi-primitive camping sites with picnic tables and fireplaces, drinking water, and pit toilets. Few offer RV hookups or similar amenities, but RV and car campers will find good commercial campgrounds scattered throughout the vicinity.

For through-hikers, the Park Service maintains primitive camping areas that it calls Hiker-Biker Overnighters. As the name implies, you're welcome to use these sites overnight, but don't plan on establishing a long-term camp. The Overnighters are intentionally located away from roads and are closed to motorized traffic other than authorized Park Service vehicles. Most sites include fireplaces or fire rings, picnic tables, and pit toilets. Pumps—turned off in winter—provide drinking water at most sites. There is no charge to use the Overnighters, and occupancy is on a first-come, first-served basis.

Most land adjacent to the towpath is privately owned. Don't camp on private land without permission.

Trail Guide:
C&O CANAL TOWPATH

Note: This guide is keyed to mileposts along the towpath, which begin at 0.0 at Rock Creek Basin. Distances are approximate and have been rounded to the nearest tenth of a mile. Only the most convenient access points are noted; check local maps for many others.

Georgetown to Great Falls (miles 0–14)

Length: *14 miles*

Elevation change: *110 feet*

Level: *easy*

USGS quad maps: *Alexandria, VA–D.C.–MD; Washington West, D.C.–MD; Falls Church, VA–MD*

The first section of the canal begins at the upper end of the tidewater Potomac, a favorite area for kayakers, boaters, and anglers. Milepost 0.0 marks Tidelock (the canal's eastern terminus) and Rock Creek Basin. This was once a busy waterfront and warehouse district, but now the basin is drained and the original towpath obliterated.

At mile 0.4, pass the first of the Georgetown locks (1–4), where narrated mule-drawn barge trips are available from mid-April through October, Wednesdays through Sundays. Access is from 29th Street one block south of M Street in Georgetown. The locks are the first of the C&O's 74 lift locks, which raise the canal 609 feet between Georgetown and Cumberland. The average lock raised a vessel 8 feet and was tended day and night by a resident lock keeper. Today, most of the lock tenders' houses are gone, and the condition of the locks varies. Lift locks in the Great Falls area are restored and operable, but those farther upstream have been drained and stripped of their hardware. The old locks tend to tilt inward, and several have been partially filled to prevent collapse.

At 1 mile, pass under the Francis Scott Key Bridge. Key's house, long since relocated and restored, once stood at the eastern end of the present-day bridge. The author of "The Star Spangled Banner" moved from his home in the 1830s, after canal construction destroyed his orchard and gardens.

The Abner Cloud House and Fletcher Boat House are just upstream from milepost 3; access is from Canal Road at its intersection with Reservoir Road. Completed in 1801, Abner Cloud's house is the oldest remaining habitable structure on the C&O Canal. The boat house offers bike, rowboat, and canoe rentals, snack food, and fishing supplies in season. From this point, the C&O follows the bed of the Little Falls Skirting Canal, a project of George Washington's Patowmack Company (see the Great Falls chapter).

Pass under Chain Bridge at 4.2 miles. Access to this area is from the George Washington Memorial Parkway; park in the large lot north of the bridge. On weekends and holidays, the lot is usually filled by mid-morning. In March and April, shad migrate upstream to spawn here, attracting hordes of anglers. The original Chain Bridge gained a bit of notoriety in 1861, when a sentry who fell asleep at his post on the bridge became the first Union soldier to be court-martialed during the Civil War. He was later pardoned by President Lincoln.

At 4.6 miles, the towpath enters Maryland, and Maryland fishing licenses are required from this point. Just ahead is Little Falls, a series of rocky rapids that marks the beginning of the piedmont (foothill) province and the end of

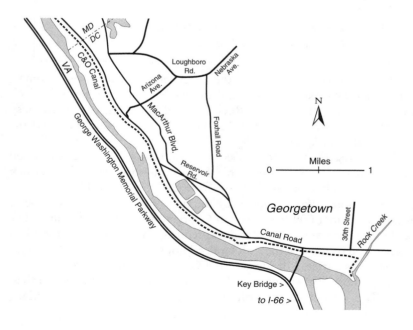

the tidewater Potomac. Access to the Little Falls area is from the southbound lane of George Washington Memorial Parkway; park in the lot near Lock 6. Pass Lock 5 and Inlet Lock 1 at 5 miles. Just upstream are Lock 6 (Magazine Lock) and Feeder Dam 1. Magazine Lock, named for a nearby federal powder magazine, was the site of the canal's ground-breaking ceremony on July 4, 1828, at which President John Quincy Adams officiated. Ruins of the Little Falls Skirting Canal (another Patowmack Company project), an old dam, and several cottages destroyed in the 1936 flood make for interesting exploring around the feeder dam.

Lock 7 (Glen Echo) lies at milepost 7. Access is from the southbound lane of the George Washington Memorial Parkway; there is a small parking area near the lock. Glen Echo was one of the earliest Washington suburbs, and social life there centered on the National Chautauqua. Nearby are Glen Echo Park (site of a former commercial amusement park now owned by the National Park Service) and the home of Clara Barton (founder of the American Red Cross), both of which can be reached from MacArthur Boulevard. Cabin John Bridge, completed in 1864 and now a registered National Historic Civil War Landmark, is a half-mile upstream.

Lock 8, at 8.3 miles, is the first of the Seven Locks, a series of closely spaced lift locks that raise the canal 56 feet in a little over a mile. Access is from the southbound lane of George Washington Memorial Parkway; there is a parking area near Lock 8. Lock 14, last of the Seven Locks, lies directly under the Capitol Beltway bridge.

Carderock Recreation Area, at 10.4 miles, is a popular picnic area with tables, toilets, and drinking water. Low cliffs above the Potomac and its side-channels attract novice rock climbers, and Stubblefield Falls, a series of rocky rapids 0.3 miles downstream, is a popular put-in spot for kayakers. To reach Carderock, take George Washington Memorial Parkway north of the Capital Beltway (I-495) and follow the signs.

At 12.3 miles, the towpath passes near a large parking area adjacent to the Old Angler's Inn on MacArthur Boulevard. There is no parking fee, but both lots are usually filled by mid-morning on weekends and holidays. This is a popular put-in spot for canoes and kayaks, as well as a convenient access point to the Berma Road and Great Falls area (see the Great Falls chapter). At mile 12.6, reach Widewater, an old channel of the Potomac that canal engineers flooded to create a long, narrow lake. Look for heron and a good variety of waterfowl here and in the swamp on the opposite side of the towpath.

Lock 15, at 13.4 miles, is the first in a series of six closely spaced locks that raise the canal as it skirts Great Falls. This scenic and heavily used section of the canal has been restored to operating condition, and the Park Service offers mule-drawn canal boat rides during the summer. At one point, the towpath perches at the edge of a sheer 60-foot drop to the rocky bed of the Potomac.

Nearby Attraction

ROCK CREEK PARK—
To reach the park, follow US-29 south from the Capital Beltway (I-495) to a right turn onto Military Road. Drive a short distance west to the park and follow the signs. From a parking area near the intersection of Parkside and West Beach Drives, a 1-mile trail leads west to Boundary Bridge. From the same area, a blue-blazed trail follows the east side of Rock Creek for about 3 miles, ending at Boulder Bridge in the park's southern end. The area between Boulder and Rapids Bridges is especially interesting where Rock Creek crosses the Fall Line (the division between the coastal plain and piedmont, and the same geological feature that forms nearby Great Falls) in a series of picturesque cascades and rapids. Although heavily used and hemmed in by highways, Rock Creek Park offers a surprisingly diverse array of plants and wildlife. White-tailed deer, raccoon, beaver, and red and gray fox manage to survive in this narrow stream valley, where the Audubon Society reports 12 varieties of snakes and 61 species of butterflies. The park is rich in both native and introduced plant species, including witch hazel, redbud, blackberry, raspberry, spicebush, sassafras, sweet cherry, more than 20 species of ferns, and at least 40 species of wildflowers. Pawpaws, one of the few native North American edible fruits, grow near Boulder Bridge. Within the park are the National Zoo, a working grist mill, bike and horse trails, tennis courts, a golf course, and picnic areas. Unfortunately, most of the park is within earshot of the Rock Creek and Potomac Parkways, and Rock Creek itself is polluted by silt and storm-drain runoff.

Great Falls to Seneca Creek (miles 14–23)

Length: *9 miles*
Elevation change: *40 feet*
Level: *easy*
USGS quad maps: *Rockville, MD; Seneca, MD–VA*

This scenic and varied section heads into more rugged terrain as it approaches the Fall Line, the dividing point between the coastal plain and piedmont. The wild nature of the Potomac gorge belies its proximity to the bustling Washington metropolitan area.

Great Falls Tavern and Visitor Center is at mile 14.3. To reach the visitor center from the Capital Beltway (I-495), exit at the George Washington Memorial Parkway and follow the parkway to its junction with MacArthur Boulevard. Bear left (north) and continue to the visitor center parking area

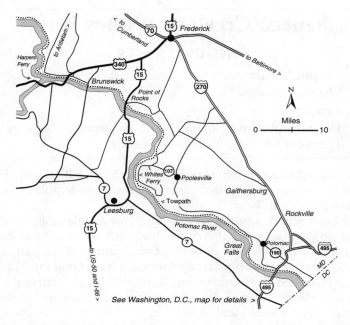

See Washington, D.C., map for details >

at the end of the boulevard. A parking fee is charged. The visitor center building was completed in stages between 1829 and 1831 and served at various times as a tavern, hotel, lockhouse, and grocery store.

Currents in the vicinity of the main falls and upstream dam are treacherous, and swimming and boating are prohibited. The nearest safe canoe put-in is downstream from the main falls, at the parking area opposite Old Angler's Inn (see mile 12.3). See the Great Falls chapter for further information on this area.

Access to the remaining locks in this section is from River Road (Route 190) north of I-495.

Lock 21 (Swain's Lock) is at 16.6 miles. Parking, drinking water, and a public telephone are provided, and a concession stand operates during the summer. Lock 22 (Pennyfield Lock), at mile 19.6, can be reached from Pennyfield Lock Road, off of River Road (Route 190). The lockhouse remains standing but isn't open to the public. The Seneca Rapids area, just upstream, is a scenic area marked by huge mica schist outcroppings and rocky rapids in the Potomac. With Dierssen Waterfowl Sanctuary and Blockhouse Point Regional Park nearby, this is a popular area for bird-watching, canoeing, and kayaking.

Lock 23 (Violettes Lock), Intake Lock 2, and Feeder Dam 2 follow in quick succession above mile 22.1. To reach Violettes Lock, which marks the upstream end of the canal's restored and watered portion, follow River Road 7 miles west of Potomac, MD, to a left turn on Violettes Lock Road.

13

Seneca Creek to Whites Ferry (miles 23–35)

Length: *12 miles*
Elevation change: *35 feet*
Level: *easy*
USGS quad maps: *Seneca, MD–VA; Sterling, VA–MD; Leesburg, VA–MD; Waterford, VA–MD*

This section provides a pleasant stroll through rolling hill country. The area is rich in evidence of Indian inhabitancy and saw considerable troop movement during the Civil War.

Lock 24 and Seneca Aqueduct (Aqueduct 1) are at mile 22.8. To reach the aqueduct, follow Route 190 (River Road) 8.5 miles northwest of Potomac, MD, turn left onto Rileys Lock Road, and continue to the parking area. Seneca Aqueduct was heavily damaged during a local flood in 1971 but has since been stabilized. The Seneca Stone Cutting Mill, just upstream from the aqueduct, produced much of the red and gray sandstone used in the lower canal structures. Groceries and supplies are available at nearby Poole's General Store. This is a popular and often crowded recreation area, and motorboat use along this section of the river, with its accompanying noise and exhaust fumes, degrades the natural setting.

At milepost 25, look for Tenfoot Island in the Potomac River. During Prohibition, Earl Blatt reportedly ran a moonshine still on the island. He was said to number many Washington officials among his clientele, perhaps explaining why his still was never raided. The nearby Winslow Archeological Site, at mile 25.7, has yielded hundreds of Early-to-Late Woodland Period artifacts (c. 500 B.C.–A.D. 1500). The site is now closed, and unauthorized digging or removal of artifacts from National Park Service property is prohibited.

Horsepen Branch Hiker-Biker Overnighter, at milepost 26, is the first of many primitive walk-in campsites along the canal (see Camping in the introduction to this chapter). McKee-Beshers Wildlife Management Area, at mile 27.2, comprises 1,500 acres of varied habitat in Hughes Hollow, and beaver, red fox, and white-tailed deer are common here. This is a popular spot for watching wildlife, but be forewarned that hunting is allowed in season.

At 30.8 miles, pass Lock 25 (Edwards Ferry). To reach the lock, drive 4.5 miles west from Poolesville, MD, on Edwards Ferry Road to a parking area with boat ramp and toilets. This was an important river crossing for Union and Confederate troops alike during the Civil War. Ruins of the Goose Creek River Locks, which admitted boats from the Virginia side of the Potomac, are a short distance downstream. Broad Run Trunk, at mile 31.9, is the only wooden aqueduct on the canal. The trunk was pressed into service after the original stone structure collapsed in 1846.

14

Pass Harrison Island at 33.3 miles. The Piscataway (Canoy) tribe fled to this island in the 1690s and built a fortified village at its upstream end. Decimated by a smallpox epidemic in 1705, the tribe was forced from the island by a band of Tuscarora, who remained there until 1713. The island and surrounding area have yielded rich evidence of native American occupation. The Battle of Balls Bluff, one of the first of the Civil War, took place in October 1861 on the Virginia shore opposite Harrison Island. Turtle Run Hiker-Biker Overnighter is upstream, at mile 34.4.

Whites to Point of Rocks Ferry (miles 35–48)

Length: *13 miles*

Elevation change: *35 feet*

Level: *easy*

USGS quad maps: *Leesburg, VA–MD; Waterford, VA–MD; Poolesville, MD–VA; Buckeystown, MD–VA; Point of Rocks, MD–VA*

The canal continues through hill country, but occasional views of Catoctin Mountain hint at more rugged land ahead. This section lies in the heart of Civil War country, and an understanding of what happened along the Potomac in those days will greatly enhance your enjoyment of this area.

Whites Ferry, site of the last operating ferry on the upper Potomac, is at mile 35.5. To reach the ferry, follow Route 107 (Whites Ferry Road) 6 miles west from Poolesville, MD, to the ferry landing. The *Jubal A. Early* runs year-round from 6 A.M. until 10 P.M. (hours may vary). A general store near the landing offers groceries and supplies. Upstream are Marble Quarry Hiker-Biker Overnighter (mile 38.2), Lock 26 (Woods Lock) (mile 39.3), and Lock 27 (Spinks Ferry) (mile 41.5).

Monocacy Aqueduct (Aqueduct 2) is at mile 42.2, on Mouth of Monocacy Road north of Dickerson, MD. Largest of the C&O Canal aqueducts, Monocacy was completed in 1833. Hurricane Agnes inflicted major damage on the aqueduct in June 1972. In the vicinity is Monocacy National Battlefield, a Civil War battlefield park that is still under development (see Appendix I). Indian Flats Hiker-Biker Overnighter is just upstream, at mile 42.4.

At mile 44.6 is Nolands Ferry. Excavations in this area and throughout the Monocacy Valley confirm the presence of a native population from the Early through Late Woodland Periods (c. 500 B.C.–A.D. 1500). At a nearby site, closed to the public, archaeologists have unearthed a Late Woodland village surrounding a central plaza and have discovered good examples of cord-marked pottery. The first documented settlement by Europeans in this area began in 1708. Nolands Ferry may be the site of a crossing on the Monocacy Trail, a corridor granted by the Treaty of Lancaster of 1744 to allow passage of Indian tribes from the Susquehanna River in Pennsylvania to Virginia and the Carolinas. By 1758, settlers had driven the natives from the area and constructed a ferry, making this an important crossing in trade between the Maryland and Virginia colonies.

Calico Rocks Hiker-Biker Overnighter is at mile 47.7. The Calico Rocks, which begin about a mile downstream from the camp area, are conglomerate outcroppings that once were quarried for use in the pillars of the Capitol's rotunda and other public buildings. Heater Island, in the Potomac opposite the Overnighter, was occupied by native tribes until the early 1700s. It is now privately owned.

Point of Rocks to
Harpers Ferry Area (miles 48–60)

Length: *12 miles*
Elevation change: *35 feet*
Level: *easy*
USGS quad maps: *Point of Rocks, MD–VA; Harpers Ferry, VA–MD–WV; Charles Town, WV–VA–MD*

This section marks the beginning of mountain country as the Potomac breaches Catoctin Mountain at Point of Rocks.

Point of Rock Station, a picturesque Victorian depot listed on the National Register of Historic Places, is at mile 47.8. To reach the station from Frederick, follow I-70 west, turn south on US-340, and continue to a junction with US-15. Follow US-15 south to Point of Rocks. If you're coming from Washington, D.C., take Route 7 west to Leesburg, VA. From Leesburg, follow US-15 north and cross the Potomac to Point of Rocks. The station offers limited Amtrak service to Washington and Harpers Ferry.

At mile 48.4, the canal skirts the foot of Catoctin Mountain. Point of Rocks Railroad Tunnel, Lock 28 (Mountain Lock), and the Catoctin Railroad Tunnel follow each other in quick succession along a narrow shelf at the base of the ridge. Catoctin is a northern outlier of the main Blue Ridge; Camp David, the presidential retreat, lies on the ridge farther to the north.

Bald Eagle Island Hiker-Biker Overnighter is at mile 50.3, and Lock 29 (Catoctin Lock) is a half-mile upstream. At mile 51.5 is Catoctin Creek Aqueduct (Aqueduct 3). To reach the aqueduct, take Route 464 to Lander Road and turn west. Follow Lander Road to the point where it turns to parallel the railroad. Parking is limited; pull off wherever you can do so safely, without blocking the road, and hike upstream. A portion of the aqueduct collapsed in 1973, but the structure has been stabilized.

Brunswick Recreation Area is at mile 54. To reach the recreation area, follow Route 464 south of Brunswick, MD, to the parking area. Operated by the town of Brunswick, the recreation area offers a picnic ground, drinking water, toilets, and a boat ramp and rentals. Camping is permitted; obtain permits at the campground in season (generally Memorial Day through Labor Day) or at the Brunswick Town Hall. A town that has gone by several names, Brunswick occupies a 1753 royal land grant originally known as Hawkins Merry Peep-o-Day. The town was platted as Berlin in 1780, and a ferry crossed here by 1822. The town's name was changed to Barry with the opening of a post office in 1832, and finally to Brunswick when the Baltimore & Ohio Railroad moved its eastern switching yard and repair shops here in 1890. Brunswick prospered as a hub of railroad activity into the 1960s, but cutbacks in rail operations during the past several decades forced this single-industry town into a decline from which it is only now emerging.

The next 2 miles of towpath beyond Brunswick make for an unpleasant hiking experience. Parts of the towpath are used by cars and motorcycles for access to a stretch of riverside cabins, and the area is marred by ramshackle structures and illegal dumping. Appropriately, this was the site of a large "hobo jungle" during the Depression years.

At mile 57.8, an unmarked and inconspicuous path leads from the towpath to the remains of the Weverton Manufacturing Company. Casper W. Wever constructed a large factory here in the 1830s, intending to rent part of it to other manufacturers, but his rents were high and most of the building lay idle. At the outbreak of the Civil War, the site was occupied by the Weverton Cotton Mills, which took the revolutionary step of providing communal living for its workers in buildings equipped with running water, a luxury unheard of at that time. The commune operated only briefly before its buildings were seized for barracks by Union troops. The canal company acquired the site in 1877 and demolished Weverton's feeder dam, which had caused flooding problems on the canal for many years. Subsequently abandoned, the town has since vanished, washed away by floods or buried beneath the silt of the Potomac floodplain. Only the walls of the Weverton factory's water intake remain.

Lock 31 (Weverton Lock) is just upstream. To reach the lock, take the Route 67 exit from westbound US-340, immediately turn left and cross US-340, then follow the road for approximately a half-mile to a parking area at the railroad crossing.

Just upstream from milepost 58, the Appalachian Trail (AT)—which has made a steep descent from the crest of South Mountain and Weverton Cliffs to this point—merges with the C&O towpath. For the next 2.5 miles, the southbound AT follows the C&O towpath upstream to Harpers Ferry. To hike the

AT northbound from here, follow the blazes across the highway and climb steeply to Weverton Cliffs, which afford a spectacular view across the Potomac. From the cliffs, the trail continues its climb on switchbacks to the ridge-line of South Mountain, the northern extension of the main Blue Ridge, where it will remain for most of its course through Maryland (see the Appalachian Trail chapter).

Reach the village of Sandy Hook at 59.6 miles. To arrive at this settlement opposite Harpers Ferry by road, follow US-340 south from Frederick and turn east onto Route 180 at a blinking light just before the Potomac River bridge. Pass a motel and a liquor store, then turn right onto Harpers Ferry Road, which descends steeply to Sandy Hook. Lock 32 (Sandy Hook Lock) is a short distance upstream. Once a busy railroad and canal town, Sandy Hook is now a quiet one-road settlement in Maryland, directly across the Potomac from Harpers Ferry. Pick up groceries and supplies here if you are planning to hike any distance upstream.

Because road, railroad, and canal squeeze along a narrow shelf at Sandy Hook, parking is very limited. Unlike their neighbors across the river, Sandy Hook's residents gain very little from tourism, yet they have had to contend with careless tourist parking for years. Thus, if your car blocks the road or private drives, it will probably be towed very quickly. The same warning applies to former parking pullouts along Harpers Ferry Road beyond Sandy Hook, which have been closed by the Park Service. If you find that you can't park safely along the canal—and that will be the case far more often than not—backtrack to US-340, park at the Harpers Ferry visitor center, take the shuttle into the historic district, and cross the footbridge back to the towpath in Maryland (see the Harpers Ferry chapter).

Harpers Ferry Area to Shepherdstown Area (miles 60–72)

(See the Harpers Ferry chapter for additional information on this area.)

Length: *12 miles*

Elevation change: *40 feet*

Level: *easy*

USGS quad maps: *Harpers Ferry, VA–MD–WV; Charles Town, WV–VA–MD; Shepherdstown, WV–MD*

The Appalachian Trail leaves the towpath at mile 60.6, crossing the Potomac to Harpers Ferry, WV, on the downstream railroad bridge. From Harpers Ferry, the AT crosses the Shenandoah River and continues south into Shenandoah National Park. Even if you aren't visiting Harpers Ferry or hiking the AT, climb the stairs to the railroad bridge for a spectacular view of the Shenandoah and Potomac confluence. Just ahead is Lock 33 (Harpers Ferry Lock). The small tunnel built into Lock 33 is a bypass flume designed to carry excess water around the lock. The flume is interesting to explore, but be wary of the poisonous copperhead snakes that frequent the rocks in this area. The roofless ruin above Lock 33 is all that remains of the Salty Dog Tavern. According to some canal veterans interviewed by Thomas Hahn, the Salty Dog name isn't historically accurate; at least two boatmen recalled the name of the tavern as Spencer's.

Maryland Heights, a northern spur of the Blue Ridge, towers above Lock 33. The railroad tunnel was begun in the 1890s (the 1931 date on its portal refers to later work), and the old tooth-powder billboard on the cliffs above has been a landmark for nearly a century. Stay out of the tunnel; rail traffic is heavy through Harpers Ferry.

At 61.3 miles, a footbridge crosses the canal to an old military road, now called the Overlook Cliff Trail, that climbs to a spectacular viewpoint on Maryland Heights. Lock 34 (Goodheart's Lock) lies just ahead, at mile 61.6; there is very limited parking where Harpers Ferry Road makes a sharp uphill turn. John Brown's raiders made their way down this steep lane on the way to their ill-fated raid of October 16, 1859. Beyond Lock 34, the canal follows the bed of the Patowmack Company's Long Canal, a forerunner of the C&O. A stone foundation marks the site of the former lock tender's house, which collapsed in the 1936 flood.

Feeder Dam 3 and Locks 35 and 36 follow in rapid succession above mile 62.3. The first dam at this site was built in 1799 to supply water power to the Harpers Ferry Armory. When the canal company suspended operations in 1924, many of its remaining boats were loaded with rocks and sunk behind the dam, which now lies in ruin. The brick shell standing below the towpath in this section is all that remains of a lock tender's house destroyed in the 1936 flood. The frame house above Lock 36—now sealed by the Park Service—has a tantalizing history of hauntings, most of which involve sightings of strange lights and fireballs. Farther uphill is the site of Fort Duncan, built by Union troops to protect Harpers Ferry in 1862. Huckleberry Hill Hiker-Biker Overnighter is a short distance upstream, at mile 62.9.

Dargan Bend Recreation Area, at mile 64.9, offers picnic tables, toilets, and a boat ramp, but camping is not permitted. To reach the recreation area, turn sharply uphill on Harpers Ferry Road at Lock 34 and continue to a left turn on Shinhan Road. Drive downhill (bearing left at the fork) to an area with ample car and trailer parking.

Mountain Lock Recreation Area, at mile 67.2, is a small park offering picnic tables and fireplaces, drinking water, and toilets. To reach Mountain Lock, follow directions for Dargan Bend Recreation Area (above), but bear right at the fork onto Limekiln Road. Lock 37 (Mountain Lock) is a short distance downstream from the recreation area.

Antietam Aqueduct, at mile 69.3, carries the canal across Antietam Creek. Just upstream, the National Park Service maintains a popular campground and recreation area that can be reached from Harpers Ferry Road, approximately midway between Sandy Hook and Sharpsburg.

Near the end of this section is Packhorse Ford (mile 71.4), a once-important river crossing that was often used by Indian tribes. This was the site of the Confederate retreat from Antietam on September 18–19, 1862.

Nearby Attraction

ANTIETEM NATIONAL BATTLEFIELD (SHARPSBURG, MD)—
Site of one of the bloodiest battles of the Civil War, Sharpsburg today is a quiet rural town. Antietam Village, 3 miles south of Sharpsburg along Harpers Ferry Road, is practically deserted now but was once an important manufacturing center. The entire Monocacy Valley is well worth exploring if you're interested in Civil War history. To reach the battlefield, follow Route 34 southwest from Boonsboro, MD, to Sharpsburg and adjacent Antietam National Battlefield. Well-placed signs direct you along a self-guided auto tour of the battlefield, which is broken into several sections bordering Sharpsburg.

Shepherdstown to McMahons Mill (mile 72–88)

Length: *16 miles*
Elevation change: *35 feet*
Level: *easy*
USGS quad maps: *Shepherdstown, WV–MD; Williamsport, MD–WV*

Shepherdstown claims to be the oldest inhabited community in what is now West Virginia. Founded by German immigrants in the early 1730s, the town was incorporated as Mecklenburg in 1762 and in 1798 was legally chartered as Shepherdstown in honor of Thomas Shepherd, an early settler. James Rumsey conducted the first successful public demonstration of a steam-powered boat here on December 3, 1787. Home to Shepherd College, the town boasts an eclectic mixture of businesses catering to locals, students, and tourists. A small museum at German and Princess Streets displays an interesting collection of local artifacts, some dating to the eighteenth century. Shepherdstown lies approximately midway between Charles Town and Martinsburg, WV, at the junction of Routes 45 (from Martinsburg) and 230 (from US-340 at Bolivar, just west of Harpers Ferry). If you are coming from

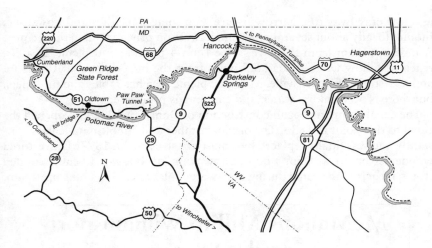

Maryland, follow MD-34 southwest from Boonsboro or Sharpsburg and cross the Rumsey Bridge into Shepherdstown. Canal access is from the last road on the Maryland side of the Rumsey Bridge.

The Shepherdstown River Lock and Lock 38 lie at mile 72.6. Now partially filled, the Shepherdstown River Lock once admitted boats from the West Virginia side of the Potomac. The stone piers upstream are all that remain of the Shepherdstown Bridge, which washed away in the 1936 flood. The mansion overlooking Lock 38 is Ferry Hill Plantation, built by Colonel John Blackford in 1813. Robert E. Lee's son was brought to Ferry Hill after being wounded at the Battle of Antietam. The National Park Service now owns the site, which is not open to the public.

Pass Lock 39 at mile 74. At mile 75.3 is the Killiansburg Cave Hiker-Biker Overnighter, which marks the beginning of a small "cave district." Several caves occur along a stretch of cliffs on the berm side of the canal. All are muddy and slippery; old clothes are recommended, and a reliable rope and flashlight are required for safe exploration. The first cave is a narrow, winding crawlway extending back 200 feet. A short distance beyond this cave are two more shallow openings 40–50 feet above the towpath. The openings aren't obvious and can be reached only by a steep climb. Several other shallow openings occur in the cliff face upstream. Caves in this area served as refuges for local citizens during the Battle of Antietam. Snyder's Landing, at mile 76.6, is the site of a small museum and general store.

At mile 79.4 is Lock 40, with the Horseshoe Bend Hiker-Biker Overnighter a short distance upstream. This was once a fairly isolated portion of the canal, but real estate development now encroaches.

The Dam 4 Cave is at mile 83.3. The cave's entrance, in Conococheague limestone at canal level, leads to a 200-foot-long passage that passes a pool before narrowing and continuing to a small room. The passage then continues as a low crawlway to a narrow fissure with some stalactites and flowstone. Inquire locally about several other small caves on private land in the vicinity. A mile upstream from the cave is the Dam 4 parking and picnic area. To reach it, follow Dam 4 Road 5.5 miles from the intersection of Routes 63 and 632 south of Downsville, MD. The picnic area has tables and pit toilets, but there is no drinking water, and camping is prohibited.

The canal company began construction of Dam 4 in 1832 and opened the canal to this point in 1833. The original timber-and-rubble dam leaked constantly and was finally replaced by a masonry structure in 1877. The restored wooden structure at Dam 4 houses a winch used to lower a heavy wooden stop-gate across the canal during high water. Inlet Lock 4 is a mile upstream.

McMahons Mill to Williamsport (miles 88–99)

Length: *10 miles*
Elevation change: *30 feet*
Level: *easy*
USGS quad maps: *Williamsport, MD–WV*

McMahons Mill, at mile 88.1, marks the beginning of another limestone cave district. To reach the McMahons Mill area, follow Route 632 south from Hagerstown to Downsville, MD. From Downsville, continue south on Dam 4 Road for 0.7 mile to a right turn on Dellinger Road, then follow Dellinger Road 0.7 mile to a left turn. There is parking near the mill, which is not open to the public.

Just upstream from the mill is Howell Cave, now largely blocked by a rockfall. Look for several smaller openings in the limestone nearby. The section of towpath beyond the caves is often flooded when flow is above normal in the Potomac. The Opequon Hiker-Biker Overnighter is farther upstream, at mile 90.9.

The entrance to Dellinger's Cave lies above the canal at mile 92.1. At the time of writing, this small cave was still open to the public, although it is difficult to locate and is recommended for experienced and properly equipped spelunkers only. Cross the canal bed and follow a deep ravine uphill to a barbed-wire fence. Turn right at the fence and work your way to the top of the cliff on an obscure, unmarked path. The cave entrance is an inconspicuous hole at the top of the cliff. From the opening, it's a steep 25-foot drop into a fairly large chamber; you'll need a rope to enter and return safely. From the main room, a low crawlway gradually widens into a larger passage before narrowing and finally becoming impassable. Most of the cave's formations have been broken or removed.

Mile 92.25 marks the canal's midpoint. Just upstream, beyond Lock 43, the towpath is paved and passes a nondescript "summer community" of cabins and shacks.

Reach Falling Waters at mile 94.4. This was the site of General Robert E. Lee's retreat following the Battle of Gettysburg in July 1863. Lee, pursued by Union General Meade to this point and finding the Potomac nearing flood stage, ordered nearby structures demolished to provide timber for pontoon bridges. His army crossed the river successfully on the night of July 13, evading Meade's laggardly forces and possibly prolonging the war. The Cumberland Valley Hiker-Biker Overnighter is a short distance upstream, at mile 95.2.

Williamsport to Fort Frederick (miles 99–112)

Length: *13 miles*
Elevation change: *40 feet*
Level: *easy*
USGS quad maps: *Williamsport, MD–WV; Hedgesville, WV–MD; Big Pool, WV–MD*

Present-day Williamsport, MD, occupies the site of a former Conococheague settlement and was an important frontier outpost in the mid-1700s, serving as a supply point for General Braddock during the French and Indian Wars. In 1790 the town campaigned for selection as the new national capital, but George Washington personally rejected the site because it lay above the navigable portion of the Potomac. Williamsport suffered through two cholera epidemics and a series of armed skirmishes between canal workers in 1832 and 1833. State militia were called in to quell the violence in January 1834, and the warring factions signed a formal peace treaty under the watchful eye of armed troops from Baltimore. Following the opening of the canal in 1834, Williamsport flourished as a commercial center. The town saw some minor action during the Civil War, including passage of Lee's troops to and from Gettysburg.

Williamsport Lock (Lock 44) lies at mile 99.3. There is good access to this section of the canal from Williamsport Riverfront Park (mile 99.8). To reach Williamsport Riverfront Park and the Conococheague Aqueduct, take I-81 to the Williamsport exit and follow US-11 (East Potomac Street) for 1 mile to the center of town. Turn left on West Salisbury Street, go one block to a right turn, and continue to the park. There is ample parking with a picnic area, toilets, a beach, and boat ramps. Overnight camping is allowed with proper registration. Conococheague Aqueduct, carrying the canal for 210 feet over Conococheague Creek, was completed in 1834. The aqueduct has been battered repeatedly over the years by man and nature alike. One arch was destroyed by Mosby's Raiders during the Civil War, and masonry in the berm wall was destroyed when a canal boat breached the wall and crashed to the creek below in 1920. Floods have left the already weakened aqueduct in poor condition. Jordan Junction Hiker-Biker Overnighter is 1.4 miles upstream from the aqueduct, at mile 101.2.

Millers Bend, at mile 104.3, once offered rich evidence of Indian occupation and was famous for its riverside accumulation of tomahawk heads. Today the relics are rare, and it is illegal to remove artifacts from Park Service property. High limestone cliffs on the opposite shore are the remains of Nestles Quarry, site of Indian Church Cave, where many artifacts were once unearthed.

Above Millers Bend, the next 4.3 miles are a pleasant stroll through rolling hill country, passing Feeder Dam and Inlet Lock 5 (mile 106.8) and Locks 45 and 46 (mile 107.3). At mile 108.6, enter the Four Locks Recreation Area (Locks 47–50). To reach the recreation area from I-70, take the Clear Spring exit, drive to the center of Clear Spring, then turn south on Big Spring Road. Continue 2.7 miles to Big Spring, turn left on Four Locks Road, and continue to the parking area. Four Locks has picnic tables, toilets, water, and a boat ramp. The canal veers from the Potomac here to make a shortcut across Prather's Neck, bypassing a 4-mile river bend but requiring the closely spaced series of locks.

At the end of the Prather Neck bypass is McCoys Ferry Recreation Area (mile 110.4). To reach McCoys Ferry from I-70, take the Big Pool exit, turn south on Route 56, and continue for nearly 3 miles to a right turn onto McCoys Ferry Road. Continue on McCoys Ferry Road to the parking area. The recreation area has a picnic area, toilets, a boat launch ramp, and a limited number of camper and trailer parking spaces.

Fort Frederick to Hancock (miles 112–124)

Length: *12 miles*
Elevation change: *45 feet*
Level: *easy*
USGS quad maps: *Big Pool, WV–MD; Hancock, WV–MD–PA*

Fort Frederick State Park and the Big Pool area lie above mile 112. To reach Fort Frederick, take I-70 to the Big Pool exit and follow Route 56 south for 1.5 miles to a right turn onto Route 44. Follow Route 44 to the state park entrance.

Built during the French and Indian Wars in 1756, Fort Frederick was one in a chain of forts stretching through the valley-and-ridge province and along the eastern foot of the Allegheny Front. George Washington visited Fort Frederick in 1756 and 1758, but the structure was never attacked. It served as a British prisoner-of-war camp during the Revolution and was occupied by Union troops protecting the canal during the Civil War. One of the best-preserved pre-Revolutionary forts in the country, Fort Frederick has massive outer walls restored by the Civilian Conservation Corps during the 1930s. Other buildings at the site are largely reconstructions. Big Pool, just upstream from Fort Frederick, is a placid 1.5-mile man-made lake on the canal.

At mile 116 is Licking Creek Aqueduct. The aqueduct, built between 1835 and 1839, used an inferior grade of local stone, and its walls were cracked and bulging by 1870. The aqueduct remains standing but is in poor condition.

Millstone Point, at mile 118.9, was once a stagecoach stop on the old National Road, which had to be rerouted slightly during canal construction. The historic roadbed now lies beneath I-70. At mile 122.6 are Locks 51 and 52 and the Tonoloway Creek Aqueduct, all completed in 1839. The canal company removed the upper stone courses from the aqueduct to reduce pressure on the structure's weak arch, so the towpath crosses the aqueduct on an elevated wooden walkway.

Hancock to Little Orleans (miles 124–140)

Length: *16 miles*
Elevation change: *45 feet*
Level: *easy*
USGS quad maps: *Hancock, WV–MD–PA; Bellegrove, WV–MD–PA; Artemas, MD–PA–WV*

Beginning as a small frontier settlement near Fort Tonoloway, a 1755 blockhouse, Hancock eventually claimed its place as an important transportation center along competing canal, railroad, wagon, and stage routes. From its beginning, the town was notorious for its gambling houses and taverns. The Confederate army under Stonewall Jackson threatened to bombard Hancock in 1862, but legend holds that the Confederates spared the town after learning that many residents were Southern sympathizers. With its strategic location at an important highway junction and river crossing, Hancock has weathered economic hard times better than many western Maryland towns. The area offers a good array of lodging, restaurants, stores, and services and is a popular starting point for short- and long-distance canal hikes.

To reach Hancock, follow I-70 to its junction with US-522. A small picnic and boat-launch area lies near the US-522 bridge. The northern terminus of the Big Blue Trail, an alternate route to the Appalachian Trail, is on the West Virginia side of the US-522 bridge, at Little Tonoloway Park (see the Big Blue Trail chapter). Maryland is less than 2 miles wide at this point, squeezed between the Mason-Dixon Line (Pennsylvania) to the north and the Potomac River (West Virginia) to the south.

Ruins of the Round Top Cement Mill, at mile 127.4, are all that remain of a once-important quarry and mill that began operations in 1837 as Shafer's Cement Mill. The Devil's Eyebrow, a large sandstone anticline, is located just a short distance downstream. Cement rock was mined from Roundtop Hill immediately behind the mill. The hill is honeycombed with old tunnels and openings, all unstable and dangerous to enter.

Beyond the cement mill, the canal continues through isolated hill country, passing Leopards Mill Hiker-Biker Overnighter and Lock 53 at mile 129.9 and Cacapon Junction Hiker-Biker Overnighter at mile 133.6. Beginning at mile 134, Lock 54, Dam and Guard Lock 6, and Lock 55 follow each other in quick succession. Canal construction halted here when funds ran out in 1842, and for eight years Dam 6 marked the western terminus of the C&O Canal. Today, the dam is little more than a pile of rubble. A short distance upstream from Lock 55, a road on the berm side of the canal leads uphill to the private Woodmont Rod and Gun Club, founded in 1870 and host to Herbert Hoover, Franklin Roosevelt, Babe Ruth, and Gene Tunney, among other celebrities.

Pass Lock 56 at mile 136.2. A short distance upstream from the lock is the 1848 Sideling Hill Aqueduct, which is now missing its upstream parapet wall. The Indigo Neck area, beginning at mile 138.1, is rich in Devonian marine fossils; look for them in the exposed rock strata around the Indigo railroad tunnel. A mile upstream (139.2) is the Indigo Neck Hiker-Biker Overnighter.

Nearby Attraction

SIDELING HILL ROAD CUT—

A deep cut made during construction of I-68 revealed spectacular rock strata in the Sideling Hill syncline, the sort of exposure rarely seen in the heavily forested and weathered eastern mountains. The cut proved to be such a traffic-stopper that the state eventually opened a new visitor center at the site. To view the cut, drive west of Hancock on I-68 and park at the visitor center. Parking or stopping along the highway shoulder in the cut will guarantee you a ticket.

Little Orleans to Paw Paw Tunnel (miles 140–155)

Length: *15 miles*

Elevation change: *40 feet*

Level: *easy*

USGS quad maps: *Artemas, MD–PA–WV; Great Cacapon, WV–MD; Paw Paw, WV–MD*

In a secluded setting at the mouth of Fifteenmile Creek, Little Orleans was the site of several Indian camps when European explorers first arrived. A tavern was operating here by 1795, and completion of a road linking Fort Frederick and Cumberland brought an influx of settlers in the early 1800s. Little Orleans was the scene of a riot in May 1838 by Irish canal laborers, who had not been paid. They continued to skirmish throughout the summer as canal contractors attempted to replace them with British and German immigrants. The violence came to a head in August 1838, when three companies of Maryland state militia were dispatched to suppress a riot at the nearby Paw Paw Tunnel construction site.

Completion of the National Road well to the north of Little Orleans eventually drew traffic away from the settlement, which today is far removed from the main tourist routes. Fifteenmile Creek Recreation Area offers limited parking, picnic tables, fireplaces, drinking water, pit toilets, and a paved boat ramp. This is a popular take-out point for canoe and raft trips coming downstream from Paw Paw. Groceries, supplies, boat rentals, and fishing licenses are available at nearby Little Orleans Store. Fifteenmile Creek Aqueduct, completed in 1850, is just upstream from the recreation area.

Little Orleans and the Fifteenmile Creek Recreation Area lie upstream from mile 140.8. To reach the area, take I-68 to Little Orleans Road and follow the road south through Green Ridge State Forest for 6 miles.

Lock 58, at mile 144.0, was the first of 13 "economy" locks, so called because they were originally faced with wooden sheathing instead of more expensive finished stone. The wooden sheathing proved to be false economy, requiring constant maintenance, and much of it was later replaced with concrete, as seen here. Devil's Alley Hiker-Biker Overnighter is a half-mile upstream, and Locks 59 and 60 are another half-mile beyond.

Robey Hollow, at mile 151.2, is the site of Busey Cabin, one of the few structures surviving from the canal construction period. Lock 61 is 2 miles upstream from the hollow.

Lock 62, at mile 154.2, marks the downstream end of Tunnel Hollow, a deep cut blasted into an existing ravine to form the approach to Paw Paw Tunnel.

The hollow, in an isolated and rather eerie setting, is well worth taking the time to explore. Just upstream from Lock 62, the canal turns away from the river and begins its route up the hollow, reaching the tunnel's downstream portal in a mile. At Lock 66 (the last before the tunnel) are the remains of a canal carpenter shop and other structures scattered in the brush on the berm side of the canal. Just ahead, an old tunnel construction road veers uphill from the towpath, crossing Tunnel Hill to the upstream portal. The trail makes an interesting alternate route to the tunnel; see details in the following Paw Paw Tunnel section.

Upstream from Lock 66, the towpath follows an elevated boardwalk through the deep, sheer-sided canyon. Walls on both sides of the canal are subject to rock slides; look for old iron pins placed by the canal company to stabilize the rock (known locally as "slickenslide") above the towpath. The downstream (north) portal of the Paw Paw Tunnel is directly ahead.

Nearby Attraction

GREEN RIDGE STATE FOREST—

Main access is from I-68 between Hancock and Cumberland. The forest comprises 38,811 acres of state-managed land straddling Town Hill, Polish Mountain, and Green Ridge Mountain. Green Ridge offers boat launches and primitive camping areas as well as a network of forest roads and trails. Hunting and fishing are allowed with proper licenses.

Paw Paw Tunnel to Oldtown (miles 155–166)

Length: *11 miles*
Elevation change: *45 feet*
Level: *easy*
USGS quad maps: *Paw Paw, WV–MD; Oldtown, MD–WV*

The Paw Paw Tunnel was an engineering marvel in its day, blasted and hand-dug through 3,118 feet of solid rock to avoid a series of meanders and sheer cliffs along the Potomac. Although construction began in 1836, with a projected completion date of July 1838, the tunnel didn't open to canal traffic until 1850. Two sets of vertical shafts, sunk from the crest of Tunnel Hill to tunnel level, provided ventilation and additional digging faces. Excavated rock was hauled through the shafts and dumped in moraine-like heaps that you'll see if you hike the old construction road over Tunnel Hill. Later filled and sealed, the shafts can be detected in the roof of the tunnel where water drips from the brick lining.

Unrest among Irish immigrant laborers at the site in 1837 escalated into a full-scale strike in May 1838, after canal contractors failed to meet their payrolls and attempted to replace the Irish with English and German laborers. In August of that year, Maryland state militia were called in to suppress rioting at the tunnel site. Work at the tunnel stopped again in 1842, when the canal company collapsed financially. Although broken through, the tunnel sat unfinished and unusable.

Construction resumed under new management in 1847, and the tunnel and upper canal were finally opened to traffic in 1850. From the start, the Paw Paw Tunnel attracted sightseeing as well as cargo vessels, and angry disputes occasionally arose over right-of-way through the narrow passage. The tunnel gradually fell into disrepair after the canal suspended operations in 1924, but restoration in the 1960s returned the tunnel to its former glory.

To reach the Paw Paw Tunnel from Cumberland, MD, and points west, follow Route 51 southeast for approximately 25 miles to the well-marked Paw Paw Tunnel parking area. From Berkeley Springs, WV, and points east, follow US-522 to Berkeley Springs, go west on WV-9, and drive approximately 25 miles to Paw Paw, WV. This scenic route winds past Berkeley Castle, Prospect Peak overlook, and a placid stretch of the Cacapon River. Cross the Potomac at Paw Paw and continue a short distance on MD-51 to the parking area.

Advice: Take a flashlight. The light you see at the end of this tunnel doesn't penetrate very far from either portal, and you'll quickly find yourself engulfed in total darkness. You can feel your way through safely (the handrail is solid enough), but some find the experience unnerving. Inside, look for rope burns along the old towpath rail and evidence of the sealed vertical shafts in the brickwork overhead. During the winter, the Park Service seals both tunnel portals to prevent frost damage. You can enter the tunnel through doors in the barricades, but the barricades completely darken the tunnel's interior. On rare occasions, the tunnel entrance is locked, as it was following the 1985 and 1996 floods, and you'll have to detour over Tunnel Hill to continue your hike (see description at mile 155.8 below).

Note: If you hike to the tunnel from the parking area on Route 51, you will be walking downstream, in the opposite direction from this guide. Therefore, read this section in reverse order, beginning at mile 156.2 below.

The Paw Paw Tunnel's downstream approach was cut through soft shale that tends to slide. As you approach the tunnel, look for the natural arch above it, which protects the tunnel from cave-ins that might otherwise occur in the unstable rock. Climb the portal's steps for a dramatic view down Tunnel Hollow. In early spring, melting snow forms spectacular waterfalls down the sheer cliffs. The towpath follows a ledge through the tunnel, about 6 feet above water level.

The tunnel's upstream (south) portal is at mile 155.8. Climb the stone steps for a close look at the fossil-bearing shales and the engraved keystone commemorating Charles B. Fisk, the canal's engineer. From the towpath, a rough, unmarked trail leads uphill to an excellent rocky viewpoint above the portal. From there, the trail ascends steeply on a switchback, turns, then intersects a wide dirt road on the crest of Tunnel Hill. Cross the road and continue north on the unmarked trail. At one point, the trail descends to cross a ravine, climbs slightly, then begins a long descent to the tunnel's north (downstream) portal. The crest of Tunnel Hill presents a confusing maze of dirt roads and paths, some long abandoned and most unmarked. You may get lost, although not seriously so. If you hike over the hill, take a compass and detailed topographic map. General direction of travel is north and south.

C&O Canal, MD —
Paw Paw Tunnel

The Paw Paw Tunnel parking area is at mile 156.2, just off of MD-51. From the parking area, the tunnel is downstream (to your right). The large building near the parking area was the Canal Section Superintendent's house. Thousands of bricks unearthed along this section some years ago were probably an inferior local product rejected for use in the tunnel. Indian spear points have also been discovered here. The Paw Paw Tunnel Hiker-Biker Overnighter is a short distance downstream.

Little Cacapon River enters on the West Virginia side of the Potomac, opposite mile 159.6. This was an important river crossing during the French and Indian Wars and is mentioned in General Braddock's orders for May 7, 1755.

Lock 67 is at mile 161.8. Access to the lock is from MD-51, where there is limited parking. Cross the railroad tracks to reach the towpath. From Lock 67, it's a half-mile to Town Creek Aqueduct. Several water-powered mills operated here in the last century, and scattered foundations remain above the railroad trestle. The aqueduct was rebuilt in 1976–1977, unfortunately with little regard for authenticity. Town Creek Hiker-Biker Overnighter is a short distance downstream.

At mile 164.8 is Lock 68 (Crabtree's Lock) and the Potomac Forks Hiker-Biker Overnighter. Potomac Forks marks the division of the Potomac into its north and south branches. The fork was a source of contention for years in establishing the Maryland-Virginia boundary. Eventually, the North Branch (now commonly referred to simply as the Potomac) was accepted as the "true" Potomac; had the South Branch been accepted, Maryland would have been a much larger state. The South Branch, which has its headwaters high in the Virginia mountains, flows northward through West Virginia to reach this point.

Oldtown to Cumberland
(miles 166–184)

Length: *19 miles*
Elevation change: *35 feet*
Level: *easy*
USGS quad maps: *Oldtown, MD–WV; Patterson Creek, MD–WV; Cresaptown, WV–MD; Cumberland, MD–PA–WV*

The canal passes through rugged mountain terrain in its final stretch. Oldtown may have been the site of the Warrior's Path, a historic Indian trail, although some historians dispute this claim. A group of Shawnee settled here in 1692, but by the time that Thomas Cresap and other white settlers arrived here in the 1740s, the natives had moved on. Nevertheless, the area was known as Shawnee Old Town for some time afterward. Like many early houses in this region, Cresap's resembled a fort more than a home. The structure was a landmark on the road to Fort Cumberland, and a teenaged George Washington spent five nights there in March 1748 while high water on the Potomac delayed his surveying chores. Only a stone chimney remains of Cresap's original house, but his second home, partially restored, still stands on Main Street in Oldtown.

Locks 69 (Twiggs Lock) and 70 (Oldtown Lock) lie above mile 166.4. To reach the Oldtown area from Cumberland, follow Route 51 southeast. From Lock 70, a road leads to the only privately owned bridge across the Potomac, a low-slung single-lane wooden structure that may test your nerve a bit. The owners collect their modest toll in an old tin can welded to an iron handle.

Pass Lock 71 at mile 167.0 and Pigmans Ferry Hiker-Biker Overnighter at mile 169.1. Spring Gap Recreation Area, at mile 173.3, offers primitive camping sites, a picnic area, and a boat ramp. A post office and general store are nearby on MD-51 in Spring Gap.

At mile 174.4 is Lock 72 (the Narrows), which can be reached from MD-51. Canal, highway, and railroad squeeze through this gap, not to be confused with the better-known Narrows near Cumberland. A mile upstream from the Narrows are Locks 73–75 and the Irons Mountain Hiker-Biker Overnighter. Lock 75 is the last numbered lock on the canal as it approaches Cumberland.

Evitts Creek Aqueduct, at mile 180.7, is the last and smallest of the canal aqueducts, completed in 1840. The structure is in poor condition, with both ends partially collapsed.

At mile 181.7 the towpath enters an unattractive area bordered by a sewage disposal plant, and hiking the remaining towpath into Cumberland can be a disappointing experience. Beyond mile 183.5, little remains of the old canal structure, most of which was obliterated by a 1950s flood-control project.

The Cumberland Basin, at mile 184, was drained and filled many years ago and is now host to some nondescript industrial development. But in the last century, Cumberland Basin was a boisterous waterfront district catering to canal and railroad workers, and many canal families lived on their boats here during the winter months. The original towpath is long gone; follow the railroad right-of-way to the canal's end.

C&O Canal, MD —
Lock 18 near Great Falls

The C&O's western terminus comes at mile 184. All that remains of this historic point are ruins of the guard and inlet locks, now mostly buried under a railroad trestle. Access is just downstream from the Western Maryland railroad station, which offers scenic rail tours.

Platted in 1787, Cumberland was an important stop on the National Road. The early road took various routes, but in 1834 it was extended up Wills Creek and through the Narrows, the route still followed by present-day US-40. The Cumberland portion of the C&O Canal opened in October 1850, more than two decades after construction began at Georgetown. The railroad had reached Cumberland eight years earlier, rendering the canal obsolete even before it opened. Tentative plans to extend the canal to Pittsburgh were scuttled after 1874, when it was determined that the projected canal right-of-way had already been claimed by the rival Baltimore & Ohio Railroad.

Once a bustling mining, manufacturing, and transportation center, Cumberland fell victim to hard times during the Depression and again in the 1970s and 1980s when several major industries moved away. Today, with a population of 23,000, Cumberland shows signs of economic recovery, fueled to some extent by tourist dollars.

Nearby Attractions

THE NARROWS—

On Route 40-A west of Cumberland, this rugged water gap through the front ridge of the Alleghenies has been an important transportation corridor since pioneer time. Public access to the cliffs is now uncertain; inquire locally.

ROCKY GAP STATE PARK—

Six miles east of Cumberland on I-68, Rocky Gap is a high-profile park that Maryland is attempting to promote as a major tourist and convention destination. The park boasts a 243-acre man-made lake, swimming beaches, boat rentals, picnic areas, developed campground (reservations recommended), and hiking trails.

DANS MOUNTAIN STATE PARK—

A somewhat underused park on Route 36, 2 miles southeast of Lonaconing, MD, Dans Mountain offers fishing, a swimming pool, a picnic area, and hiking trails. Unfortunately, Dans Rock, a prominent sandstone ledge affording sweeping views from the Allegheny Front, is outside of the park boundaries, and public access is now uncertain; inquire locally.

Great Falls, MD — C&O Canal runoff below Rocky Island

Chapter 2

GREAT FALLS (MARYLAND/VIRGINIA)

The parks at Great Falls straddle the Fall Line, the rocky ledge marking the end of the level coastal plain and beginning of the hilly piedmont region. Here the Potomac drops 76 feet within a quarter-mile in a series of wild falls and rapids.

The Maryland and Virginia parks at Great Falls are separate entities—the Maryland side is actually a part of the C&O Canal National Historical Park—and there is no link directly connecting the two parks. To visit both, you'll need to backtrack to the Capital Beltway (I-495). Both parks are open year-round from 9 A.M. until dark; neither allow camping or overnight stays. Although both sides offer outstanding scenery, the best view of the main falls is from Virginia.

The area's rugged setting may belie its proximity to the nation's capital, but the crowds will quickly remind you of where you are. Arrive early to ensure a parking space on holidays and weekends in all but the worst weather. A weekday or wintertime visit is usually more rewarding.

History

In the autumn of 1631, Henry Fleet anchored his vessel in the river somewhere near present-day Georgetown and rowed a shallop upstream to within earshot of Great Falls. There, the English sailor pronounced, "this place without all question is the most pleasant and healthful place in all this country. The Indians in one night commonly will catch thirty sturgeons. ... As for deer, buffaloes, bears, turkeys, the woods do swarm with them, and the soil is exceedingly fertile." Other European newcomers shared Fleet's enthusiasm, and expanding settlement soon drove away the native Anacostia, an Algonquin-speaking tribe that controlled trade at the head of the navigable Potomac.

George Washington established the Patowmack Company in 1784 with the intention of skirting the worst obstacles on the Potomac and opening its upper reaches to navigation. Work began on canals skirting Maryland's Little Falls and Virginia's Great Falls in 1785, and for the next seventeen years the Patowmack Company dredged channels and built other short canals around impassable falls and rapids on the upper Potomac. When work was finally completed, boatmen were able to float rafts and flat-bottom barges from western Maryland to Georgetown in several days. The Patowmack Company, however, had failed to provide a practical route for the return trip, and the boatmen usually scuttled their vessels at Georgetown and returned home on foot or horseback rather than battle heavy currents. Today, the Patowmack Company's canal bed and several lift-locks remain on the Virginia side of Great Falls; on the Maryland side, part of the Little Falls canal was incorporated into the later Chesapeake & Ohio structure.

Opening of the C&O Canal in the 1830s attracted industry to the Great Falls area, and a small gold strike brought another brief flurry of development along the Maryland side in the nineteenth century. But by 1900 it was obvious that the canal could not compete with the railroad. As the mines and mills closed, a tourist industry developed in their stead, and in 1913 a trolley excursion line was run to the falls from Washington. The canal's structures began to deteriorate, and operations were finally suspended after the disastrous 1924 flood. Today, a portion of the C&O Canal south of Great Falls Tavern has been restored to operating condition, and mule-drawn barges now haul sightseers instead of coal or grain.

Natural Features

Rock at the falls is primarily metagraywacke, a fine-grained and highly erosion-resistant blue-gray metamorphic rock that was shattered and weakened during a period of uplift approximately 2 million years ago. As sea levels fell and the weakened underlying rock was uplifted, the Potomac crashed down an increasingly steep slope, carving the deep, sheer-sided canyon known to-

Great Falls, MD —
Rocky Island erosion patterns

day as Mather Gorge. The power of the ancient Potomac must have been awe-inspiring; geologists have traced some of the massive boulders below Mather Gorge to outcroppings more than 30 miles upstream.

The gorge extends along a fault line for more than a mile downstream from Great Falls before widening as the Potomac approaches the tidewater region. As the river cut deeper, old side-channels were left on slopes high above the present-day riverbed. You can see one of these abandoned channels at Widewater on the C&O Canal, where engineers flooded an old ravine to create a long, narrow lake.

Despite its proximity to a sprawling metropolitan area, Great Falls offers a tremendous variety of flora and fauna. A mature eastern hardwood forest flourishes on the upper slopes, while sycamore, elm, boxelder, and jimson weed dominate the floodplain. The scattered islands support chestnut oak, Virginia pine, cedar, and other vegetation that can survive in thin, sandy soil. Marshes, ponds, and side-channels are home to heron and an interesting population of waterfowl, reptiles, and amphibians. Poisonous copperheads, as well as many nonpoisonous snake species, are common here.

Nearby Attractions

CABIN JOHN TRAIL—

This greenbelt trail winds its way through the suburban sprawl surrounding the Cabin John Creek Valley. The trail begins at the junction of MacArthur Boulevard and Cabin John Parkway, leading to a point near the junction of Montrose Road and Washington National Pike.

RIVER BEND PARK—

Administered by Fairfax County, River Bend adjoins the northern border of Great Falls Park in Virginia and boasts a marina and nature center. To reach the park, follow the directions to Great Falls, but continue past the entrance to Great Falls Park on Route 193 to a right turn onto River Bend Road. Follow River Bend Road to the park entrance.

ROCK CREEK PARK—

See the C&O Canal chapter.

Access

To reach the Maryland park, take I-495 (Capital Beltway) to George Washington Memorial Parkway, the last exit on the Maryland side of the Potomac. Follow the Parkway west, eventually merging onto MacArthur Boulevard, and continue along MacArthur to its end at the visitor center. A parking fee is charged. If you want to avoid the parking fee, use the free parking area on MacArthur Boulevard opposite the Old Angler's Inn, about 3 miles north of I-495. There are also small parking pull-outs scattered along the south side of MacArthur Boulevard. On holidays and weekends, these spots are often filled by mid-morning.

To reach the Virginia side, take the first exit on the Virginia side of the Potomac (Route 193, Georgetown Pike). Drive 6 miles north, turn right at the well-marked park entrance on Old Dominion Drive, and continue another 1.3 miles to the visitor center. A parking fee is charged.

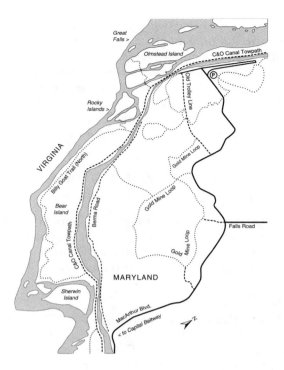

Trail Guide:
GREAT FALLS (MARYLAND SIDE)

Berma Road

Length: *1.5 miles*
Elevation change: *none*
Level: *easy*
USGS quad map: *Falls Church, VA*
Access: *Southern terminus is at the western end of the parking area opposite the Old Angler's Inn on MacArthur Boulevard. Northern terminus is reached via a footbridge just upstream from Lock 16 on the C&O Canal towpath. The road is closed to motorized vehicles.*

The Berma road is a pleasant path through open woods on a bluff above the C&O Canal, offering a less-crowded alternative to the C&O towpath. (The name—shown incorrectly as "Burma" on some maps—is probably a corruption of the word "berm," the side of a canal opposite the towpath.)

This wide, level road follows the top of a nineteenth-century masonry conduit supplying water to Washington, D.C., and passes near the site of a modest nineteenth-century gold strike. Streams in the region still occasionally yield flakes and tiny nuggets. Old quarries and mine shafts (now sealed), evidence of Civil War gun emplacements, and a network of abandoned trails and railroad grades make this a fascinating area to explore.

From the parking area on MacArthur Boulevard, the Berma Road leads west through open woods overlooking the C&O Canal. At 0.2 mile, pass a yellow-blazed side trail that leads a half-mile uphill to the Gold Mine Trail (see entry in this chapter). The road then skirts high above Widewater and passes another yellow-blazed connector to the Gold Mine Trail at 1.2 miles. Continue an additional quarter-mile to the footbridge near restored Lock 17 and the ruins of an 1837 lock keeper's house. Return the way you came, or cross the canal and return on the towpath.

Billy Goat Trail

Length: *1.6 miles (northern section), 1.4 miles (central section), 1.6 miles (southern section)*

Elevation change: *less than 100 feet*

Level: *easy (southern and central sections); moderately difficult (northern section)*

USGS quad map: *Falls Church, VA*

Access: *Northern section—Park at the visitor center and walk approximately 0.5 miles south on the C&O Canal towpath. The north trailhead is just south of milepost 14; the south trailhead is near milepost 13, opposite Widewater. Central section—North trailhead is on the C&O towpath near the parking areas opposite the Old Angler's Inn on MacArthur Boulevard. South trailhead is on the C&O towpath north of milepost 11. Southern section—North trailhead is on the C&O towpath near milepost 11. South trailhead is on the towpath opposite the U.S. Naval Reservation and 0.3 miles north of Lock 14.*

The Billy Goat Trail is actually three separate riverside trails linked by short stretches of the C&O Canal towpath. The sections can be hiked individually or combined for a strenuous one-way hike of 6 miles.

The northern section is the oldest and most scenic portion of the Billy Goat Trail, winding through varied, rugged terrain in Mather Gorge. From its north trailhead, the path enters open woods above the head of the gorge. Wander off the main trail for spectacular views of the river and cliffs from boulders

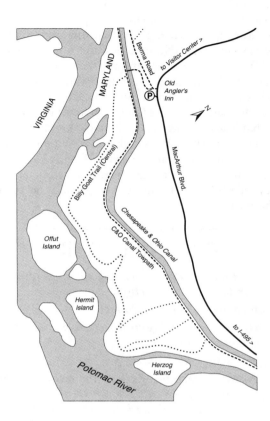

scattered among the trees. A rough unmarked trail leads down the cliffs, providing access to the Rocky Islands (see entry) when water levels are low. The Billy Goat Trail then turns east on the sheer cliffs above Mather Gorge. This section requires some elementary rock scrambling, and at some points you can work your way to spectacular rocky perches high above the river. The trail eventually descends to a sandy beach, where portions of the trail may be impassable in times of high water. From the beach, the trail makes a steep climb up a slippery ledge and then meanders, with many ups and downs, among massive boulders and intriguing marshes and side-channels. An informal network of short, unmarked side trails will encourage you to explore. At 1.3 miles, the trail swings north to join the C&O Canal towpath opposite Widewater. Back at the towpath, turn left for an easy stroll along the canal and back to the Great Falls Visitor Center parking area, or continue downstream on the towpath to the trail's central section.

The central section of the Billy Goat trail is not as difficult as the northern, although the path is often muddy and may be hard to follow in spots.

But you can't really get lost, being wedged between river and canal. The trail passes several small inlets and islands before making a sharp switchback at midpoint to skirt a ravine opposite Hermit Island. Near its end, the trail turns sharply to the north to rejoin the towpath. At the towpath, turn left to return to the visitor center or right to continue to the southern section of the Billy Goat Trail.

The southern section is an easy stroll through the popular Carderock Recreation Area. From its north trailhead, the path skirts a quiet side-channel of the Potomac, then descends to river level at Stubblefield Falls, a series of rapids popular with kayakers. This section of the trail is also popular with anglers and may be crowded on weekends and holidays. The trail continues downstream from Carderock, mostly near the shoreline, before making a sharp turn to the north to reconnect with the C&O Canal towpath near Lock 14.

C&O Canal Towpath—
See the C&O Canal chapter

Gold Mine Trail

Length: *2 miles (excluding access trails)*

Elevation change: *less than 100 feet*

Level: *easy*

USGS quad map: *Falls Church, VA*

Access: *The Gold Mine Trail is a loop that can be reached by several access trails: (1) two yellow-blazed trails on the Berma Road (see entry), one at 0.2 mile from the MacArthur Boulevard parking area, and the other at 1.2 miles from the parking area; (2) several yellow-blazed trails on the south side of MacArthur Boulevard; (3) the blue-blazed Old Trolley Line Trail (see entry), which begins near Lock 20 and the Great Falls Visitor Center. This area contains a maze of game paths, trails, and old roads, many unmarked. Although it is too compact an area to get seriously lost in, a reliable map and compass may prove handy.*

The Gold Mine Trail is an easy stroll, with only minor ups and downs, through open woods. The site of a nineteenth-century gold mine lies at approximately midpoint on the loop, near the junction of MacArthur Boulevard and Falls Road, although little evidence of the operation remains.

Old Trolley Line Trail

Length: *0.6 mile*

Elevation change: *less than 100 feet*

Level: *easy*

USGS quad map: *Falls Church, VA*

Access: *East trailhead is on MacArthur Boulevard 0.6 miles west of Falls Road. West trailhead is near Lock 20 and the Great Falls Visitor Center (parking fee required).*

This is an easy stroll linking the Gold Mine Trail and C&O towpath. As its name implies, the trail follows the railbed of an old excursion trolley line that ran from Washington to Great Falls until 1921. From the visitor center, the trail makes a short, steep climb to the site of the trolley turnaround, then follows the level right-of-way through mostly open woods. At a half-mile from the visitor center is a junction with the Gold Mine Trail. The MacArthur Boulevard trailhead, a short distance beyond the Gold Mine junction, is a popular access point for park visitors wishing to avoid the visitor center parking fee.

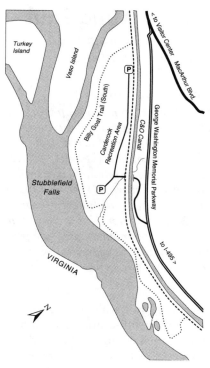

Olmstead–Falls Islands Trail

Length: *0.5 mile*
Elevation change: *50 feet*
Level: *easy*
USGS quad map: *Falls Church, VA (not shown)*
Access: *From the C&O Canal towpath between Locks 17 and 18, south of the visitor center. The January 1996 flood washed away the bridges linking this trail to the shore. They will eventually be rebuilt, but as this guide goes to press, the trail remains inaccessible.*

This trail crosses rugged, wooded terrain on Olmstead and Falls Islands to a spectacular overlook of the main falls.

Rocky Islands Scramble

Length: *0.5–2 miles*
Elevation change: *50 feet*
Level: *moderately difficult*
USGS quad map: *Falls Church, VA (not shown)*
Access: *From the north end of the Billy Goat Trail (see entry).*

Precautions: The Park Service discourages this hike, but so far it hasn't restricted access to the islands. Don't attempt this crossing unless the water level is exceptionally low and you can make the entire crossing on dry rocks. Currents here are treacherous in times of normal and above-normal flow, and many drownings have occurred. Swimming, wading, and boating are prohibited. River levels can rise quickly after a storm, leaving you stranded. The Park Service now charges for rescue services at Great Falls.

This is a rough and potentially dangerous scramble to two rugged islands in the Potomac. Read the precautions above and proceed only if you have the skills and common sense to continue safely. Begin on a primitive unmarked footpath leading steeply downhill from the cliffs at the northern end of the Billy Goat Trail. At river's edge, if water levels are low, you will see an obvious, rocky route to the islands. During normal flow, the rocks are mostly submerged. Don't cross unless the route is clearly above water and the rocks are dry. The rocks are dangerously slippery when wet.

The Rocky Islands are two jagged outcroppings in the Potomac that offer outstanding opportunities for bushwhacking, rock scrambling, or just escaping the crowds. There's no formal trail; once on the islands, you can explore at will. Views from the exposed spines are unlike any others in the park. You'll see evidence of floods along the island's highest ridges, where the Potomac has left behind sand, logs, shells, and debris.

Trail Guide:
GREAT FALLS (VIRGINIA SIDE)

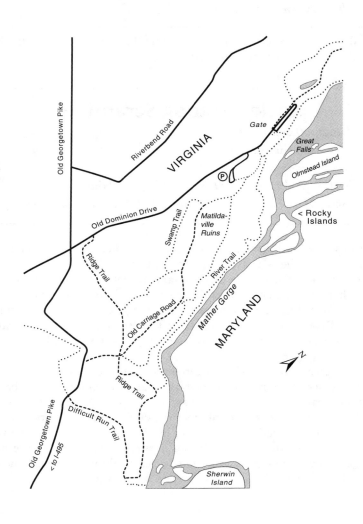

Difficult Run Trail

Length: *1.2 miles (from Old Dominion Drive trailhead)*
Elevation change: *150 feet*
Level: *moderate*
USGS quad map: *Falls Church, VA*
Access: *Trailheads are located on Old Dominion Drive and Old Georgetown Pike. Limited parking is available at both trailheads.*

From the trailhead on Old Dominion Drive, the Difficult Run bears east through open woods, crossing Old Georgetown Pike at 0.6 mile. Beyond Old Georgetown Pike, the trail joins an old fire road for a short distance, then descends steeply along Difficult Run on a rough footpath leading to a narrow beach at river's edge. Return as you came, or turn onto the Ridge Trail for a longer return loop.

Old Carriage Road

Length: *1.8 miles*
Elevation change: *insignificant*
Level: *easy*
USGS quad map: *Falls Church, VA*
Access: *From the Great Falls Visitor Center.*

The Old Carriage Road is an easy loop hike past the ruins of Matildaville. "Light Horse Harry" Lee, hero of the Revolutionary War, invested heavily in the Patowmack Company project, anticipating a development boom along the canal in Virginia. In 1790 he platted the town of Matildaville, named for his wife, and the town flourished for a time. But the Patowmack Company suspended operations as the C&O Canal neared completion across the river in Maryland, and Matildaville eventually fell into ruin.

At the Matildaville site, the trail forks. To the right, it leads south through open woods, makes a sharp bend at an old quarry site, then loops north along the Patowmack Company Canal, on the bank opposite the River Trail. At about a half-mile from the quarry site, the trail returns to the fork at Matildaville.

Ridge Trail

Length: *1.8 miles*
Elevation change: *50 feet*
Level: *easy*
USGS quad map: *Falls Church, VA*
Access: *From Old Dominion Drive approximately 0.2 mile north of Route 193. Parking is limited.*

From Old Dominion Drive, a short spur of the Ridge Trail leads northwest to end in a half-mile at River Bend Road. The main trail leads east toward the river through open woods. At about three-quarters of a mile from the trailhead, the Ridge Trail makes a short jog to the north, turns east again, then veers to the southeast to end at Difficult Run near its confluence with the Potomac.

River Trail

Length: *1.8 miles (south section); 1.5 miles (north section)*
Elevation change: *insignificant*
Level: *easy*
USGS quad map: *Falls Church, VA*
Access: *From the visitor center parking area, walk toward the river. You will intersect the River Trail, which follows George Washington's Patowmack Canal both north and south from this point.*

South of the visitor center, the River Trail parallels the old canal for a half-mile, then crosses it to continue south along the high cliffs of Mather Gorge. This is a popular, and often crowded, section of the trail, affording fine views across the gorge. Technical climbing is allowed, subject to Park Service regulations; check in at the visitor center. A mile from the visitor center, a spur trail descends to a sandy beach in Mather Gorge. The main trail continues south to Cow Hoof Rock, a popular overlook, then continues a short distance to its intersection with the Ridge Trail.

North of the visitor center, the River Trail follows the Patowmack Canal for a half-mile to its intake at the Potomac. From there, the trail follows the Potomac shore above the main falls, providing spectacular views of the river and Rocky Islands. The trail continues north into adjacent River Bend Park, ending at the nature center.

Part Two

THE
LONG TRAILS

Appalachian Trail, Shenandoah N.P. — Mount Marshall

The Long Trails

Two long-distance trails—the Appalachian and the Big Blue—wind through the mountains west of Washington, D.C. Both trails are suitable for hikes of any length, from an easy afternoon stroll to a grueling backpacking trip. Both are works-in-progress, and minor rerouting occurs from time to time.

The Maine-to-Georgia Appalachian Trail presents a 2,000-mile challenge that only a hardy few have completed. In Maryland and northern Virginia, the AT stays at or near the top of the Blue Ridge, dipping only briefly to follow the Potomac near Harpers Ferry. Its passage through Shenandoah National Park leads to panoramic views and links hundreds of miles of side trails.

The Big Blue was conceived as an alternative to the AT at a time when that trail's route through northern Virginia seemed threatened by development and private land closure. Beginning at the C&O Canal near Hancock, MD, the Big Blue makes a 144-mile trek to connect with the AT in Shenandoah National Park. Although not as popular as the AT, the Big Blue has some spectacular moments as it passes through rugged and isolated terrain along the western edge of the Shenandoah Valley.

The guide provides a general overview of both trails, with the most convenient access points noted. Long-distance hikers should contact the Potomac Appalachian Trail Club (see Appendix I) for the latest updates and more detailed information.

Appalachian Trail, Shenandoah N.P. — Blackrock

Appalachian Trail, Shenandoah N.P. — Blackrock

Chapter 3

THE APPALACHIAN TRAIL
(MARYLAND TO CENTRAL VIRGINIA)

Arguably America's most famous footpath, the Appalachian Trail (AT) follows the spine of the eastern mountains for 2,000 miles, linking Stone Mountain, GA, to Katahdin, ME. Conceived by Benton MacKaye in 1921, the trail caught the imagination of a public that was growing concerned about the loss of America's eastern wilderness. By the mid-1920s, volunteers were at work on a project that is still under way.

In the six decades that have passed since then, the integrity of the Appalachian Trail has been threatened by private landowners, developers, and members of Congress. And yet the trail survives, with occasional minor rerouting, kept in shape by a devoted corps of volunteers and supported by countless millions who have set foot on it, if only briefly, and decided that it is something worth preserving.

The AT in Maryland follows the low, narrow ridge of South Mountain through pleasant open woodland before making a steep drop to the Potomac at Weverton Cliffs. From there, the trail abruptly changes character, following the C&O Canal towpath for 2.5 miles to Harpers Ferry, WV. After passing through the town (headquarters of the Appalachian Trail Conference), the AT finds its way back to the ridge top on Loudoun Heights. There follows a section that is being badly squeezed by real estate development, but the trail eventually reenters more isolated surroundings. South of Manassas Gap and I-66, the AT has been forced onto roads in spots, but the situation improves south of Front Royal as the trail makes a steep climb to regain the ridge at Compton Gap in Shenandoah National Park. The trail through the park, much of it originally blazed in the 1920s and 1930s, is a Blue Ridge classic that everyone should experience.

Trail Guide:

Pen-Mar Park to C&O Canal

Length: *40.5 miles*

Elevation change: *1,580 feet*

Level: *moderate*

USGS quad maps: *Harpers Ferry, VA–MD–WV; Keedysville, MD*

Access: *Northern access is from Pennsylvania Route 16 near the crest of South Mountain east of Waynesboro, PA. Southern access is from Lock 31 on the C&O Canal (see next section). Other convenient access points in Maryland are Greenbrier State Park near I-70, Washington Monument State Park near Alternate Route 40, and Gathland State Park north of US-340. There are many other access points on back roads; inquire locally.*

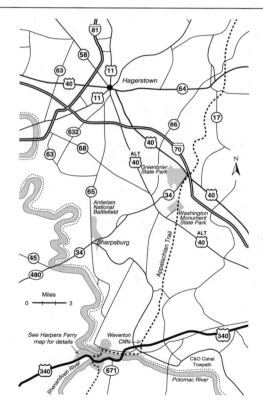

From Pen-Mar Park, just north of the Pennsylvania-Maryland border, the Appalachian Trail enters Maryland and swings east to climb 2000-foot Quirauck Mountain, highest point on the trail between Maryland and northern Connecticut. From Quirauck, it drops to 1,300 feet to resume its southward course along the crest of South Mountain, where it will stay for most of its trek through Maryland. After passing through boulder-strewn Devil's Racecourse, the trail has some ups and downs as it crosses Raven Rock Hollow, Warner Gap, and Harman Gap.

From Harman Gap, the AT continues 13 miles to Turner's Gap, crossing I-70 and passing through Washington Monument State Park. A popular day-use area, the park is the site of a stone tower said to be the first monument built to Washington. The structure, which resembles the old lime kilns and blast furnaces common to this area, is a Depression-era reconstruction and offers a panoramic view from the western slope of South Mountain. South of the park, the AT crosses Alternate Route 40, a portion of the historic National Road.

South of Alternate 40, the AT continues to Crampton Gap, site of some intense Civil War fighting. The trail descends to Gathland State Park, then regains the ridge for a 6-mile stretch to Weverton Cliffs. The cliffs offers a spectacular view across the Potomac and mark the end of the Blue Ridge in Maryland. Continue downhill on steep switchbacks below the cliffs and, once on relatively level ground, follow the blazes south to the C&O Canal towpath.

C&O Canal
to Loudoun Heights

Length: *approximately 6 miles*

Elevation change: *800 feet*

Level: *moderate*

USGS quad maps: *Harpers Ferry, VA–MD–WV; Charles Town, WV*

Access: *Northern access is from Lock 31 (Weverton Lock), at mile 58.1 on the C&O Canal towpath. To reach the lock, take the Route 67 exit from westbound US-340, immediately turn left and cross US-340, then follow the road for approximately a half-mile to a parking area near the railroad crossing. Southern access is from the Shenandoah River bridge on US-340 near Harpers Ferry National Historical Park (see the Harpers Ferry chapter).*

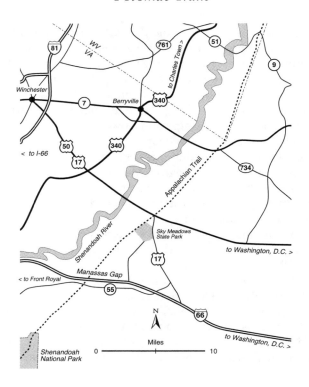

Having dropped to river level from Weverton Cliffs, the AT joins the C&O Canal towpath for the next 2.5 miles. At the foot of Maryland Heights, the AT leaves the towpath to cross the Potomac on a pedestrian walkway on the downstream railroad bridge. The walkway was closed after the January 1996 flood. In the event that it hasn't been rebuilt by the time you read this, you will have to backtrack to the Potomac River bridge and follow US-340 to the Shenandoah River bridge.

Once in Harpers Ferry, the well-marked AT follows a graveled footpath into the main historic district. Once there, it turns left on Shenandoah Street and right on High Street. From High Street, the trail climbs a set of rough steps chiseled into the bedrock and then follows a low cliff paralleling the Shenandoah. Jefferson Rock, the former Storer College campus (founded in 1867 to educate freed slaves), Harper Cemetery, and other historic points of interest lie just off the trail. The AT then drops to US-340 and crosses the Shenandoah River on the highway bridge. At the far end of the bridge, the trail turns uphill to regain the ridge for the first time since leaving Maryland. Loudoun Heights, the southern continuation of the main Blue Ridge, is also the unmarked Virginia–West Virginia border, which you will follow for some distance in the next section.

54

Loudoun Heights to Shenandoah National Park

Length: *48 miles*

Elevation change: *1,400 feet*

Level: *moderate*

USGS quad maps: *Ashby Gap, VA; Front Royal, VA; Harpers Ferry, VA–MD–WV; Charles Town, WV–VA; Round Hill, WV–VA*

Access: *Northern access is from US-340 on the Virginia side of the Shenandoah River bridge. Southern access is at Compton Gap (mile 10.4 on Skyline Drive) in Shenandoah National Park. Other convenient access points are Route 7 midway between Leesburg and Berryville, VA; Sky Meadows State Park, south of US-50; I-66 in Manassas Gap; and Route 522 south of Front Royal, VA.*

In this section, the AT continues south along the main spur of the Blue Ridge. Views from the ridge show how seriously the trail is threatened by nearby development. In some areas the trail right-of-way is in danger of becoming little more than a narrow easement between housing developments.

Twelve miles from Harpers Ferry, the AT passes the Blackburn Trail Center, which offers campsites to Potomac Appalachian Trail Club members only. Beyond the center, the AT climbs into more rugged country before entering Virginia. Beyond Route 7 and Snickers Gap, the AT is routed well down the slope to avoid military installations on the crest of the Blue Ridge. The trail continues south, crosses US-50, then passes through Sky Meadows State Park and the Thompson Wildlife Management Area, both of which offer primitive campsites.

South of Route 55, parts of the AT have been diverted onto back roads, making for some monotonous walking. But after crossing US-522, the AT regains the high country, making a steady climb to the crest of the Blue Ridge and entering Shenandoah National Park just below Compton Gap. Continue to climb to the AT's first of many crossings of Skyline Drive, the scenic ridge-top road that connects to the Blue Ridge.

The Appalachian Trail in Shenandoah National Park

Once on the crest of the Blue Ridge in Shenandoah National Park, the Appalachian Trail crosses Skyline Drive at least 29 times before finally leaving the park north of Rockfish Gap. The drive's presence is a mixed blessing, detracting from the trail's wilderness qualities but allowing easy access to the park's outstanding network of side trails. In this section, access points are keyed to Skyline Drive mileposts, which are placed along the drive at every mile beginning with 0.0 in Front Royal. They are included as a convenient way of locating trail crossings, but they do not reflect actual trail distances.

Shenandoah National Park (North Section): Compton Gap to Thornton Gap

Length: *32.5 miles*

Elevation change: *2,915 feet*

Level: *moderate (strenuous in spots)*

USGS quad maps: *Bentonville, VA; Chester Gap, VA; Front Royal, VA; Thornton Gap, VA*

Access: *From Skyline Drive at mile 10.4 (Compton Gap), 12.4 (Jenkins Gap), 14.2 (Hogwallow Flats), 15.9, 17.6 (Gravel Springs Gap), 18.9, 19.4, 21.1, 23.9 (near Elkwallow Wayside), 28.5 (Beahms Gap), and 31.4 (Thornton Gap at US-211).*

The Appalachian Trail regains the crest of the Blue Ridge at Compton Gap, which marks the junction of the main Blue Ridge with Dickey Ridge, the outlier that carries Skyline Drive from Front Royal. After crossing the Drive at mile 10.4, the AT makes a 0.8-mile climb to Compton Peak, where a short spur leads to a good viewpoint. The trail then descends to Jenkins Gap; avoid an eroded and overgrown trail branch leading steeply downhill to private land. The AT continues to Hogwallow Flats before climbing North Mount Marshall, where a short unmarked trail leads to an open outcropping with a spectacular view southward along the main spine of the Blue Ridge. From there, the AT makes an easy descent to Skyline Drive.

The AT crosses Skyline Drive at mile 15.9, in the saddle between North and South Mount Marshall, before climbing to the summit of South Mount Marshall. Although there are no views from the heavily wooded summit, a short side-trail below the peak leads to a good view similar to that from North Mount Marshall.

Gravel Springs Gap, at Skyline Drive mile 17.6, was once famous for the moonshine whiskey produced nearby. The old trail intersecting the AT here is the Browntown–Harris Hollow Road, a historic mountain crossing now maintained as an access road to Gravel Springs Shelter. The Jinney Gray Fire

Road, on the opposite side of Skyline Drive at mile 19.4, leads south toward Fork Mountain and can be used for access to Little Devils Stairs. The AT continues west, following Skyline Drive, to Little Hogback Mountain, with its sweeping views of the Browntown and Shenandoah Valleys backed by the long ridge of Massanutten Mountain.

The AT crosses Skyline Drive again at mile 21.1, on Hogback Mountain. This is your access to the Overall Run Trail and the southern terminus of the Big Blue Trail. From Hogback, the AT takes off to the east, skirting well away from Skyline Drive for nearly 3 miles in one of its longest uninterrupted stretches within the park. It returns to Skyline Drive at mile 23.9, near the Elkwallow Wayside, then shifts to the western slope, passing access to the Jeremy's Run Trail, the Neighbor Mountain Trail, and Byrd's Nest Shelter #4.

At the Beahms Gap crossing (mile 28.5 on Skyline Drive), the AT returns to the eastern slope, skirting well to the east of Skyline Drive for the next 3 miles. This section crosses the summit of Pass Mountain, passing occasional viewpoints, before descending to Thornton Gap at the end of the park's north section. The AT crosses Skyline Drive and passes the Panorama development on US-211 (restaurant, restrooms, telephone, gift shop, drinking water, and gas station in season). US-211 descends to Sperryville to the east and Luray to the west.

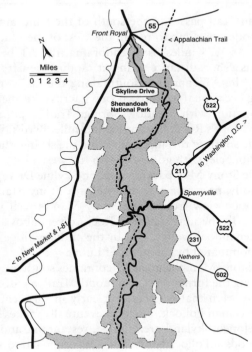

Shenandoah National Park (Central Section): Thornton Gap to Swift Run Gap

Length: *34 miles*
Elevation change: *1,350 feet*
Level: *moderate (strenuous in spots)*
USGS quad maps: *Big Meadows, VA; Fletcher, VA; Old Rag, VA; Thornton Gap, VA*
Access: *From Skyline Drive at mile 31.5, 37.9 (via Shaver Hollow Shelter service road), 39.1, 43.3, 44.4, 45.5 (Hawksbill Gap), 49.4 (Fishers Gap north of Big Meadows Campground), 51.4 (via service road), 52.8, 55.1, 56.5 (Bearfence Mountain), 59.5 (via Pocosin Fire Road), 60.2, 61.8, 62.8, 63.1 (via South River Shelter service road), and 65.5 (Swift Run Gap at US-33). The trail also connects to the Big Meadows and Lewis Mountain campgrounds.*

The Appalachian Trail passes to the south of the Panorama parking area, then begins a moderate climb to regain the crest of the Blue Ridge south of Thornton Gap. At 1.75 miles from Panorama, the AT bears south (left), while a spur leads a short distance to an outstanding view from Mary's Rock. From that fork, the AT continues south along the main spine of the Blue Ridge, affording occasional overgrown views across the Shenandoah Valley, and passes a junction with Meadow Springs Trail, a popular route from Skyline Drive to Mary's Rock, in another half-mile. Byrd's Nest Shelter #3 is another half-mile south of this junction. From the shelter, the AT crosses the summit of the Pinnacle, with good views to the west.

From the Little Stony Man parking area on Skyline Drive (mile 39.1), the trail climbs steadily, passing a side trail to Little Stony Man Cliffs within a half-mile. The open view from Little Stony Man is well worth the short additional climb. To the north, Mary's Rock towers above Thornton Gap; to the west is Shenandoah Valley, split by the outlying ridge of Massanutten Mountain and dominated by the town of Luray.

Beyond Little Stony Man, the main AT continues south toward the Skyland development along the former Passamaquoddy Trail, a cliff-hanging path at the foot of Stony Man that was laid out early in this century by Skyland owner George Freeman Pollock. The trail eventually makes its way through the heavily developed Skyland area (lodge, restaurant, and stables) before reentering the woods at Pollock Knob. Pollock's original resort, which boasted some wonderfully eccentric architecture, was demolished in the 1930s and 1940s in favor of the drab government buildings you see today.

Crescent Rock, on Skyline Drive at mile 44.4, was the site of outdoor religious revival meetings before the coming of the park. The practice continued for some time under Park Service management; thus, the sprawling parking lot. A mile beyond Crescent Rock is Hawksbill Gap (mile 45.5 on Skyline Drive). From the gap, the AT makes a steady ascent, passing the first of several interesting talus slopes about a half-mile west of the parking area. At 1.4 miles from the parking area, a spur leads north to Nakedtop, an isolated knob affording only overgrown views but some level backcountry campsites. From the Nakedtop Trail junction, the AT makes a steady ascent to the summit of Hawksbill Mountain, highest point in the park (4,050 feet). Hawksbill offers a 360-degree view, but Park Service development and hordes of tourists rob the peak of any wilderness quality.

The AT crosses Skyline Drive at Fishers Gap at mile 49.4. The AT has approached the gap from the north, passing excellent viewpoints along the lower tier of Franklin Cliffs. South of Fishers Gap, the AT veers west and begins a steady, moderate climb to Big Meadows Campground. The trail skirts the Big Meadows development along the western edge of Blackrock Mountain (not to be confused with Blackrock in the park's southern section). Near the campground amphitheater, Lewis Falls Trails branches west, leading downhill to an interesting (but sometimes nearly dry) waterfall on Hawksbill Creek. Continue south for excellent views of the Shenandoah Valley and Blue Ridge from a high outcropping just off the AT near Big Meadows Lodge.

South of Big Meadows, the AT crosses Skyline Drive at Milam Gap, a former orchard area where some old apple trees still survive. A surprising number still bear fruit despite decades of neglect. South of Milam Gap, the AT skirts the summit of Bearfence Mountain, where a short side-trail leads to an easy scramble over the rocky summit of Bearfence, affording good views from a high outcropping. With easy access from the road, this is a popular short hike, and the area is often crowded on weekends and holidays.

South of mile 57.5, the AT skirts the former Lewis Mountain Campground, opened in 1940 and originally operated as a campground "for Negroes," to quote from early park literature. The campgrounds were later integrated, and today Lewis Mountain is a quieter and more intimate alternative to the sprawling Big Meadows complex. Two miles south of the campground, the trail crosses Pocosin Fire Road, which descends southward to the ruins of Pocosin Mission, a small Episcopal mission and settlement that was abandoned after the park acquired the land in the 1930s. A few scattered foundations remain.

Near mile 63 on Skyline Drive, the AT passes the South River picnic area and South River Falls Trail, a popular trail that leads to an attractive waterfall. Just ahead, the AT crosses South River Fire Road, which leads east into an undeveloped and secluded state wildlife area. The AT continues an additional 1.5 miles to cross US-33 on the Skyline Drive overpass at Swift Run Gap, the southern end of the park's central section. Stanardsville is to the east on US-33, Elkton and Harrisonburg to the west.

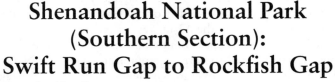

Shenandoah National Park (Southern Section): Swift Run Gap to Rockfish Gap

Length: *40 miles*

Elevation change: *1,685 feet*

Level: *moderate (strenuous in spots)*

USGS quad maps: *Browns Cove, VA; Fletcher, VA; McGaheysville, VA; Waynesboro East, VA*

Access: *From Skyline Drive at mile 66.7, 68.6 (Smith Roach Gap), 69.9 (Powell Gap), 73.2 (Simmons Gap), 75.2 (Pinefield Gap), 77.7, 81.1 (Doyle River parking area), 83.0 (Browns Gap), 84.2, 87.2 (near Blackrock Gap), 88.9, 92.1 (Riprap Hollow parking area), 92.4, 94.1 (Turk Hollow), 96.8 (via fire road at Jarman Gap), 99.5 (Beagle Gap), 102.1 (near McCormick Gap), and 105.2 (southern park boundary, at junction of Skyline Drive, Blue Ridge Parkway, and I- 64).*

From the US-33 crossing at Swift Run Gap, it's 1.5 miles to the summit of Hightop, thought by some to be the point at which explorer John Lederer first reached the crest of the Blue Ridge in 1669. There's no view from the overgrown summit, but a short side trail leads to an open ledge with an outstanding view across the Shenandoah Valley. From Hightop, the AT continues with many ups and downs, crossing Smith Roach Gap, Powell Gap (from which it makes a 3-mile arc to the east, one of its longest uninterrupted stretches within the park), Simmons Gap, and Pinefield Gap.

Near Skyline Drive milepost 80, the AT passes several good viewpoints on Loft Mountain before turning south to skirt Loft Mountain Campground (which, despite its name, is actually on Big Flat Mountain to the south of Loft). A mile beyond the campground, reach the Doyle River parking area, where a popular side trail to Doyle River Falls begins. Browns Gap, at Skyline Drive milepost 83, saw considerable troop movement during the Civil War.

From the Skyline Drive crossing at mile 84, it's an easy 1-mile hike to Blackrock, a spectacular pile of shattered Hampton quartzite affording a 360-degree view from its bare summit. A side trail leaves from the western edge of the summit for Trayfoot Mountain. The AT continues southward with many more ups and downs. Although average elevations are lower in this section, the terrain can be more challenging.

Just north of Skyline Drive milepost 97, in Jarman Gap, is a fire road linking the AT to the drive. This was once the southern boundary of Shenandoah National Park and the end of Skyline Drive, but the park was later extended an additional 8 miles south to Rockfish Gap. Those last 8 miles of park, however, are nothing more than a 200-foot-wide right-of-way along Skyline Drive, and the AT crosses several sections of private land south of the gap. Hikers are welcome to use the trail, but camping is not permitted.

At a Skyline Drive crossing at Beagle Gap (mile 99.5), the trail enters an especially interesting section as it crosses high, open meadows on Bear Den Mountain, a marked contrast to the heavy forest through which the trail has tunneled to this point. Look for catnip, mountain oregano, and other herbs and wildflowers throughout the summer. From Beagle Gap, the AT continues 6 miles to finally exit the park at Rockfish Gap (junction of Skyline Drive, Blue Ridge Parkway, and I-64).

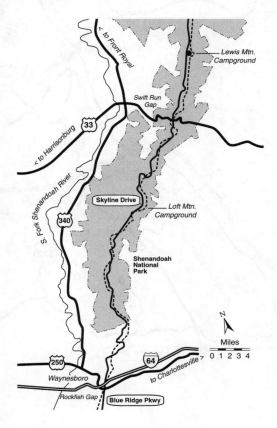

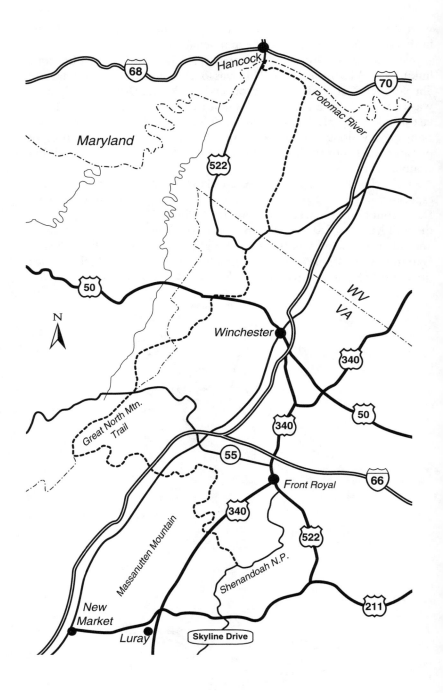

Chapter 4

THE BIG BLUE TRAIL

In the mid-1960s, the Appalachian Trail through northern Virginia was under pressure from private landowners and developers. Realizing the threat, the Appalachian Trail Conference began to scout an alternate route along the western edge of the Shenandoah Valley that would bypass the northern Blue Ridge. The result was the birth of the Big Blue Trail.

Work on the Big Blue began in 1967, and the route was finally completed late in 1981. But as the trail planners were to discover, they were several decades late in undertaking such a project. Despite generous donations of land, easements, and rights-of-way, the same pressures from landowners that threatened the Appalachian Trail were at work throughout northern Virginia and the eastern panhandle of West Virginia. As a result, the Big Blue never materialized as a continuous woodland trail but instead was forced onto existing public roads at many points. Today, the Big Blue is a patchwork of public and private roads and trails leading 144 miles from the C&O Canal at Hancock, MD, to the Appalachian Trail in Shenandoah National Park.

In the end, a concerted effort saved the Appalachian Trail in northern Virginia and in the process condemned the Big Blue to relative obscurity. It's easy to dismiss the Big Blue as a failed project that requires too much monotonous road walking and crosses too much private land, especially in its northern sections. But that overlooks the fact that the Big Blue also crosses some of the most rugged and isolated terrain in northern Virginia. Built and maintained by the Potomac Appalachian Trail Club (PATC), the Big Blue remains very much a work-in-progress as the club continues its efforts to route the trail away from roads. Changes in the route occur from time to time, and you would do well to check with the PATC for the latest updates if you plan to hike any distance on the trail.

The PATC divides the trail into eleven short sections, each with its own distinct personality. Taken singly, or combined for overnight trips, each section has something to offer the hiker.

Note: The Big Blue Trail is not shown, or is shown inaccurately, on most USGS quad maps. The PATC's map series for this trail is highly recommended (see Appendix I).

Potomac Section

Length: *10.2 miles*
Elevation change: *360 feet*
Level: *easy to moderate*
USGS quad maps: *Hancock, WV–MD–PA; Cherry Run, MD–VA–PA*
Access: *North trailhead is on the C&O Canal towpath at Hancock, MD. Follow I-70 west to Hancock and exit on MD-144, which becomes Main Street. From Main, turn left (south) on Penn Street. Go one block on Penn Street, then bear right and cross the C&O Canal to the parking area at Little Tonoloway Park. (The southern terminus of the Tuscarora Trail lies 8 miles to the east on the towpath. The trail continues the Big Blue's northeasterly course through Maryland and Pennsylvania.) South trailhead is on WV-9, a half-mile west of Spruce Pine Roadside Park. From I-81 at Martinsburg, WV, take WV-9 west for 14 miles to Spruce Pine Roadside Park, where there is limited parking. Hike a half-mile west to the trailhead.*

The Big Blue makes an inauspicious start under a highway bridge before entering more pleasant surroundings in the Ruth Morris Forest. Like most of the northern sections of the Big Blue, much of the Potomac section crosses private land and has been pieced together from county roads and existing trails.

From the parking area at Little Tonoloway Park, follow the C&O Canal towpath a short distance upstream to the US-522 bridge. Cross the dry canal bed when you see the blue blazes, then climb the highway embankment and cross the highway bridge into West Virginia. Once across the bridge, turn left onto River Road, which the Big Blue follows for its first leg.

At approximately 4 miles, the Big Blue veers right at a double blue blaze and enters Ruth Morris Forest, where camping is permitted. The trail makes an easy stream crossing before climbing the ridge. Continue, with some ups and downs and another easy stream crossing, for about a mile through Morris Forest before exiting onto private land, where camping is prohibited.

At 6 miles, the trail passes the remains of an old farm on private land. For the next 1.5 miles, the Big Blue is patched together from a combination of footpaths and backroads. At 7.9 miles, the trail crosses Sleepy Creek, beyond which it is routed primarily over country roads on private land. Watch for vehicles (although these roads carry little traffic) and respect the rights of property owners. The junction with WV-9, at 9.3 miles, marks the end of the Potomac section.

Sleepy Creek Section

Length: *22.7 miles*

Elevation change: *1,375 feet*

Level: *moderate*

USGS quad maps: *Cherry Run, MD–WV–PA; Big Pool, WV–MD; Stotlers Crossroads, WV; Glengary, WV–VA*

Access: *To reach the north trailhead, follow WV-9 west from I-81 for 14 miles to Spruce Pine Roadside Park. The trailhead is a half-mile farther west on WV-9. To reach the south trailhead, follow WV-45 west from I-81 to Glengary. At 2.5 miles beyond Glengary, look for a parking area and trail crossing where the road makes a sharp left turn. To reach the Sleepy Creek area, take WV-9 from I-81 for 6 miles, pass through Hedgesville, and follow County Road 7 south for 7 miles to WV-7/9 (Sleepy Creek Road). Follow Sleepy Creek Road west for 6 miles and pass the Public Hunting Area Office to a fork in the road. Go right at the fork and continue 0.7 mile to a parking area at the end of the road. There is trail access from the Lower Campground.*

From the parking area at Spruce Pine Roadside Park, walk a half-mile west to the blue-blazed trailhead. Enter the woods, turn left, and follow Meadow Branch through dense rhododendron and hemlock for a short distance. You'll need to rock-hop or wade the stream at about a half-mile from the trailhead. The first 2 miles of this section cross private land; stay on the trail.

The trail makes a short, steep climb to follow the remains of an old millrace once owned by George Washington's brother Charles. The Potomac Appalachian Trail Club maintains a primitive campsite on the level area beyond the millrace. Beyond the levels, the trail climbs and then turns left onto a dirt road across private land.

At 1.6 miles, the trail leaves the road and narrows to a footpath, climbing steeply on switchbacks. There are occasional overgrown views through the trees and a good open view from a power-line clearing near the top of the ridge. The large operation visible to the northwest is the Pittsburgh Plate Glass Company sand quarry on US-522 north of Berkeley Springs.

Approaching the ridge top, the Big Blue bears right and reaches the crest near Devil's Nose, a prominent rock outcropping. This is the beginning of the Sleepy Creek Public Hunting and Fishing Area, a state-owned parcel managed primarily for the benefit of sportsmen. Within the area is a 205-acre pond stocked with bass, bluegill, channel catfish, crappie, and sunfish. You are welcome to hike and camp in the area, but it's best avoided during hunting season, generally from mid-October through December. Camping is prohibited except at designated primitive sites, which are generally under-used. You must register and pay a small fee to camp, and stays at any one site are limited to 7 days. Horses and vehicles (including mountain bikes) are prohibited on the trails. At 3.4 miles the trail passes through the first of several wildlife clearings.

Reach Whites Gap at 6.6 miles and turn left (downhill) at the fork; the spur straight ahead leads a short distance to a fire-tower clearing with good views. This portion of the Big Blue follows Meadow Branch Run Trail, and there are two easy stream crossings in the next mile. A third stream crossing at Rocky Ford (8.7 miles) may be difficult, requiring wading in knee-deep water; don't attempt the crossing if water levels are high. Two more stream crossings, somewhat less difficult, lie ahead.

At 9.5 miles, just beyond the last stream crossing, the Big Blue passes through a gate and skirts the Lower Campground primitive camping area. At 11 miles, it skirts Piney Point Campground. Just beyond the campground, bear right to continue on the Big Blue, or left to register for a campsite. Upper Campground is directly ahead. Beyond Upper Campground, the Big Blue passes through two game clearings before joining a 1.5-mile stretch of rough and often muddy jeep road (shown on some maps as the Old Still Trail) along Meadow Branch. There are two fairly easy stream crossings in this segment.

Shenandoah N.P., VA —
Blue Ridge from Mt. Marshall

At 17 miles, turn right and follow a road a short distance to a junction with Shanghai Beacon Trail, a jeep road that leads a mile south to an airway beacon on the highest point in the Sleepy Creek area (2,172 feet). Continue straight ahead on Big Blue for 0.8 mile, then turn left onto a jeep trail at Locks of the Mountain. This is an especially popular section during hunting season, and car camping is permitted along the road from mid-October through December. The Big Blue leaves the Sleepy Creek Public Hunting and Fishing Area at 22 miles. Beyond the area boundaries, bear left at a fork and follow Old Pack Horse Road, a route that is reputed to have changed little since colonial times. A junction with WV-45 and the end of the Sleepy Creek section comes at mile 22.7.

Dresel Wayside

Length: *16.5 miles*

Elevation change: *300 feet*

Level: *easy*

USGS quad maps: *Glengary, WV–VA; White Hall, VA–WV; Gore, VA–WV*

Access: *The north trailhead is on the west side of WV-45, 2.5 miles west of Glengary, with limited parking along the road where it makes a sharp turn to the south. To reach the south trailhead, take US-50 west from Winchester, VA, to VA-751 at Gore and park across from the C&S Grocery. This section is largely on private land and requires more road walking than other portions of the Big Blue.*

The Big Blue follows WV-45 south. At 1.3 miles, cross the West Virginia–Virginia border, where WV-45 becomes VA-681. Continue south along VA-681 to a junction with VA-671. Bear right onto VA-671, then almost immediately turn left onto VA-690. At 4.6 miles, VA-690 merges with VA-600. Cross the bridge over Brush Creek; reportedly, there is a reliable spring just before the bridge. South of the bridge, the trail leaves the road and turns left into the woods to follow Brush Creek for a short distance before turning right to climb on an old jeep road.

At 5 miles, the trail bears right and leaves the jeep road. Cross over a barbed wire fence into a field, where there are good views to the east. Continue across the field, crossing another barbed wire fence, and descend into a wooded ravine. At 5.7 miles, cross paved VA-600; for the next 1.6 miles, the Big Blue passes through woods alternating with occasional overgrown meadows.

Reach the Dresel Wayside area at 7.3 miles. Dresel Wayside Campsite #1 is west of the trail, with Campsites #2 and #3 farther south, in deep woods. All are primitive sites, with tent pads and fire rings, and they are the only legal campsites along this section of the Big Blue. The remainder of this section is on private land, and camping is prohibited.

At 7.5 miles, pass a junction with the Fish Pond Trail, then cross a gas-line clearing and watch carefully for the blue blazes. At the far side of the clearing, turn downhill (southeast), avoiding an old unblazed trail that continues straight ahead. At approximately 8 miles the trail merges onto a rough road through an attractive farming area, joining VA-689 in another mile. At the junction of VA-689 and VA-600, turn right on paved VA-600. The Big Blue follows VA-600 to the south for 1.5 miles to its intersection with US-522.

Cross US-522 and continue south on VA-600 a short distance to a junction with VA-684. Turn right on VA-684 and follow it through the village of Gainsboro.

Beyond Gainsboro, turn southwest onto VA-688, which the Big Blue follows for 3 miles through pleasant farming country. At 15 miles, turn west (right) on US-50 and follow the highway for about a mile toward Gore, VA. At Gore, turn left onto VA-751, where there is ample parking. This is the end of the Dresel Wayside section.

Devils Backbone

Length: *13.5 miles*

Elevation change: *1,900 feet*

Level: *moderate (climb to Pinnacle Ridge is strenuous)*

USGS quad maps: *Gore, VA–WV; Hayfield, VA; Capon Springs, WV–VA*

Access: *To reach the north trailhead, follow US-50 west of Winchester to Gore, VA. At Gore, turn left onto VA-751 and park opposite the C&S Grocery. The trailhead is at the junction of VA-741 and VA-853. To reach the south trailhead, drive 14 miles west of Winchester on US-50, turn south on WV-259, and continue 7.3 miles south to Lehew Road (WV-23/3). Turn left on Lehew Road, pass Shiloh Church, turn left at the end of the cemetery, and continue about 0.7 mile to a parking area where the road makes a sharp left turn.*

At Gore, turn south on paved VA-853, which becomes a dirt road in approximately a half-mile. A short distance beyond, follow the blue blazes into the woods and begin a gradual climb. For the next 6.5 miles the Big Blue is pieced together from a combination of old roads and footpaths leading generally southward.

At 6.7 miles, the Big Blue enters Deep Hollow at the foot of Cat Rock cliffs. This deeply shaded hollow is especially pleasant in late summer, when wild blueberries are plentiful. At 7.2 miles, pass Pinnacle Spring and make an easy crossing of the headwaters of Laurel Run; in dry weather, the streambed may be dry. A short distance beyond the crossing, the trail passes the first of several intersections with the orange-blazed Frye Path, a historic pioneer route across the Great North range. A portion of this path, which dates to the French and Indian Wars, is maintained by the Potomac Appalachian Trail Club and is well worth exploring if you have the time and energy. From this intersection, the Big Blue climbs steadily on switchbacks to Pinnacle

Ridge, an eastern outlier of the Great North Mountain range. Turn left at the ridge top and scramble to the top of Pinnacle Rocks for an outstanding view to the west. Pinnacle Ridge Campground, a primitive hike-in site, lies just to the east of the rocks.

Pass the highest point in the Devils Backbone section (2,600 feet) at 8.5 miles. Just ahead, several outcroppings provide good views above the dense ridge-top thicket of scrub oak, laurel, and pine. At 10.4 miles, the Big Blue enters West Virginia, then descends steeply on switchbacks, crossing the unmarked Virginia–West Virginia border several more times, only to end in Virginia once again at the foot of the mountain.

At 11.3 miles, the Big Blue enters Lucas Woods, a gift to the Potomac Appalachian Trail Club from the Nature Conservancy. The PATC maintains a primitive campsite here, in an attractive and isolated hollow. The trail leaves Lucas Woods after a short stretch and once again enters West Virginia. For the next 1.3 miles, the Big Blue follows jeep roads through heavy forest; watch carefully for the blue blazes. Adjacent land is private, and camping is not permitted. At 13.5 miles, the trail turns left onto an unmarked gravel road, crossing Lohman Branch to reach the end of the Devils Backbone section.

Jemina Section

Length: *11.3 miles*

Elevation change: *400 feet*

Level: *moderate (strenuous at south end)*

USGS quad maps: *Capon Springs, WV–VA; Yellow Springs, WV–VA; Wardensville, WV–VA; Mountain Falls, WV–VA*

Access: *To reach the north trailhead, follow US-50 west of Winchester for 14 miles to a junction with WV-259. Turn south (left) on WV-259 and continue 7.2 miles to Lehew Road (WV-23/3). Turn left on Lehew Road, pass Shiloh Church, and turn left at the corner of the cemetery. Continue 0.6 miles to a sharp left turn and park along the side of the road. To reach the south trailhead, follow VA-55 west from Strasburg, VA, for 16 miles to a well-marked right turn at Hawk Recreation Area sign. Follow the Forest Service road downhill for 3 miles to a left turn, then continue about a half-mile to a parking area near the trailhead. Go a half-mile and turn right for parking.*

This section of the Big Blue is named for Jemina Farmer, whose grave and abandoned homestead lie along the trail. Beginning in a narrow valley along

Lohman Branch, the trail wanders among the foothills before making a steep climb to the Hawk Recreation Area on the eastern flank of Great North Mountain. Although elevation change is not great, there are many ups and downs as the trail passes through rolling hill country. Most of the trail is on private land (camping prohibited), and parts of it are difficult to follow.

From the north trailhead, leave the blacktop road and cross Lohman Branch on a gravel road, which follows the stream for some distance. At approximately 2.8 miles, turn left (uphill) at a junction with an unmarked gravel road, then almost immediately bear right onto a footpath that climbs the hill on switchbacks. At the top of the hill, turn left onto a dirt road.

At 3 miles, the trail becomes obscure as it crosses private land. The next 1.5 miles, patched together from roads, old farm lanes, and footpaths, are

Shenandoah N.P., VA —
Blue Ridge from Mt. Marshall

especially hard to follow; watch carefully for the blue blazes and be sure to close all farm gates behind you. At 4.7 miles, cross a power-line clearing and continue to an easy stream crossing. Turn left onto an unmarked dirt road just beyond the stream crossing. At 5.5 miles, bear right at a fork, then make a second right (downhill) on a footpath. Just ahead is the gravestone of Jemina Farmer and the ruins of the Farmer homestead on private land.

At 6.4 miles, the Big Blue makes a fairly easy crossing of Dry Run, then crosses the railroad right-of-way. Beyond the railroad, the Big Blue turns right and begins a steep climb on switchbacks to the crest of Middle Ridge, then descends to cross a bridge over Capon Spring Run and Capon Springs Road at 7.5 miles. Beyond the crossing, follow a dirt road steeply uphill, and at 7.8 miles bear left at a fork. The area ahead presents a confusing maze of old roads, trails, and spurs that requires special attention. Stay on what appears to be the main dirt road; with luck, you'll reach the top of the ridge at 8.5 miles.

From the ridge top, the Big Blue makes a steep descent on switchbacks to a crossing of Hawk Run near a small waterfall. Two other crossings, both fairly easy, lie just ahead. The trail follows Hawk Run on an attractive old mountaineer road for about a half-mile before turning uphill to begin a steep climb into George Washington National Forest.

At 11 miles, the Big Blue crosses Hawk Road, makes a sharp turn, and joins the road a short distance ahead, passing a parking area. This is the end of the Jemina section.

County Line Section

Length: *12.2 miles*

Elevation change: *1,200 feet*

Level: *moderate*

USGS quad maps: *Wardensville, WV–VA; Mountain Falls, VA–WV*

Access: *Access to the north trailhead is from Hawk Campground on US-55, 16 miles west of Strasburg, VA. Turn right (north) at the well-marked Forest Service road and follow it to a parking and picnic area. Hawk is a primitive and secluded site that makes a good base camp for exploring the surrounding country. You can also pick up the trail on US-55 at the crest of Great North Mountain, above Hawk Campground. To reach the south trailhead, follow US-55 for 20 miles west of Strasburg to Wardensville, WV. Just before reaching WV-259, turn left on an unmarked paved road, go approximately a half-mile, then turn left on another unmarked road. Go less than 0.2 mile and turn onto unmarked Waites Run Road (Route 5/1). Follow Waites Run Road for approximately 5 miles, crossing the stream three times, and look for the trailhead just beyond the third bridge.*

Most of the County Line section follows the rocky spine of Great North Mountain. This entire section lies within George Washington National Forest, and backcountry camping is permitted, although level sites are scarce. Wild berries are plentiful in late summer, but except for Terrapin Spring (mile 10), there are no reliable water sources along the ridge.

From the trailhead on Hawk Road, near the campground turnoff, follow the blue blazes along the road to a footpath and begin a moderate climb. At 0.8 mile, cross the Hawk Recreation Area Road and begin a steady 1-mile climb on switchbacks to the crest of Great North Mountain. Once on the ridge, turn left and follow the rocky footpath southward. Views along the trail are better in the winter, when the leaves have fallen.

Pass a microwave relay tower at 2 miles. The ridge narrows ahead, offering some good wintertime views. At 3.3 miles, the trail merges with a dirt road and begins a short, steady descent to US-55. Cross the highway and regain the ridge after a short climb. This section of the Big Blue, also known as County Line Trail, follows the crest of Great North Mountain southward toward the Wolf Gap area. You'll pass occasional viewpoints along the next 2 miles.

At 6.2 miles, cross the marked border into Virginia. The Paul Gerhard Memorial Shelter, maintained by the Potomac Appalachian Trail Club (see

Appendix I), lies 1.5 miles ahead. A blazed side-trail to the left leads from the shelter to FS-93, which in turn connects with US-55. From the shelter, the trail climbs to an abandoned orchard, where there are some overgrown views.

Pass Terrapin Spring at 10 miles. The spring is reliable except in the driest weather, but is unprotected; boil or treat the water. A short distance beyond the spring, the trail bears right; avoid the faint path straight ahead, which is a long-abandoned section of the original County Line Trail. The Big Blue makes a steep, rocky 1,100-foot drop to Waites Run, where it turns sharply and merges with a dirt road, which it follows for a short distance to a Forest Service gate at Waites Run Road. This is the end of the County Line section. Turn right on Waites Run Road to continue.

Sugar Knob Section

Length: *9.0 miles*

Elevation change: *1,685 feet*

Level: *moderate (some stream crossings may be difficult)*

USGS quad maps: *Wardensville, WV–VA; Wolf Gap, WV–VA; Woodstock, VA–WV*

Access: *The north trailhead is on Waites Run Road (Route 5/1) south of Wardensville, WV. To reach the south trailhead, take I-81 to the Toms Brook exit. Follow Route 651 northwest for 1.4 miles to Route 623. Follow Route 623 for 4 miles to Route 600, and follow Route 600 over Fetzers Gap to Route 603. Follow Route 603 southwest, bearing left at a fork where Route 713 intersects, and eventually pass the Van Buren Furnace ruins. Continue beyond the furnace to a Forest Service gate and park. Continue beyond the gate on foot for approximately a half-mile to the trailhead and turn north.*

The Sugar Knob section of the Big Blue Trail is a challenging route through steep, remote terrain in the George Washington National Forest. There are connections to the excellent Wolf Gap trail system (see Wolf Gap Recreation Area chapter) and many outstanding backcountry campsites. Be prepared for numerous stream crossings in this section.

From the north trailhead on Waites Run Road, the first 2.5 miles of this section (also known as the Pond Run Trail) are often wet, and there are at least eight stream crossings that require some wading in all but the driest weather. During early spring snowmelt, the trail becomes a quagmire.

Reach the top of the ridge at 2.5 miles and bear left. (To the right, the yellow-blazed Halfmoon Trail descends to Trout Run Valley.) A good backcountry campsite, with a reliable spring, lies just ahead. At 3.3 miles, reach a junction with Mill Mountain Trail, which continues southward 6 miles to Wolf Gap Campground. The Big Blue goes straight ahead, merging with a rough dirt road that leads to an intersection of the Big Blue, Little Stony Creek, and Peer Trails. The Big Blue continues straight ahead, climbing for a short distance before making a steep descent.

At 4.8 miles, reach the intersection of the Big Blue, Little Sluice Mountain, and Racer Camp Hollow Trails and begin a steady 1-mile climb to the crest of Little Sluice Mountain. Once on the crest, the trail turns south, passing the White Rocks Trail, a short spur leading to a good overlook above the Cedar Run Valley. The Big Blue continues along the ridge top, intersecting several dirt roads. Keep straight ahead, following the blue blazes. At 7 miles, the Big Blue turns right and begins a sharp descent on what is shown on some maps as the Little North Mountain Trail. A small, sheltered hollow at 8.2 miles provides a good backcountry campsite. Beyond the campsite, go right at a fork and make an easy stream crossing. The trail becomes a dirt road in another half-mile and continues south to a parking area at the Forest Service gate on Route 603, the end of the Sugar Knob section.

Fetzers Gap Section

Length: *11.6 miles*

Elevation change: *1,400 feet*

Level: *moderate*

USGS quad maps: *Woodstock, VA–WV; Toms Brook, VA*

Access: *To reach the north trailhead, follow the rather complicated directions to the south trailhead in the previous section. There is also trail access from Route 600 at Fetzers Gap. The south trailhead is on US-11 near its junction with Route 740. From I-81, take the Toms Brook exit, turn left on Route 651, and follow it for a mile to US-11. Turn right on US-11, drive 2 miles south to Maurertown, and park along the highway near its intersection with Route 740. Walk up Route 740 a short distance to the trailhead.*

Approximately half of the Fetzers Gap section follows county roads through Shenandoah Valley farm country. Although the views from the roads are pleasant enough, the last 6 miles can make for monotonous walking. Unless you're hiking the entire Big Blue, there is little reason to hike this section.

From the north trailhead, turn south and follow the Big Blue downhill to an easy stream crossing. Beyond the crossing, the trail turns right to follow Cedar Creek. Within a short distance, the trail crosses the creek, a difficult crossing in high water. The section ahead is often muddy.

The trail begins a climb up Tea Mountain a half-mile from the trailhead. For the next 1.3 miles, the Big Blue is strung together from old roads and footpaths, and there are several potentially confusing intersections with other trails. Follow the blue blazes carefully. At 1.9 miles, a short side trail on the flank of Tea Mountain leads to a good view of Little Sluice Mountain. The trail reaches the ridge crest at 2.8 miles, and many ups and downs lie ahead. In winter there are views through the trees, and at 3.7 miles the trail passes a sweeping panorama across the Blue Ridge, Massanutten Mountain, and the Shenandoah Valley.

Where the footpath ends at 5.8 miles, turn northeast onto a gravel road. In a short distance, cross paved Route 600 and continue northeast on the gravel road, approaching a television tower. At the tower, bear right, continue downhill, and at 6.8 miles merge with a dirt road. The area ahead presents a confusing maze of unmarked forks and intersections. Watch carefully for blazes and stay on what appears to be the main dirt road.

Most of the remainder of this section follows county roads. At 7.6 miles, reach a gate and turn northeast onto Route 656. At 8.1 miles, turn southwest onto Route 623, then turn left onto Route 655 (8.6 miles) and right onto Route 652 (9 miles). At 9.7 miles, turn left on Route 642, and at 10.2 miles reach a junction with Route 657. Route 642, on which you've been traveling, turns left here; continue straight ahead on Route 657 and cross I-81 in a half-mile.

At 11.3 miles, leave Route 657 and cross a stile. The trail wanders through open meadows on private land; stay on the trail and respect the rights of the property owners. Within a short distance, the trail crosses the railroad tracks to US-11, the end of the Fetzers Gap section.

Massanutten West and Massanutten East Sections (US-11 to US-340)

Length: *28.5 miles*

Elevation change: *1,640 feet*

Level: *moderate*

USGS quad maps: *Bentonville, VA; Strasburg, VA; Toms Brook, VA*

Access: *West trailhead is on US-11 at Shenandoah County Park, on the north side of Maurertown. East trailhead is on US-340 at Route 628 south of Bentonville. Other convenient access points, from west to east, are Route 678 near the Elizabeth Furnace Recreation Area and Route 613 along the eastern foot of Massanutten Mountain north of Bentonville Landing.*

The Big Blue Trail

Two sections of the Big Blue Trail—Massanutten West and Massanutten East—cross the Massanutten Range, linking both forks of the Shenandoah River and providing a challenging two- or three-day backpack trip.

The Massanutten West section of the Big Blue begins at Shenandoah County Park. From the park, hike north on the blue-blazed trail and then bear right (east) onto Route 650 at a cemetery. After a short distance, turn north onto Route 653, which turns to the east. At approximately 3.5 miles from the trailhead, turn onto a private road at Little River Farm, following the road to the north of the barn. This is private land, but the owner has granted access. Continue on the road to a bridge across the North Fork of the Shenandoah. Turn right at the end of the bridge, turn right again at a farmhouse, and pass through two farm gates, being sure to close both behind you.

At 4.4 miles, the trail leaves the road, narrowing to a footpath that climbs Doll Ridge on an old horse trail dating to the last century. Reach the crest of Three Top Mountain on the western edge of the Massanutten Range at 5.7 miles, turn left (north), and hike north at or near the ridge line for 3.3 miles to Strasburg Reservoir. Camping is prohibited in the watershed area.

North of the reservoir, the Big Blue crosses Massanutten West Trail to follow the Bear Wallow Trail. From the fork, the combined Big Blue–Bear Wallow Trail climbs to the ridge crest, where there are some good wintertime views. Continue straight ahead at an unmarked trail intersection at 10.7 miles. Low outcroppings a mile ahead provide good views overlooking the Fort Valley. At 13 miles is a junction with the Bear Wallow Spur Trail, which leads south to the Elizabeth Furnace Campground. A half-mile beyond the junction, pits along the trail are all that remain of the nineteenth-century quarries that once supplied ore to nearby Elizabeth Furnace. Turn right at 13.8 miles; a spur trail straight ahead leads to the Signal Knob parking area on Route 678. At 14 miles, cross Route 678 and continue to the Elizabeth Furnace Picnic Area parking lot. Turn right and follow the road to a Forest Service gate. This is the end of the Massanutten West section.

The Massanutten East section of the Big Blue Trail begins at the Elizabeth Furnace Picnic Area. From the parking lot, follow the trail along Passage Creek to the east. The trail eventually turns south, climbing on switchbacks to the crest of Massanutten Mountain at Shawl Gap and crossing an abandoned wagon road several times before reaching the ridge line. The old road is steep, making for a strenuous climb, but provides an easy and more direct alternate route if you're hiking in the opposite direction.

At Shawl Gap, the Big Blue intersects Massanutten Mountain Trail. (For a long but rewarding side trip to Buzzard Rock, turn left [north] on Massanutten Mountain East Trail at Shawl Gap and make a steady 2-mile descent. There are good views of the Blue Ridge and the Narrow Passage gorge from low cliffs and outcroppings along this section of the trail.) From Shawl Gap, the Big Blue joins the Massanutten Mountain East Trail for 6 miles on its southward trek to Veach Gap. Once at the gap, the Big Blue leaves Massanutten Mountain East Trail, turning onto the eastern extension of Veach Gap Trail to make a steep descent. This section follows Morgan's Road, a route laid out by the colonial army during the Revolutionary War as a possible escape route into the Fort Valley.

At 10.7 miles, turn right (south) onto Route 613 and continue along the road for 2 more miles to a bridge on the South Fork of the Shenandoah. Cross the bridge and, a short distance beyond, turn right (south) onto a steep path that connects to Route 629. Turn right (south) onto Route 629, then turn left (east) onto Route 628. Continue a mile on 628 to the eastern trailhead on US-340.

Matthews Arm Section

Length: *9 miles*

Elevation gain: *2,800 feet*

Level: *moderate (strenuous)*

USGS quad map: *Bentonville, VA*

Access: *The north trailhead is on US-340 approximately 1.5 miles south of Bentonville, VA. It is offset from the connecting Massanutten East trailhead, lying a short distance to the south. There is no safe or legal parking available in the area. The south trailhead (and southern terminus of the Big Blue) is on the Appalachian Trail a half-mile south of Hogback Overlook (mile 21 on Skyline Drive).*

This final section of the Big Blue involves a strenuous climb along Overall Run from the Shenandoah Valley to the crest of the Blue Ridge. From the north trailhead on US-340, turn left and follow an unmarked gravel road under the railroad tracks. Continue across private land for approximately a mile to the Shenandoah National Park boundary. The Overall Run area has been plagued by trail closures and friction between hikers and local landowners for some time, and the route outlined here is subject to change. Stick closely to the blazed trail and take private property postings very seriously.

Once in the park, the trail works its way across the foothills, with some ups and downs, at the western base of the Blue Ridge before reaching the Overall Run Trail at 3.4 miles. (The Lower Overall Run Falls are a short distance downstream from this junction.) From the junction, turn left and hike upstream on the combined Big Blue/Overall Run Trail. At 5.2 miles, you'll reach the base of Upper Overall Run Falls, highest in the park at 93 feet. From the falls, the trail climbs more steeply to the crest of the Blue Ridge.

After 144 miles, the Big Blue finally ends at the Appalachian Trail, south of Hogback Mountain.

Part Three
SHENANDOAH VALLEY
AND THE
BLUE RIDGE

Shenandoah N.P.—Whiteoak Canyon

Northern Virginia has been a playground for Washingtonians since late in the last century, when George Freeman Pollock opened his Stony Man Camp on one of the highest peaks in the Blue Ridge. Pollock attracted an affluent, adventure-seeking clientele, and in time he upgraded his accommodations and renamed his resort Skyland. It was a confounding mixture of the rustic and the overly polite, the sort of place where one might spend the morning scrambling down Whiteoak Canyon, only to return in time to attend a masked ball or seven-course banquet.

The Shenandoah Valley and northern Blue Ridge retain much of that contradictory quality today. Lush, well-tended horse farms coexist with house trailers; expansive wilderness areas vie for attention with tacky souvenir stands and RV parks named after cartoon characters. Rappahannock County, on the eastern slope of the Blue Ridge, battles to prevent subdivision and retain its rural character, while the citizens of nearby Haymarket remain split after a battle to reject a theme park that would have peddled sanitized Civil War history to hordes of tourists.

The contradictions aside, this section of Virginia holds some of the most compelling scenery and challenging wilderness to be found in the middle Atlantic states. A hiker could explore Shenandoah National Park for years without covering every trail in the park. Lesser known but equally spectacular areas, like Massanutten Mountain, are here for the more adventurous.

An encouraging sign is a grass-roots drive to create new natural areas in the upper Shenandoah Valley. Parts of Shenandoah National Park are badly overused; the Park Service tactfully tries to steer visitors to its lesser-used trails and has finally begun to ration access to Old Rag Mountain, one of the most overused areas in the park. One response to pressure for new wilderness areas is the proposed Shenandoah Primitive Recreation Area (SPRA). Advocated by two independent groups—Virginians for Wilderness and Preserve Appalachian Wilderness—the proposed SPRA would encompass 65,000 acres within the George Washington National Forest that harbor several rare and endangered species. In a sign of things to come, the coalition advocates user fees and entry permits, proceeds from which would be applied toward administration and maintenance costs. If approved, the SPRA would be the largest single wilderness area in the central Appalachians.

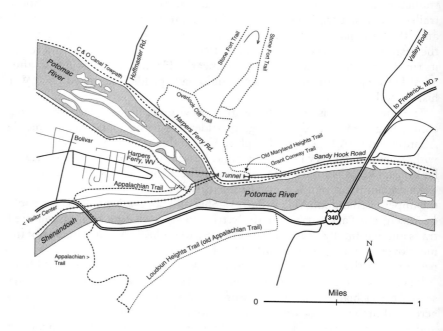

Chapter 5

HARPERS FERRY
(WEST VIRGINIA/VIRGINIA/MARYLAND)

Guarding a rugged break in the Blue Ridge where the Potomac and Shenandoah Rivers collide, Harpers Ferry presents an idyllic appearance that belies its tragic past. The town was the site of John Brown's ill-conceived raid on the Federal Armory, the spark that ignited the Civil War.

Over the past four decades, the National Park Service has done an impressive job of returning what had been a decaying rural slum to something vaguely resembling its Civil War–era appearance. Unfortunately, the restoration suffers a bit from what has been termed the Williamsburg Syndrome—a tendency to prettify the past without regard for strict historical accuracy. The Harpers Ferry that photographers captured in the 1860s—a gritty industrial town surrounded by barren, clearcut slopes—was a far cry from the pastoral little village that the Park Service has created in its stead.

That complaint aside, the Harpers Ferry area provides some outstanding day hikes. Lying at the approximate midpoint on the Maine-to-Georgia Appalachian Trail, it's the site of Appalachian Trail Conference headquarters. The Appalachian Trail, C&O Canal towpath, and an interesting network of shorter trails on Maryland, Loudoun, and Bolivar Heights provide access to riverside as well as ridge top.

Harpers Ferry is a popular and often crowded place. The Park Service is continuing its policy of closing public parking areas in and around the historic district and now provides shuttle service to town from a new visitor center near US-340. To truly savor this area, avoid weekends and holidays, or plan to visit in colder weather.

History

In 1733, Peter Stephens began a ferry operation at the Potomac-Shenandoah confluence, at what was then called "Peter's Hole." Stephens sold his property to Robert Harper in 1747, and Harper prospered, offering lodging to the likes of Thomas Jefferson and George Washington in the 1780s. His hospitality apparently paid off: Washington ordered a federal armory established at Harpers Ferry in 1798.

Harpers Ferry evolved as a major industrial and transportation center early in the nineteenth century. A crude turnpike, opened in 1832, linked Harpers Ferry to Frederick, MD. The Chesapeake & Ohio Canal reached this point in November 1833, and the Baltimore & Ohio Railroad followed in early 1835, one of the few times that it was bested in its westward race with the canal. Abundant water power drove the factories on Hall and Virginius Islands in the Shenandoah.

But Harpers Ferry's prosperity was to be short-lived. In the summer of 1859, John Brown made his way east from Kansas and quietly took up residence across the river in Sandy Hook, MD, under the alias of Isaac Smith. The abolitionist soon rented the nearby Kennedy farm, where he assembled men and weapons for a raid on the Federal Armory. Brown's plan was to hold the armory hostage until the commonwealth of Virginia agreed to free all slaves, and he naively assumed that local slaves would rebel and come to his aid in battle. On the evening of October 16, 1859, Brown and his raiders slipped away from the Kennedy farm, reaching the Harpers Ferry railroad bridge at approximately 10:30. Brown's men quickly seized control of the armory and took hostages into the early morning hours. But by daybreak on October 17, news of the raid had spread through Harpers Ferry. Local citizens, joined first by the Charles Town militia and later by regular army reinforcements, managed to isolate Brown and cut off his escape route to Maryland. The slave rebellion that Brown had counted on never materialized, and in the early morning hours of October 18, Robert E. Lee—then representing the U.S. Army—arrived on the scene and demanded Brown's surrender. When Brown refused, troops stormed the armory's fire engine house, where Brown held his few remaining hostages, knocking him unconscious and ending the raid on Harpers Ferry.

Harpers Ferry, WV — Harpers Ferry from Maryland Heights

Brown's raid was only the beginning of Harpers Ferry's troubles. With its strategic location, the town changed hands repeatedly throughout the course of the Civil War, and by 1865 much of Harpers Ferry lay in ruin. The armory was not rebuilt, and what little industry remained washed away in the floods of 1870 and 1889.

By the time that Congress established the Harpers Ferry National Monument in 1944, the town was a decaying and largely abandoned derelict. With large land donations from West Virginia in 1955 and Maryland in 1960, restoration work began in earnest, and today the park hosts more than a million visitors annually.

Nearby Towns and Attractions

ANTIETAM NATIONAL BATTLEFIELD—
See the C&O Canal chapter.

BOLIVAR, WV—
Perched on the heights above Harpers Ferry, Bolivar is still very much a working town that remains largely undiscovered by the tour-bus crowds. A picturesque cluster of nineteenth-century structures and an eclectic array of shops line the main street. Bolivar Heights, an important strategic position during the Civil War, is nearby (see trail guide).

CHARLES TOWN, WV—
Site of John Brown's trial, Charles Town was founded in 1786 and named for George Washington's brother Charles. The town retains many historic and architectural treasures but is marred by recent suburban sprawl on its outskirts. If you're in a hurry to get elsewhere, take the highway bypass around Charles Town. Otherwise, follow old US-340 (Washington Street) into town. Good places to begin your visit include the Jefferson County Courthouse or Jefferson County Museum, both on Washington Street in the heart of the old town.

CRYSTAL GROTTOS—
A 250-million-year-old cave discovered during blasting and drilling operations on Shepherdstown Pike (Route 34) in 1918, the grottos are open for guided tours daily from March through November, or weekends only from December through February. Admission is charged.

MONACACY NATIONAL BATTLEFIELD—
Site of a Civil War battle near Frederick, MD, the park is still under development. Contact park headquarters (see Appendix I) for updates.

Access
From I-70 at Frederick, MD, bear south on US-340 to the well-marked park entrance and visitor center on Cavalier Heights, 1 mile northwest of the Shenandoah River bridge. (The former park entrance at Shenandoah Street, just northwest of the Shenandoah bridge on US-340, is now closed to unauthorized vehicles.) The visitor center is open every day except Christmas, from 8 A.M. to 6 P.M. (summer) and from 8 A.M. to 5 P.M. (winter). Entry fee is $5 per vehicle for a 7-day pass, or $3 per person for hikers and bicyclists. The Park Service provides a shuttle from its new visitor center to the historic district, and parking within the main historic district is restricted or prohibited. Amtrak provides limited rail service from Washington, D.C., along a scenic route that parallels the C&O Canal.

Camping

There are no campgrounds within the Harpers Ferry historic district, and backcountry camping and open fires are prohibited throughout the park, which includes large tracts of land along both rivers, the C&O Canal, and on adjacent Bolivar, Loudoun, and Maryland Heights overlooking the main historic district. Backcountry camping is permitted on the Appalachian Trail beyond the park boundaries and on the C&O Canal at designated hike-in sites (see the C&O Canal chapter). Inquire locally about commercial car campgrounds in the area.

Trail Guide:
HARPERS FERRY AREA

Note: The Park Service has made many changes in trail routes, access, and parking regulations at Harpers Ferry since the late 1980s. Guides and maps published before 1993 are generally no longer accurate.

Appalachian Trail—
See the Appalachian Trail chapter

Bolivar Heights Trail

Length: *less than 1 mile*
Elevation change: *none*
Level: *easy (wheelchair-accessible)*
USGS quad map: *Harpers Ferry, VA–MD–WV*
Access: *From US-340, turn north at the traffic signal 1 mile west of the Shenandoah River bridge and follow the Park Service signs to Bolivar Heights.*

Bolivar Heights Trail is a level loop through a grassy meadow above Harpers Ferry, passing Civil War earthworks and restored artillery pieces. Bolivar Heights was an important defensive position during the Civil War, and it was here that 12,500 Union troops surrendered to Stonewall Jackson's Confederate forces on September 15, 1862. Two weeks later, Union forces retook the area, and on October 2 President Lincoln and General McClellan reviewed Union troops on the heights. Civil War–era photographs show a treeless landscape on Bolivar Heights, but today a mature forest blocks most views.

Chesapeake & Ohio Canal Towpath—

See the C&O Canal chapter
(miles 60–62)

Loudoun Heights Trail
(Old Appalachian Trail)

Length: *2 miles (including AT connection)*

Elevation change: *800 feet*

Level: *moderate*

USGS quad map: *Harpers Ferry, VA–MD–WV*

Access: *From the US-340 bridge across the Shenandoah River, follow the Appalachian Trail steeply uphill to the crest of Loudoun Heights.*

From the rerouted Appalachian Trail, turn left (northeast) onto the former AT at the top of the ridge and make a moderate descent along the crest of Loudoun Heights to a short side path leading to several rocky overlooks. Beyond the overlooks, the trail crosses private land, and public access is now uncertain. Check with Park Service or Appalachian Trail Conference personnel for current status.

Maryland Heights Trails

Maryland Heights are the sheer cliffs on Elk Ridge that overlook Harpers Ferry below the confluence of the Shenandoah and Potomac Rivers. The formation marks the south end of a spur of the Blue Ridge that extends to near Keedysville, MD. The main Blue Ridge continues north into Pennsylvania on South Mountain, a low ridge immediately to the east of Elk Ridge.

With its commanding view of Harpers Ferry, Maryland Heights was an important objective during the Civil War. In 1862, Confederate forces drove Union troops off the Heights and forced the surrender of Harpers Ferry. The Union army soon regained control of the town, and President Lincoln inspected troops on the Heights on October 2, 1862. Today, only scattered earthen breastworks hint at the army's presence.

Maryland Heights is formed of Weverton quartzite, an erosion-resistant metamorphosed quartz sandstone. The rock above the railroad tunnel has been blackened from a century of exposure to soot, diesel exhaust, and coal dust from trains passing through the Harpers Ferry tunnel. The cliffs are a favorite roost for ravens and buzzards, not to mention tourists. With some luck you may see feral goats, descendants of escaped farm animals that grazed on the Heights during the last century.

The view from Maryland Heights is one of the most striking in the mid-Atlantic states. Harpers Ferry and the Potomac lie directly below, with the Shenandoah River to your left. The farthest set of stone piers is all that remains of the Shenandoah Bridge, a weak structure that stood for only seven years before being swept away in the 1889 flood. Bridge and railroad configuration has changed considerably since the Civil War, and the present-day tunnel and bridges are all post–Civil War structures. The original Harpers Ferry bridge that John Brown crossed was completed in 1837 and stood on the low stone piers downstream from the present railroad bridges. The piers have survived remarkably well, although they haven't carried a bridge since the last was swept away in the 1936 flood. The high ridge to your left is Loudoun Heights, the main spine of the Blue Ridge along the Virginia–West Virginia border. Beyond Harpers Ferry is the gently rolling northern end of the Shenandoah Valley, with peaks along the eastern edge of the valley-and-ridge province visible in the distance.

Hikers can reach the Maryland Heights cliffs by any of the routes listed below, although two of the older trails are no longer marked or maintained. Recent closures of parking areas along Harpers Ferry Road make access inconvenient. Legal parking is now virtually impossible to find on the Maryland side of the river, but if you'd like to try, turn east at the blinking signal on US-340 just uphill from the Potomac River bridge. Continue a short distance past a motel and liquor store and make the first right, to Sandy Hook. Otherwise, continue on US-340 to the Harpers Ferry Visitor Center and take the shuttle to the historic district. Follow the well-marked Appalachian Trail, which crosses the Potomac on the downstream railroad trestle. You will end up on the C&O Canal towpath at the foot of Maryland Heights.

Technical climbing is allowed on Maryland Heights, subject to Park Service restrictions. Climbers must register at the Harpers Ferry National Historic Park ranger station or information center, and permits will be issued only to climbers with approved equipment. Check-out is also required.

(1) Overlook Cliff Trail

Length: *1.4 miles to Maryland Heights (2.1 miles including access from Harpers Ferry)*
Elevation change: *500 feet*
Level: *moderate*
USGS quad map: *Harpers Ferry, VA–MD–WV (marked, but unidentified)*

Access: *Trailhead is on Harpers Ferry Road 1.75 miles west of Sandy Hook. Parking is limited to several cars, and cars parked illegally along Harpers Ferry Road will be towed. Unless you arrive very early, you'll find the pull-out filled during weekends and holidays. If that's the case, try your luck at the small parking area near Lock 34 at Hoffmaster Road, or backtrack to the Harpers Ferry Visitor Center and follow the directions above.*

This old military road is the "official" route to Maryland Heights. Although the road passes a few mildly interesting Civil War breastworks along its ascent, this route is lacking in character compared to the old Maryland Heights or Grant Conway trails. At a half-mile from the trailhead is a junction with the Stone Fort Trail, which can be combined to make a longer loop hike on Maryland Heights (see the next entry); continue straight ahead. After climbing steadily for a little more than a mile, the Overlook Cliff comes to a four-way intersection. Turn right and continue downhill for another 0.4 mile to the Maryland Heights cliffs.

(2) Maryland Heights Loop

Length: *6 miles (round trip)*
Elevation change: *1,040 feet*
Level: *moderate (strenuous)*
USGS quad map: *Harpers Ferry, VA–MD–WV (marked, but unidentified)*
Access: *Follow the directions to Overlook Cliff Trail (1).*

Follow the Overlook Cliff Trail uphill through open woods (see the previous entry). At a half-mile from the trailhead, turn left onto the Stone Fort Trail, an old military road that climbs steadily to the northeast along the western flank of Elk Ridge. At midpoint, pass the remains of some Union fortifications before making a U-turn. Pass the remains of a Union blockhouse on the crest of the ridge, then continue south. The Stone Fort Trail splits into two for a short stretch before reconnecting with the Overlook Cliff Trail at a point uphill from and 0.2 miles beyond its western trailhead. From here, you can turn right (east) and continue downhill to the Maryland Heights cliffs for the full 6-mile loop. Return the way you came.

(3) Old Grant Conway Trail

Length: *0.8 mile*
Elevation change: *400 feet*
Level: *moderate*
USGS quad map: *Harpers Ferry, VA–MD–WV (marked, but unidentified)*
Access: *The unmarked trailhead is on Harpers Ferry Road 0.6 mile west of the base of the US-340 bridge, opposite Lock 32 on the C&O Canal. This is no longer an "official" trail, so it is unmarked and receives no maintenance.*

From the obscure trailhead, the old Grant Conway Trail makes a steady climb to the Maryland Heights cliffs through open woods along the ridge's south flank. There are good views across the Potomac from scattered outcroppings and a power-line clearing.

(4) Old Maryland Heights Trail

Length: *0.6 mile*
Elevation change: *400 feet*
Level: *moderate*
USGS quad map: *Harpers Ferry, VA–MD–WV (not shown)*
Access: *There are rumors that the Park Service plans to officially close this trail, but on last visit it was still open. The unmarked trailhead is on Harpers Ferry Road, immediately east of the Harpers Ferry tunnel's rear portal. The Park Service discourages use of this historic old trail, which isn't shown on current National Park Service or USGS maps, and has blocked parking areas in the vicinity. Rather than risk parking illegally along Harpers Ferry Road, back-track to Harpers Ferry and cross the AT footbridge to the C&O Canal towpath in Maryland. Cross the dry canal bed at Lock 33 opposite the footbridge and scramble up the adjacent berm wall to Sandy Hook Road. Turn right and follow the road toward Sandy Hook for about a half-mile to the eastern portal of the railroad tunnel. The road is narrow and has no shoulder; watch carefully for oncoming traffic. The trail itself is probably less hazardous than the situation that the Park Service has created in its attempt to block access.*

This historic trail isn't marked or maintained, but it's a classic, well worn from more than a century of use, and is the most scenic and challenging route to Maryland Heights. Cross the bridge over the railroad tracks at the tunnel's rear portal and look for a steep, rocky footpath leading uphill from the eastern bridge abutment. The trail begins as a nearly vertical scramble above the railroad cut, becoming less steep after a short distance as it traverses the lower slope of Elk Ridge through open woods and grassy meadows. Outcroppings near the trail afford sweeping views of the Potomac-Shenandoah confluence as well as a degree of solitude that you may not find on the main cliffs above. Continue to climb steadily until you reach Maryland Heights, the large boulder-strewn clearing directly above the railroad tunnel. From Maryland Heights, return the way you came. For a longer loop hike, continue uphill to the Overlook Cliff Trail.

Virginius Island

Length: *up to 1 mile*

Elevation change: *none*

Level: *easy*

USGS quad map: *Harpers Ferry, VA–MD–WV (not shown)*

Access: *From Shenandoah Street near the shuttle stop in the main historic district, walk to the Shenandoah River and turn right. Follow the informal trail upstream, along the river. Much of this trail was badly damaged in the 1996 floods.*

This is an easy riverside walk through a historic industrial site. Virginius Island was once a major manufacturing center on the Shenandoah. Incorporated as a town separate from Harpers Ferry in 1827, it was the site of Hall's Rifle Works, a major supplier to the Harpers Ferry Armory. With its ample water power, Virginius Island eventually boasted flour, fabric, paper, and lumber mills, a tannery, foundry, and workers' housing. But water power proved to be a double-edged sword for this vulnerable strip of land; severe floods in 1870 and 1889 destroyed many of its factories. The site was eventually abandoned, and today only a few foundations and stabilized ruins remain. You can see some of these by hiking upstream along the Shenandoah River from the main historic district. The trail is a work-in-progress and may be impassable when the Shenandoah is running high. Archaeological excavations are under way on the island, and public access is restricted in some areas.

Shenandoah N.P., VA — Trayfoot Mountain from Blackrock

Chapter 6

SHENANDOAH NATIONAL PARK (VIRGINIA)

S henandoah National Park has been brought back from the dead, an environmental success story just 85 miles from the nation's capital. What the Park Service acquired in the late 1920s and early 1930s was a 180,000-acre section of the Virginia Blue Ridge devastated by a century of clear-cutting, overgrazing, soil depletion, erosion, and neglect. What has returned is a mature eastern hardwood forest that blankets deep gorges and sheer slopes rising above 4,000 feet.

Of the millions of visitors who travel Skyline Drive every year, a fair number seem oblivious to the fact that they are in the midst of a major national park. In our automobile-focused society, the road is the main attraction, and the park gets second billing. But those who get off the road and onto its trails soon discover that Shenandoah National Park holds some of the most challenging terrain in the central Appalachians.

What follows is only a brief sketch of the park. It would be impossible to do justice to a place as big and complex as Shenandoah National Park in a single chapter, but I hope that I can tempt you to park your car and start exploring.

History

Humans probably first settled in the Shenandoah Valley region 8,000 to 10,000 years ago, around the end of the last Ice Age. Between 8000 and 1000 B.C., as the Shenandoah climate warmed, the familiar eastern forest of pine, maple, oak, hickory, and chestnut slowly evolved. After 1000 B.C., native tribes developed agriculture, settled in small semi-permanent villages in the valley, and buried their dead in mounds. Hunting parties crossed the Blue Ridge, leaving arrowheads and spear points as evidence of their passing, and burned large tracts of forest to corral game animals and create open grasslands.

The first Europeans to arrive in the Shenandoah Valley found it sparsely populated by the Shawnee. In 1669, the colonial governor of Virginia dispatched

John Lederer to the Blue Ridge, deep within what was then unexplored wilderness. Led by Indian guides, Lederer reached the crest of the Blue Ridge on March 18, 1669, probably at or near Hightop Mountain in the park's southern section.

Lederer's trek went largely unnoticed, but Virginia governor Alexander Spotswood's well-publicized 1716 expedition to the Shenandoah, in the company of 63 hard-drinking "gentlemen," focused attention on the region. Settlers began to trickle into the valley from the north in the 1720s, and in time primitive roads across the Blue Ridge opened the valley to settlers from the east. "Turnpikes," little more than rutted mountain trails, crossed Jarman Gap by 1750, Thornton Gap in 1785, and Browns, Swift Run, and Fishers Gap in the early 1800s.

The valley farmers prospered as new markets opened for their goods, but problems lay ahead in the surrounding mountains. With the better valley lands claimed, poorer settlers were forced to higher and less productive land in the Blue Ridge hollows. At first, they sustained themselves fairly well by hunting and gathering, but they occupied a fragile environment. By the turn of the century, large game was extinct in the Blue Ridge and small game was becoming scarce. Lacking any knowledge of good farming practices, the mountaineers depleted the thin soil of the hollows, and families barely survived by peddling chestnut bark to local tanneries and homemade whiskey to wealthy guests at George Pollock's Skyland resort. Many mountaineer families were squatters who found themselves locked in an inescapable downward spiral of poverty and social isolation. In a controversial 1933 exposé of the mountaineer culture, Mandel Sherman and Thomas Henry focused on Corbin Hollow near Old Rag Mountain (reported pseudonymously as Colvin Hollow), where they found "the inhabitants live in scattered, mud-plastered log huts. No one in the Hollow proper can read or write. One building, closed for many years, is called a school. There is no general system of communication ... no road to the outside world. Nearly all the inhabitants are blood relatives. ... They speak a peculiar language which retains many Elizabethan expressions." Corbin was the poorest of the hollows, but conditions in many others were not much better.

The mountaineers couldn't have known, but by the mid-1920s their way of life was about to end. In 1924, the Southern Appalachian National Park Commission recommended the northern Blue Ridge as the site of a new national park, and Shenandoah National Park was authorized by an act of Congress in 1926. Construction of Skyline Drive began in 1931, the Civilian Conservation Corps began to break trails in 1933, and the new park was formally dedicated by President Franklin Roosevelt on July 3, 1936. Over 2,200 people were forced to move from the park; many resettled in new government-built communities in the valley. In a regrettable move, the Park Service demolished virtually all of the mountaineer structures.

Natural Features

Rocks in this section of the Blue Ridge are among the oldest exposed formations in North America. Ancient granites estimated to be more than 1 billion years old are exposed on the summits of Hogback, Mary's Rock, and Old Rag Mountain. Most of the rock that caps the northern and central sections of the park is somewhat younger Catoctin greenstone, the remains of ancient lava flows that poured through cracks, or dikes, in the underlying granite. You'll find greenstone dikes scattered throughout the park; one outstanding example forms a natural staircase along the Ridge Trail below the Old Rag summit. In the park's southern section, sandstone and shale predominate.

Shenandoah N.P., VA —
Old Rag along Ridge Trail

The Blue Ridge forest has recovered remarkably well from the clear-cutting and erosion that took place early in the century. Mature oaks predominate, although they are seriously threatened by gypsy moth infestation. Hickory, basswood, tulip poplar, and maple are common at lower elevations. Hemlocks predominate in the cool, moist hollows, and various species of pine are common throughout the southern section. Among the 200 to 300 wildflower species known to occur here are showy orchis, purple fringe orchid, at least two varieties of lady slipper, and trillium. More than 47 species of ferns and clubmosses grow in the park, as do many types of mushrooms, toadstools, and other fungi. Shenandoah's oak forest provides a perfect environment for the morel, a mushroom that was as highly prized by the early mountaineers as by present-day gourmets. Ginseng, another native highly regarded by the mountaineers, occurs in out-of-the-way places. In addition to native species, Shenandoah is home to many imported species—running the gamut from catnip and horehound to yucca—originally introduced by settlers.

Wildlife has also staged a remarkable comeback. The black bear, once extinct in the northern Blue Ridge, now numbers between 150 and 300 within the park. Bobcats have also returned. Your best chance of spotting this shy and nocturnal cat occurs around sunrise, in the more isolated sections of the park, although I have occasionally seen them near Skyline Drive. Virginia white-tailed deer, also once hunted to extinction here, have repopulated (or, in recent years, overpopulated) from a small herd imported from George Washington's Mount Vernon estate in the 1930s. Red fox, gray fox, striped and spotted skunk, raccoon, and chipmunk are also common. Over 200 species of birds have been reported in the park, including the turkey and black vulture, raven, wild turkey, ruffed grouse, and woodcock. Two poisonous snakes—the copperhead and eastern timber rattler—occupy the park, along with many nonpoisonous species. It is illegal to kill, injure, or harass any wild animal—snakes included—in the park.

Environmental Concerns

Shenandoah National Park may be an environmental success story, but all isn't well. The park came under attack in 1995 from Republican members of Congress who introduced legislation to freeze park boundaries, prohibit acquisition of new park land even by donation, and return roads and easements at lower elevations to the counties. The Potomac Appalachian Trail Club and other groups worked tirelessly to expose those plans and rally public protest, but we can assume the threat to be ongoing given the current political climate. Private developers covet land adjacent to the park for vacation home and resort development, and they are exerting considerable political pressure to open up those lands for their commercial gain. But Shenandoah is a narrow park, only a mile wide at some points, and its boundaries lie far up the slopes. If left unchecked, expanding development could quickly destroy Shenandoah's fragile illusion of wilderness and put still more pressure on an already overused area.

In 1979, smog topped the Blue Ridge for the first time, and air quality continues to decline with increased development and traffic in the region. In contrast, water quality has improved. In 1940, the American Viscose Corporation poisoned the Shenandoah River at Front Royal so badly that in 1946 Virginia passed one of the earliest clean-water acts. But problems remain on the river: reports of fish kills at Front Royal, chemical discharges at Waynesboro, pH disturbances at Castlemans Ferry, and the list goes on.

Equally pressing is the problem of overuse. In sixty years, traffic on Skyline Drive has increased tenfold, and the most popular park trails are badly overused. Weekend overflow parking near the Old Rag, Hawksbill, and Whiteoak Canyon trailheads shows how serious the problem has become. This raises the thorny issue of rationing access, which the Park Service belatedly began to address in 1995. Permits are now required to hike Old Rag during high-use weekends and holidays, and there are plans to close Skyline Drive to vehicles on one day each month. Additional restrictions undoubtedly loom in the near future.

Access

To reach the north park entrance and Skyline Drive, take I-66 west from Washington, D.C., turn south on US-340, and continue through Front Royal to the well-marked park entrance south of town. There are three other entrance stations: Thoroughfare Gap, on US-211 between Sperryville and Luray; Swift Run Gap, on US-33 between Stanardsville and Elkton; and Rockfish Gap, at the Skyline Drive–Blue Ridge Parkway Junction on I-64 between Charlottesville and Waynesboro.

Skyline Drive is the 105-mile scenic parkway that ties Shenandoah National Park together. Built largely with hand labor during the Depression, the Drive winds along the crest of the Blue Ridge between Front Royal and Waynesboro. Entrance stations close at sundown and generally don't re-open until 9 A.M. The road is closed when conditions on the mountain— snow, ice, or heavy fog—are judged unsafe for drivers.

Although you sometimes can't drive into the park, you can always enter on foot (barring yet another government shutdown, of course). The easiest access is at the Skyline Drive entry stations. Getting into the park from other points is trickier, since private landowners at the foot of the mountain increasingly are denying access to park trails from their property.

Nearby Towns and Attractions

BLUE RIDGE PARKWAY—

The Blue Ridge Parkway extends Skyline Drive's southerly course an additional 469 miles to Great Smoky Mountains National Park in North Carolina, passing many fine trails, natural areas, and a seemingly endless succession of overlooks along the way. Except for widely spaced concessions, there is no commercial development on the parkway, and sections of the road may be closed in bad weather. Elevations range from 649 to 6,050 feet.

FRONT ROYAL, VA—

Once so rough that it was known as Hell Town, Front Royal today is a quieter place that combines a solid industrial base with a healthy tourist industry. You'll find a wide array of restaurants, lodging, shops, and services. To its credit, Front Royal has controlled its commercial development fairly well. But if you don't like crowds and traffic, it's still best to avoid Front Royal (or, for that matter, the park itself) on weekends and holidays from May through mid-October.

GEORGE WASHINGTON NATIONAL FOREST—

Two large tracts border Shenandoah National Park. The Massanutten Mountain section, to the west, is covered in this guide. To the south, the Blue Ridge Parkway passes through another large section of national forest (not covered in this guide) that includes Crabtree Falls, Humpback Rocks, the continuation of the Appalachian Trail, and other points of interest.

LURAY CAVERNS—

See the Massanutten Mountain chapter.

SPERRYVILLE, VA—

This is the last town you'll pass through if you approach the park from the east via US-211. Nestled at the foot of Thornton Gap, Sperryville retains much of its rural character despite its proximity to the park. This is a truly eclectic little town, where local produce stands and upscale specialty shops coexist with the usual tourist traps.

Camping

With over 500 miles of trails and fire roads, Shenandoah looks like a haven for backcountry camping. Good, legal sites are plentiful at the lower elevations but scarce along the higher ridges. You'll need a backcountry permit, available at the entrance stations, visitor centers, and park headquarters. Permits are free of charge but may be denied at the rangers' discretion. Your camp must be at least 75 feet from any stream or water source, 250 yards from any paved road or park boundary, one-half mile from any man-made or developed area, and out of sight of any unpaved road, trail, shelter, "no camping" sign, or other camping party. Group size is limited to ten people. Cutting of live wood is prohibited, and from March 1 through May 15, open fires are allowed only from 4 P.M. to midnight.

Trailside shelters scattered throughout the park are for emergency use only in severe weather. The Potomac Appalachian Trail Club maintains several furnished cabins within the park and rents them to the general public (see Appendix I).

The Park Service also operates large developed campgrounds at Big Meadows (mile 57.5), Lewis Mountain (mile 57.5), and Loft Mountain (mile 79.5). The Matthews Arm Campground in the park's northern section is closed. Stays at a single site are limited to 14 days from June 1 through October 31; campgrounds are often filled during that time, and reservations are highly recommended (see Appendix I). Park campgrounds don't offer RV hookups and have only a limited number of spots for oversized vehicles, but they do have restrooms with running water. They also have crowds, traffic, and noise. If you're looking for a peaceful mountain experience, look elsewhere.

Roadside camping—and "roadside" includes overlooks, pull-outs, parking lots, and trailheads—is prohibited. If you're tempted to spend the night in your truck or camper along Skyline Drive, be forewarned that rangers patrol routinely and will move you along regardless of the hour.

Trail Guide:
SHENANDOAH NATIONAL PARK

This is only a sampling of the more than 500 miles of footpaths and fire roads in Shenandoah National Park. In general, the trails listed here are well maintained and clearly marked, with concrete guideposts at most trail junctions. For experienced hikers armed with USGS maps and a compass, there are miles of old mountaineer roads that still exist as faint footpaths, bushwhacking possibilities to rarely visited waterfalls, and thousands of acres of roadless wilderness areas. Vehicles of any kind, including mountain bikes, are prohibited on park trails and fire roads. Dogs are prohibited on many trails and must be leashed on those where they are permitted. Horseback riders and hikers alike are allowed to use the yellow-blazed bridle trails; riders have the right-of-way.

Appalachian Trail—
See the Appalachian Trail chapter

Big Run—
See Rocky Mountain–Big Run Circuit

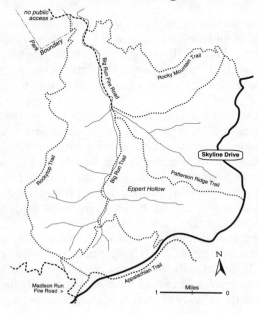

Cedar Run–
Whiteoak Canyon Circuit

Length: *7.5 miles (round trip)*
Elevation change: *2,015 feet*
Level: *moderately difficult (strenuous). This hike requires a sustained effort and several stream crossings. Allow at least 5 hours to complete the circuit.*
USGS quad maps: *Big Meadows, VA; Old Rag, VA*
Access: *Park at Hawksbill Gap (mile 45.6 on Skyline Drive). The Cedar Run trailhead is marked by a concrete post on the east side of Skyline Drive.*

This is a difficult but rewarding hike through two of Shenandoah's most spectacular gorges. From the Cedar Run trailhead marker, walk a short distance downhill, turn left on the horse trail, continue a short distance to a fork, then bear right onto the Cedar Run Trail. The trail is steep and rough throughout but isn't nearly as treacherous as some guides have portrayed it. Cedar Run flows over a rocky bed in a deep canyon, dropping over a 34-foot falls in a natural amphitheater at about 1.5 miles from the trailhead. There's no formal trail to the falls, but you can bushwhack upstream to its base. The trail passes obstructed views of two more falls, then descends on two switchbacks.

At the end of the second switchback, look carefully for an obscure trail junction to the left. (Avoid the continuation of Cedar Run Trail, which crosses private land to Berry Hollow. If you pass red or orange boundary blazes, you've gone too far.) Turn left, make an easy stream crossing, and continue north for approximately 0.9 mile on a fairly level trail to the foot of Whiteoak Canyon.

At the junction with Whiteoak Canyon Trail, turn left (to the right, the trail leads to private land, and public access is uncertain). Wade Whiteoak Creek and continue upstream 0.7 mile to another stream crossing. This stream was known as Nigger Run in earlier times, and you'll still hear the name used locally. At some point the hapless stream was renamed Negro Run, but some newer maps avoid the issue entirely by simply not labeling the stream. A short but somewhat difficult bushwhack upstream leads to a secluded falls rarely seen by the average park visitor.

From the stream crossing, Whiteoak Canyon Trail climbs steeply, passing six waterfalls within a mile. The canyon is spectacular, worth all of the time that you devote to it. Unfortunately, it attracts crowds on weekends and holidays, but off-season visitors often find the canyon virtually deserted. A visit in mid-winter, when the falls are often frozen solid, is especially rewarding.

The highest falls (86 feet) is the farthest upstream. At the head of that falls, turn left on the Whiteoak Fire Road and make a long, steady climb back to Skyline Drive at mile 45. Turn left on either the horse trail (just before reaching the drive) or the drive itself and walk back 0.6 mile to the Hawksbill Gap parking area.

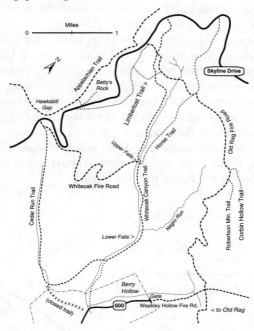

Corbin Hollow Trail —
See Old Rag Circuit Hike

Falls Trail

Length: *4.8 miles (7.8 miles including Appalachian Trail link)*

Elevation change: *1,410 feet*

Level: *moderate (strenuous)*

USGS quad maps: *Browns Cove, VA; McGaheysville, VA*

Access: *East trailhead is on Skyline Drive at the Doyle River parking area (mile 81.1). West trailhead is on the drive at the Falls Trail parking area (Skyline Drive mile 84.1).*

This boomerang-shaped route takes you down the eastern flank of the Blue Ridge, then returns to the ridge top on a strenuous trek that will reward you with views of three waterfalls. From the Doyle River parking area, the Falls Trail leads downhill to Upper Doyle River Falls, an attractive but often crowded spot. The crowds thin quickly as the trail begins a steep, rocky descent through a narrow canyon to the more secluded Lower Doyle River Falls.

Beyond the lower falls, the Falls Trail continues to lose elevation steadily, reaching its low point at the confluence of Doyle River and Jones Run. From there, the trail swings west to climb along Jones Run. This is an especially attractive stretch that passes cascades and small pools in a rocky, fern-draped ravine as it approaches Jones Run Falls, a nearly vertical drop of 42 feet. From the base of the falls, the trail follows a steep switchback, then veers away from the stream as it continues its steady climb through open woods to reach Skyline Drive. To return to your starting point, turn right on the Appalachian Trail and hike 3 miles back to the Doyle River parking area.

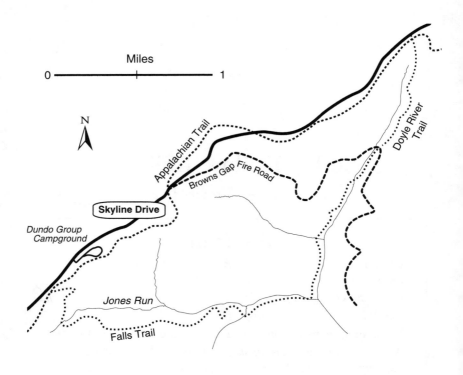

Hannah Run Trail—
See Nicholson Hollow Trail

Hawksbill Summit

Length: *1 mile*
Elevation change: *420 feet*
Level: *easy*
USGS quad map: *Big Meadows, VA*
Access: *Trailhead is at Upper Hawksbill parking area (mile 46.7 on Skyline Drive).*

From the parking area, the trail climbs steadily for approximately a half-mile to dead-end at a service road. Turn right on the dirt road and continue uphill for another half-mile to the observation platform on Hawksbill summit. At 4,050 feet, this is the highest point in the park, and the summit offers a sweeping vista across the piedmont, Blue Ridge, and Shenandoah Valley. But various Park Service "improvements"—an observation platform and shelter, a maze of roads and trails, and some unsightly cable strung along the cliffs—combine to rob this notable peak of any wilderness quality. With some effort, you can find views nearly as good in more pristine settings.

Jeremys Run

Length: *6.5 miles (including Appalachian Trail link)*
Elevation change: *2,100 feet*
Level: *moderately difficult (strenuous, with many stream crossings)*
USGS quad maps: *Bentonville, VA; Luray, VA; Thornton Gap, VA*
Access: *To reach the east (upper) trailhead, follow the Appalachian Trail northwest from its Skyline Drive crossing at mile 23.9, near the Elkwallow Wayside. If the small parking area is full, continue a short distance to Elkwallow Wayside parking lot, then backtrack. The west (lower) trailhead is on private land in the Shenandoah Valley, and public access is no longer certain.*

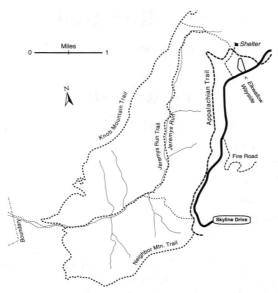

Follow the Appalachian Trail downhill from the northwest side of Skyline Drive. Just beyond the Elkwallow Shelter, the AT makes a sharp left at the head of the Jeremys Run Trail. Continue straight ahead on Jeremys Run. At 0.3 mile from the AT–Jeremys Run junction, a spur trail bears right to the Knob Mountain Trail. Bear left, remaining on the Jeremys Run Trail as it passes cascades and pools and a low waterfall in a steep, rocky canyon. You'll need to wade Jeremys Run more than a dozen times, and some of the crossings are difficult. Jeremys Run is one of the most scenic streams in the northern park, and the trail—although fairly difficult—is deservedly popular. Expect crowds on weekends and holidays in good weather, especially during trout season.

The Neighbor Mountain and Knob Mountain Trails intersect the Jeremys Run Trail near its lower end. Both provide little-traveled, but strenuous, alternate return routes. The Jeremys Run Trail crosses private land beyond the park boundary, and public access is uncertain.

Little Devils Stairs

Length: *4.5 miles one way; 8 miles via circuit hike*
Elevation change: *1,850 feet*
Level: *moderately difficult (strenuous)*
USGS quad maps: *Bentonville, VA; Thornton Gap, VA*
Access: *From the parking area at mile 19.4 on Skyline Drive.*

The Little Devils Stairs Trail is a rugged scramble through a narrow, boulder-strewn canyon. Be prepared to wade and rock-scramble; good non-slip boots are essential. Little Devils Stairs is a dangerous place when the rocks are wet, icy, or snow-covered.

From the parking area, hike 1 mile west on the Jinney Grey Fire Road through pleasant, open woods. At 1 mile, reach a junction and turn left (but see the alternate circuit hike below) onto the Little Devils Stairs Trail. The trail follows a small stream downhill, crossing it several times before entering the main gorge. Once in the main gorge, work your way downstream any way you can. There is no formal trail down the Stairs, a series of boulder-strewn cascades on Keyser Run.

At the mouth of the gorge, the trail swings away from the stream and leads to a small parking area on private land beyond the park boundary. Turn back at the trail's end and return the way you came.

If you prefer a longer but less challenging return route, turn right (west) on Keyser Run Fire Road at the end of the Little Devils Stairs Trail. The road, closed to public vehicles, leads back to the park boundary within a short distance. At about 1 mile from the gate, pass a ruined cemetery. This was once the burying ground for the Bolens, a relatively affluent mountain clan with large land holdings, who were displaced when the park was established. The cemetery hasn't been used since the 1930s and is in disrepair.

At the cemetery, turn right (north) and begin a steady uphill climb on the Jinney Grey Fire Road. Continue straight ahead at the junction with the upper end of Little Devils Stairs Trail, staying on Jinney Grey, and return to Skyline Drive.

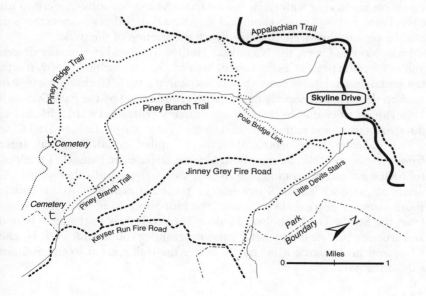

Little Stony Man Cliffs—
See the Appalachian Trail chapter

Mary's Rock—
See the Appalachian Trail chapter

Nicholson Hollow Trail

Length: *6 miles*
Elevation change: *2,055 feet*
Level: *moderate*
USGS quad maps: *Old Rag, VA*
Access: *West trailhead is on Skyline Drive, just north of a large grassy parking area at mile 38.5. East trailhead is on Route 600 at the mouth of Weakely Hollow, near the Old Rag parking area; see the Old Rag entry for directions.*

Nicholson Hollow Trail follows an old mountaineer road into what was once known as "Free State Hollow," stronghold of the Nicholson clan. The Nicholsons defended their territory from all comers, including the occasional law officer, and patriarch Aaron Nicholson laid claim to the entire hollow based on his having walked its boundaries. As the Nicholsons were to discover in the 1930s, Aaron's claim was worthless. Like other squatters throughout the region, they were displaced with the coming of the park.

From Skyline Drive, the Nicholson Hollow Trail makes a steady descent and at 1.8 miles passes Corbin Cabin. Built by George Corbin in 1909, it is the last remaining habitable mountaineer house in the park. Corbin put a new tin roof on the structure shortly before it was condemned by the Park Service in 1936, an injustice that he dwelled on for many years afterward. His cabin is now maintained and rented to hikers by the Potomac Appalachian Trail Club.

Two miles beyond Corbin Cabin, the 5.7-mile Hannah Run Trail enters from the north; it climbs steeply to Skyline Drive near Pinnacle Overlook, following an old mountaineer trail past cabin ruins and other subtle evidence of early settlement. Rock-hop or wade Hannah Run to continue; a short distance beyond the crossing, the Hot-Short Mountain Trail enters from the north. The Nicholson Hollow Trail continues to the park boundary, crossing private land for the last quarter-mile. You'll wade both Hughes River and Brokenback Run shortly before the trail ends at Route 600 outside of the park.

Old Rag Circuit Hike (via the Ridge Trail)

Length: *7.5 miles (round trip)*
Elevation change: *2,380 feet*
Level: *difficult (strenuous)*
USGS quad map: *Old Rag, VA*
Access: *This is one of the few Shenandoah hikes to begin at the foot of the mountain. To reach the trailhead, drive into Sperryville on US-211, turn south on US-522, and at 0.6 mile turn right onto Route 231. Drive south on Route 231 for approximately 7.8 miles to a right turn onto Virginia 602 (marked "Nethers"). In another half-mile, bear right onto Route 601 just after crossing the Hughes River. Follow the main road (which changes numbers, becoming first 707 and then 600) to a gate at the park boundary. Park wherever you can without blocking the road. The parking area is on private land; if you block the road or access to private drives, your car will be towed. On weekends and holidays in good weather, you may have to backtrack more than a mile to the overflow parking area.*

Note: The Park Service now requires permits to hike Old Rag on certain high-use weekends and holidays. Permits are issued only until the overflow parking area fills, and rangers are stationed at the trailhead to check permits. You can avoid this problem by hiking Old Rag during the week or in colder weather. Old Rag is one of the most heavily visited sites in the park, and during peak tourist season you may find yourself elbow-to-elbow with other hikers on the trail.

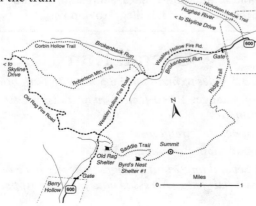

From the parking area, the Ridge Trail makes a steady ascent by switchbacks, becoming steep as it approaches the first of several rocky false summits. From there, the going gets tricky. You'll wedge yourself into a deep cleft, only to emerge onto a narrow ledge above a sheer drop-off of several hundred feet, and later make a nearly vertical climb up a slippery rock chute to the lower slope of Old Rag's true summit. At one point, the trail climbs what appears to be a natural staircase—actually an ancient lava flow—between high granite walls. For your effort, you'll be rewarded by a sweeping 360-degree view from cabin-sized granite boulders on Old Rag's barren summit. Spend as much time as you can, but plan to leave well before sundown unless you're an experienced night hiker. Camping on the summit is prohibited.

From the summit, the Ridge Trail makes a steep, rocky descent to the Old Rag saddle and Byrd's Nest Shelter #1. At the shelter, turn right onto the Saddle Trail and make an easy descent for another mile to the Old Rag Shelter and spring. Beyond the shelter, the trail continues downhill as a fire road for a short distance before intersecting Weakley Hollow Fire Road.

The four-way junction in Weakley Hollow was once the site of Old Rag village, which was demolished by the Park Service after World War II. The fire road to the left leads southwest to Berry Hollow. Straight ahead is the Old Rag Fire Road, which makes a steep climb to the head of Corbin Hollow before continuing to Skyline Drive. To return to your car, turn right and begin an easy downhill stroll on the Weakley Hollow Fire Road along Brokenback Run.

(If you have ample time and energy, make a side-trip into Corbin Hollow. The well-marked trail will be on your left about a mile from the four-way junction. Corbin Hollow was home to some of the poorest mountaineers, and even a short journey up the hollow is revealing. This was land that no one else wanted: Thin, rocky soil and nearly vertical slopes, with only an eroded footpath to connect to the outside world, locked the Corbin clan into a downward spiral of poverty and isolation. You'll still find scattered evidence of their existence—old foundations, shards, and assorted junk—if you take the time to look, but remember that it is illegal to remove artifacts from the park.)

Overall Run

Length: *3.5 miles to main falls; 6.5 miles to park boundary*

Elevation change: *1,140 feet to main falls; 2,140 feet to park boundary*

Level: *moderate (strenuous)*

USGS quad map: *Bentonville, VA*

Access: *Several important changes in access have occurred in the past few years. Access is now from the Appalachian*

Trail at Hogback Overlook (mile 21.5 on Skyline Drive). Matthews Arm Campground, once a popular access point, is now closed. The west trailhead, near US-340 on private land, has been closed by the landowner, and the Park Service no longer maintains the lower end of Overall Run Trail west of the Big Blue Trail. For directions to Overall Run from US-340, see the Matthews Arm section of the Big Blue Trail chapter.

From the Hogback Overlook, follow the Appalachian Trail south for a half-mile to the Big Blue Trail. This is the southern terminus of the Big Blue, which has come 144 miles to this point from the C&O Canal at Hancock, MD. Turn right (west) and begin a steady descent on the western flank of the Blue Ridge. At 3 miles, bear right onto the combined Big Blue/Overall Run Trail. Within a short distance, you'll pass a spur trail to the head of Upper Overall Run Falls, the highest in the park at 93 feet. The main Overall Run Trail skirts the edge of a steep ravine and beyond the main falls passes another spur, this one a rough path to the base of the falls. From there, the trail continues downhill alongside Overall Run, leveling off as it approaches the mouth of the hollow.

At 5.6 miles, the Big Blue veers away from Overall Run to continue to US-340 in the Shenandoah Valley, while the Overall Run Trail continues straight ahead and downhill. Lower Overall Run Falls are a short distance downstream from this junction. The lower hollow is especially scenic and well suited for backcountry camping, but the western end of Overall Run Trail is no longer blazed or maintained. The owner of the lower end of Overall Run is reportedly hostile to hikers, who are advised to take private property postings in the area seriously.

From the end of the blazed trail, the Beecher Ridge horse trail provides an alternative route back up the mountain. The trail has no outstanding scenic features, but it receives little use, and the environs look promising for secluded backcountry camping.

Rocky Mountain–Big Run Circuit

Length: *10 miles (round trip)*

Elevation change: *2,465 feet*

Level: *moderate (strenuous). This hike requires a sustained effort. It is best suited to a two-day backpack trip. Otherwise, allow a full day to complete the circuit.*

USGS quad maps: *McGaheysville, VA*

Access: *Starting point is the Brown Mountain Overlook on Skyline Drive (mile 76.9).*

This long but rewarding circuit features outstanding views and a hike along the park's largest stream. There are many possibilities for other circuit hikes in the Big Run area.

To start the circuit, find a break in the overlook wall, the beginning of the Brown Mountain–Rocky Mountain Trail. From the overlook, the trail descends steeply at first, levels off somewhat, and then climbs on switchbacks to the narrow crest of Rocky Mountain, where there are several limited viewpoints. From the first crest, the trail makes a moderate descent into a saddle. Just before the trail begins to climb again, bushwhack uphill and to your left through open woods to the top of a talus slope with a panoramic view back to the main Blue Ridge. Return to the main trail and continue to the second summit of Rocky Mountain, where the trail swings to the right and begins a long descent on Brown Mountain. Much of the trail is routed slightly below the ridge crest, but you can scramble to the ridge where there are occasional spectacular views from outcroppings and talus slopes. The trail becomes steeper as it approaches the Big Run Valley, finally descending on switchbacks.

The Brown Mountain–Rocky Mountain Trail ends at Big Run; you will have to wade the stream to continue. Once across the stream, turn left on the Big Run Fire Road and follow it upstream. (Downstream, the road continues to private property, and public access is uncertain.)

Big Run is the largest stream in the park, a series of cascades and large pools in a steep, rocky canyon that is now a designated wilderness. Continue up the fire road for approximately 1.5 miles to a well-marked former fire trail that leads uphill and to the east along Rocky Mountain Run, returning you to the Brown Mountain–Rocky Mountain Trail. Turn right and return to the Brown Mountain Overlook.

Stony Man Nature Trail

Length: *less than 1 mile*
Elevation change: *340 feet*
Level: *easy*
USGS quad maps: *Big Meadows, VA; Old Rag, VA*
Access: *Turn into Skyland's north entrance from Skyline Drive at mile 41.7 and almost immediately make a right turn into the Nature Trail parking area.*

This graded, well-marked trail is keyed to a descriptive brochure, which—with any luck—you'll find in an honor-system dispenser at the trailhead. The trail climbs to the summit of Stony Man (4,010 feet) and makes a short loop around the summit; look for a spur leading to the sweeping viewpoint on the exposed greenstone cliffs. Talus slopes below the cliffs offer the opportunity for rock scrambling. Several companies tried to mine copper on

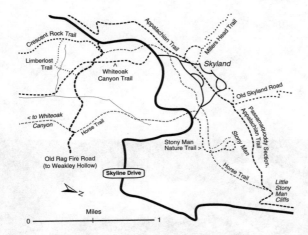

Stony Man in the last century, but the high cost of extracting the ore doomed their operations. George Freeman Pollock eventually gained title to Stony Man and in 1894 opened Stony Man Camp, forerunner of the Skyland resort. Pollock later campaigned long and hard for the development of Shenandoah National Park, finally turning Skyland over to the Park Service in 1935. His memoirs, available at the visitor centers, offer a fascinating look at turn-of-the-century life in this part of the Blue Ridge.

Whiteoak Canyon—
See Cedar Run–
Whiteoak Canyon Circuit

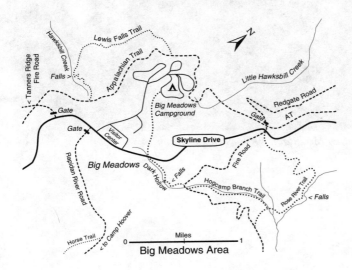

Big Meadows Area

Massanutten Mountain, VA — Strickler Knob

Chapter 7

Massanutten Mountain
(Virginia)

Massanutten Mountain is an oddity, a faintly mysterious free-standing range that rises abruptly to split the Shenandoah Valley in two from Strasburg to Harrisonburg. Sometimes regarded as a poor step-child to the Blue Ridge, the mountain remains virtually unknown among the tour-bus crowd. True, Massanutten lacks Shenandoah National Park's 4,000-foot peaks and mountain-top parkway. But it also lacks the park's traffic, crowds, and restrictive regulations. Aside from several modest recreation areas and some clear-cutting operations, the Forest Service has left its holdings on the Massanutten largely undisturbed, and you're free to roam and camp in the backcountry at will.

History

In keeping with Americans' tendency to ascribe Native American origins to any unusual place name, "Massanutten" has been presented in various accounts as an Indian word meaning "three-topped mountain," "old field," "potato field," "basket-shaped valley" … and the list goes on. But another theory holds that the name came from a corruption of an old colloquial German expression translating roughly to "great furrow." That seems reasonable, since the name originally referred only to the valley at the eastern foot of New Market Gap. The ridge was known first as Peaked Mountain, then as Buffalo Mountain, and only later took the Massanutten name. The earliest settlers were Germans, who probably arrived here by way of Pennsylvania around 1726.

George Washington surveyed the northern end of Massanutten Mountain in 1748 or 1749, working his way up Passage Creek gorge to Mudhole Gap and returning along the eastern crest of Massanutten Mountain, on a course followed today by the Massanutten East Trail. Impressed by the natural fortifications surrounding the gorge and the Fort Valley, Washington later considered sheltering his troops at Massanutten following the disastrous winter at Valley Forge, but he never put his plan into action.

Battles raged around the base of Massanutten during the Civil War, although no significant action took place on the high ridges. Signal Knob, however, served as an important Confederate relay station from which messages were flashed to high points in the Blue Ridge and then on to Richmond.

Massanutten Mountain, VA — New Market Gap

At nearby New Market, hundreds of teenaged boys were ordered into battle in 1864, and in autumn of that year General Sheridan made good on his boast that "when this is completed, the valley ... will have but little in it for man or beast" as his troops looted and burned their way across the Shenandoah Valley.

Massanutten was once an important iron-making area, and well-preserved nineteenth-century blast furnaces still stand at Elizabeth Furnace Recreation Area in the northern section and at Catherine Furnace in the southern section. But by the turn of the century, the familiar Appalachian cycle of mining, clear-cutting, erosion, and abandonment was nearing its end, and much of the ruined land was eventually acquired by the Forest Service.

In the 1920s, a group of Virginia businessmen promoted Massanutten as the site of a newly proposed national park. What they hadn't counted on was the opposition of Skyland owner George Freeman Pollock, who battled ferociously to have the proposed park situated in the main Blue Ridge near his popular Skyland resort. In the ensuing struggle, Pollock mounted a smear campaign so effective that even today a tendency lingers to regard Massanutten as somehow inferior to the Blue Ridge. In his memoirs, Pollock recalled, "We drove into the Fort Valley ... and even this brief excursion made it obvious that comparison with the Blue Ridge was absurd. ... I laid the facts on the table, cold and hard. 'You are betting on a lame horse. ... My home in the Blue Ridge is 1,200 feet higher than the highest peak in the Massanuttens.'"

Pollock's view prevailed. The Blue Ridge was selected as the site of Shenandoah National Park, but Massanutten still had its supporters. By the early 1930s the Forest Service had incorporated several large Massanutten tracts into the George Washington National Forest, and Camp Roosevelt—the first Civilian Conservation Corps settlement—opened there on April 4, 1933. Today, Massanutten's northern half is largely in the hands of the Forest Service and boasts a well-developed trail system and several popular semi-primitive campgrounds and recreation areas. Forest Service holdings in the southern half remain largely undeveloped but are facing pressure from nearby private development on the mountain.

Natural Features

Despite Massanutten's proximity to the Blue Ridge, its geology is more closely related to the valley-and-ridge formations farther to the west. Hard sandstone caps the highest ridges, forming low cliffs and small talus slopes. An east-west cross-section of the range reveals three parallel, northeasterly trending ridges, true to valley-and-ridge form. Major streams flow north and south, while many of the east-west streams tend to be intermittent.

Largely clear-cut at the turn of the century, a typical eastern hardwood forest has returned and reached maturity at the lower elevations, with pine and mountain laurel intermixed on the higher ridges. White-tailed deer, once extinct in the area, are now plentiful, and the black bear reportedly is making a modest comeback in the more isolated areas.

Access

To reach the northern end of Massanutten Mountain, follow Route 55 west from Front Royal or east from Strasburg and turn south on Route 678 at Waterlick, approximately midway between the two towns. Route 678 is a narrow, scenic drive that winds through the rocky gorge of Passage Creek and then climbs to Fort Valley.

To reach Massanutten's northern half from Luray, follow US-211 west of Luray to Route 675, which climbs steeply to Camp Roosevelt Recreation Area before intersecting Route 678. A more interesting alternative is to continue up US-211 to the crest of New Market Gap and turn north on Forest Service Road 274, a rough dirt road that eventually becomes paved Route 678 south of Fort Valley. The unpaved portion of the road is passable to ordinary passenger cars in good weather, but a four-wheel-drive vehicle is recommended.

To reach Massanutten's southern section, follow US-340 for 1.4 miles south of Newport and turn right (west) on Route 685. Continue to the Catherine Furnace Recreation Area and Cub Run Road, which turns south and continues 12 miles to Runkles Gap, near the town of Shenandoah. Read the cautionary note at the beginning of the trail guide if you're planning to explore Massanutten's southern section.

Nearby Towns and Attractions

CAVES—

The Shenandoah Valley, with its underlying limestone base and slightly acidic groundwater, is honeycombed with caverns. Most undeveloped sites are on private land, but several commercially developed caverns in the area are worth a visit. Largest and best known is Luray Caverns, an often crowded attraction west of Luray on US-211. Two smaller but equally interesting caves, at the very foot of Massanutten's western slope, are Shenandoah Caverns (4 miles north of New Market off I-81 at exit 269) and Endless Caverns (take exit 257 from I-81 and continue 3 miles south on US-11). The latter is marked by a none-too-subtle sign spread Hollywood-style across Massanutten's lower flank. Skyline Caverns, at the foot of the Blue Ridge and known for its delicate anthodite formations, is on US-340 just south of Front Royal.

FORT VALLEY—

Sheltered by steep ridges, this valley high in the Massanutten once offered refuge to an array of outlaws and shady characters. One such individual was named Powell, and for a time after his arrival in the 1730s the region was known as Powell's Fort Valley in honor of his fortified home. Largely clear-cut in the last century, the valley today is peaceful farming and grazing country. Most of the valley along Route 678 is privately owned; enjoy your drive, but respect property rights.

GEORGE WASHINGTON NATIONAL FOREST VISITOR CENTER—

On US-211 at the crest of New Market Gap, between Luray and New Market, the center is a good source of more detailed information on the Massanutten area.

NEW MARKET BATTLEFIELD—

On May 15, 1864, a desperate Confederate General Breckinridge ordered 247 teenaged cadets from Virginia Military Institute into battle here. Many were killed in action. On the grounds are several restored buildings and the New Market Battlefield Military Museum.

STRASBURG, VA—

One of the oldest settlements in the Shenandoah Valley, Strasburg lies at the foot of Massanutten at the junction of Routes 55 and 11. The town boasts a small museum (E. King Street) and a modest but interesting assortment of shops, restaurants, and historic structures.

Camping

An extensive and well-maintained trail system on Massanutten's northern half leads to any number of good backcountry sites, and permits are not required. You'll find springs along many trails, but boil or treat all drinking water. Open fires are allowed by state law only between 4:00 P.M. and midnight from March 1 through May 15. The Forest Service maintains several attractive, semi-primitive car campgrounds in the area. Elizabeth Furnace (on Route 678 south of Waterlick) and Camp Roosevelt (on Route 675 northwest of Luray) offer level campsites with fire rings, picnic tables, drinking water, and pit toilets. Hazard Mill Recreation Area, on the Shenandoah River at the eastern foot of the mountain, also offers semi-primitive sites and is popular with canoeists. Car-camping is also allowed at informal roadside pull-outs throughout the national forest unless posted otherwise.

Trail Guide:
MASSANUTTEN MOUNTAIN

The following trails lie on Massanutten Mountain's northern half, between Strasburg and New Market Gap. Most are clearly blazed and fairly well maintained. In contrast, Massanutten's southern section presents such an array of problems that I can't recommend the area to the casual hiker. Many of the trails south of US-211 receive little or no maintenance and when last hiked were overgrown and hard to follow. Others have been degraded by ORV and ATV use (legal and otherwise) or present access problems because of nearby private development and inholdings. To make matters worse, hikers have reported incidents of harassment, vandalism, and theft in the area, and hunters overrun the mountain in autumn. If none of this dissuades you, stop by the Forest Service visitor center on US-211 to obtain more information about trails in the southern section.

Big Blue Trail (Massanutten West and Massanutten East Sections)—
See the Big Blue Trail chapter

Duncan Hollow Trail

Length: *9 miles*
Elevation change: *1,400 feet*
Level: *moderate*
USGS quad map: *Hamburg, VA*
Access: *North trailhead is on Route 675 just east of Camp Roosevelt. South trailhead, with ample parking, is on US-211 in New Market Gap, 1.8 miles east of the Forest Service visitor center.*

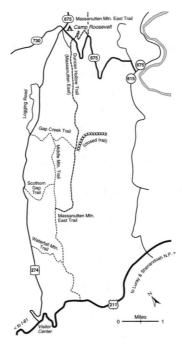

Duncan Hollow Trail is a continuation of the Massanutten Mountain East Trail's southward course, and newer maps now show it as Massanutten Mountain East Trail.

From Camp Roosevelt, hike a short distance uphill to the trail, which follows an abandoned dirt road for a mile before narrowing to a footpath. Three miles south of the trailhead, reach Peach Orchard Gap and a junction with the Gap Creek Trail, which leads west to Crisman Hollow Road (FS-274). Avoid an abandoned road that leads east to private property. At 1.75 miles beyond the Gap Creek Trail junction, the trail crosses the crest of Middle Mountain. From here, it's possible to make a bushwhack due south along the narrow ridge to a high outcropping on Strickler Knob, overlooking New Market Gap. The going is fairly rough, but you can't really get lost if you remain on the spine of the ridge.

From the crest of Middle Mountain, the trail descends to a junction with the Middle Mountain Trail, which leads north to a junction with the Scothorn Gap Trail, another connector to FS-274. Turn left (south) and continue steadily downhill through open woods on the eastern flank of Waterfall Mountain. When last hiked, this section of the trail was in rough condition and hard to follow in spots. Watch carefully for the orange blazes and avoid a short stretch of abandoned trail that still shows a few old blazes. The trail improves considerably before ending at a parking area on US-211.

Gap Creek Trail—
See Duncan Hollow Trail

Indian Grave Ridge Trail

Length: *2.5 miles*
Elevation change: *1,500 feet*
Level: *moderate*
USGS quad map: *Rileyville, VA*
Access: *East trailhead is at the top of a ridge on Route 717 west of Luray, VA. West trailhead is on the Massanutten Mountain East Trail.*

From its somewhat obscure eastern trailhead on Route 717, the Indian Grave Ridge Trail begins as an old dirt road. The Indian burial mound—long since plundered and now little more than scattered piles of rock—is 1 mile from the trailhead. Beyond the mound, the trail turns right, skirting a small pond, and begins a steep climb up the eastern flank of Massanutten Mountain. The last quarter-mile before the junction with the Massanutten Mountain East Trail is especially rough.

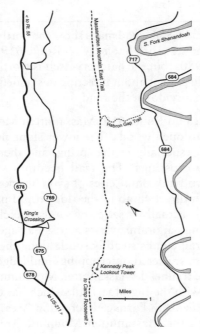

Kennedy Peak Trail—
See Massanutten Mountain East Trail

Massanutten Mountain East Trail

Length: *23 miles*
Elevation change: *1,570 feet*
Level: *moderate*
USGS quad maps: *Bentonville, VA; Rileyville, VA; Strasburg, VA*
Access: *To reach the north trailhead, follow US-55 to Waterlick, midway between Front Royal and Strasburg. Turn south onto Route 678 and continue approximately 1.3 miles to a left turn onto Route 619. Follow 619 to a large parking area at the trailhead, approximately a mile east of the state fish hatchery. The south trailhead is on Route 675 in George Washington National Forest about 1.5 miles west of Camp Roosevelt Campground. From Camp Roosevelt, the Duncan Hollow Trail (see earlier entry) serves as a southward continuation of the Massanutten Mountain East Trail.*

Note: Older guides and USGS quad maps show the north end of Massanutten Mountain Trail at the state fish hatchery on Route 619. That trailhead was closed in the early 1980s, but the hatchery itself is worth a visit, and its staff have been remarkably patient about directing misguided hikers to the "new" trailhead a short distance down the road.

From the parking area on Route 619, Massanutten Mountain Trail crosses a grassy meadow into open woods. The lower slope near the trail's beginning is wet in spots, especially in the spring, and there are several minor intermittent stream crossings. The trail becomes steeper as it climbs Massanutten's eastern flank on a series of switchbacks, eventually turning to the southeast for a direct climb to the ridge top. Buzzard Rock, 2 miles from the trailhead, is actually a series of sandstone cliffs along a narrow hogback ridge offering panoramic views across Passage Creek gorge. From Buzzard Rock, the trail climbs steadily south along the narrow ridge, with good viewpoints from scattered outcroppings and ledges.

At 4 miles from the trailhead, Massanutten Mountain Trail reaches Shawl Gap and a junction with the Big Blue Trail, which has climbed eastward to this point from the Elizabeth Furnace Recreation Area. From this junction, Big Blue merges with the Massanutten Mountain Trail, which it follows south for the next 6.7 miles to Veach Gap. Beyond Shawl Gap, the combined Massanutten Mountain/Big Blue Trail makes a short, steep climb to High Peak and continues southward, with minor ups and downs, to the crest of Little Crease Mountain (2,265 feet). From there, the trail drops into Mill Run Valley, eventually reaching Veach Gap and the Little Crease Shelter (bunks, tables, fireplace, and pit toilet).

Beyond Little Crease Shelter, the trail climbs to regain the ridge top and then splits a mile beyond the shelter, with the Big Blue leading downhill and to the east, while the Massanutten Mountain East Trail continues southward along the ridge top. At 3.3 miles beyond this fork, reach a junction with the Milford Gap Trail. To the east, the Milford Gap Trail leads down the mountain to Hazard Mill Recreation Area on the South Fork of the Shenandoah; to the west, it leads a short distance to a parking area at the Chalybeate Spring in Fort Valley. At 1.5 miles beyond Milford Gap, reach an intersection with the Indian Grave Ridge Trail, which leads downhill to Route 717 near the Shenandoah River. The ridge was named for an Indian burial mound, long since plundered, near the foot of the mountain.

The next section of the Massanutten Mountain East Trail is especially scenic, following a narrow ridge with sweeping views across the Shenandoah Valley. At 8.5 miles beyond Milford Gap, look for a short side trail to the observation tower on 2,560-foot Kennedy Peak. From the Kennedy Peak Trail junction, Massanutten Mountain Trail continues 2.2 miles to its south trailhead on Route 675. From Route 675, the Duncan Hollow Trail (see earlier entry) serves as a continuation of the Massanutten Mountain East Trail, ending at US-211 in New Market Gap.

Massanutten Mountain West Trail

Length: *17 miles*

Elevation change: *450 feet*

Level: *fairly easy*

USGS quad map: *Strasburg, VA*

Access: *North trailhead is at the end of the Signal Knob Trail. South trailhead is on Route 675 in Edinburg Gap.*

This long trail leads through varied environments on the western flank of Massanutten Mountain, starting in the Little Passage Creek Valley and climbing to the narrow western ridge of Three Top Mountain.

To begin your hike from the north, follow the Signal Knob Trail to Signal Knob and turn left (south) onto the orange-blazed Massanutten Mountain West Trail. The trail drops into the valley between the western and middle ridges of Massanutten, reaching Strasburg Reservoir in about 2 miles. Camping is not permitted in the watershed. Below the dam, the trail follows Little Passage Creek on a dirt road that may be wet or muddy at times.

*Massanutten Mountain, VA —
Passage Creek Gorge*

At 4.2 miles pass the Powell Fort special-use campground (not open to the general public). Leave the road a short distance beyond the campground, bearing right onto an orange-blazed footpath. Reach an intersection with the Big Blue Trail at 5 miles. The Big Blue descends to the west, while the Massanutten Mountain West Trail continues south along the western crest of Massanutten, known here as Three Top Mountain. There are good views for the next 5 miles from the narrow ridge.

At 10 miles, reach route 758 and the Woodstock Observation Tower, which provides a sweeping panorama of the western Shenandoah Valley and Great North Mountain. South of the tower, the trail continues at or near the ridge top for approximately 5 miles, then begins a moderate descent, skirting behind Waonaze Peak at 6 miles and then dropping more steeply to an intersection with Peters Mill Run Road at 16.8 miles. To complete the hike, turn right (south) on Peters Mill Road and continue a short distance to the parking area on Route 675 in Edinburg Gap.

Milford Gap Trail

Length: *3.1 miles*

Elevation change: *1,200 feet*

Difficulty: *moderate*

USGS quad maps: *Bentonville, VA; Rileyville, VA*

Access: *East trailhead is at the Hazard Mill Recreation Area. To reach the recreation area, take Route 613 over the South Fork of the Shenandoah, bear left, and continue 3 miles south to the campground. The west trailhead is on Route 758, east of Route 678, in the fort valley. If you plan to use this trailhead, be forewarned that unpaved Route 758 is in poor condition, and there have been reports of friction between landowners and hikers in this area.*

From the Hazard Mill Campground, the Milford Gap Trail climbs the eastern slope of Massanutten Mountain through open woods with occasional wintertime views. At 1.9 miles from the campground, the Tolliver Trail enters from the south. Continue to climb, crossing the Massanutten Mountain East Trail at 2.5 miles from the campground. From this junction, it's a steep 0.6-mile hike downhill to the western trailhead at Chalybeate Spring.

Mudhole Gap Trail

Length: *5.2 miles*
Elevation change: *400 feet*
Difficulty: *moderate (with difficult stream crossings)*
USGS quad map: *Strasburg, VA*
Access: *East trailhead is at the parking area on Route 678 opposite the Elizabeth Furnace Campground. West trailhead is on the Massanutten Mountain West Trail south of Strasburg Reservoir.*

This challenging trail follows an abandoned dirt road along Little Passage Creek in a steep and secluded section of Green Mountain. From the parking area, follow a graveled logging road for 3.5 miles to an unattractive clearcut area, where the route becomes obscure. From the end of the logging road, continue straight ahead and downhill through open woods toward Little Passage Creek, where you should find an old dirt road leading upstream. At 4.5 miles from the trailhead, turn right and follow Narrow Passage Creek through Mudhole Gap, a steep and narrow gorge that will force you to make several potentially difficult stream crossings. Don't attempt the crossings at all if water levels are high. From Mudhole Gap, the trail continues to a junction with the Massanutten Mountain West Trail.

Sherman Gap Trail

Length: *5.3 miles*
Elevation change: *1,400 feet*
Level: *moderate (strenuous)*
USGS quad map: *Strasburg, VA*
Access: *East trailhead is on Route 613, 2.5 miles south of its junction with Route 619. The unmarked trailhead is on private land, and the nearest legal parking is at Shawl Gap, about a mile to the north. West trailhead is at the Elizabeth Furnace Picnic Area, via the Botts Trail.*

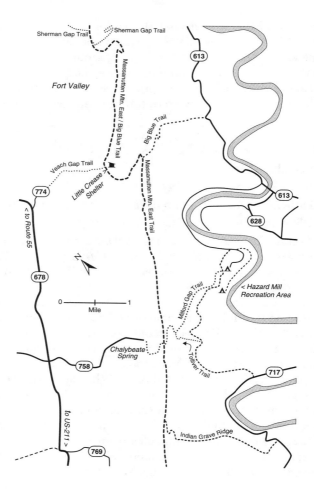

The Sherman Gap Trail follows a historic route across the eastern ridge of Massanutten Mountain. Once an important wagon road, today it serves primarily as a horse trail. Hikers are welcome to use the trail, but horses have the right-of-way. From its obscure east trailhead, the Sherman Gap Trail makes a steady 2.5-mile climb up the eastern flank of Massanutten Mountain, intersecting the Massanutten Mountain East Trail at the crest. From there, it follows the ridge-top trail north for a short distance before making a steep westward descent to end at the Botts Trail opposite the Elizabeth Furnace Campground. To reach the campground, you will have to wade Passage Creek, a difficult crossing when the creek is running high. To avoid wading, turn north onto the Botts Trail and follow it another mile to the Elizabeth Furnace Picnic Area.

Signal Knob Trail

Length: *4 miles*

Elevation change: *1,400 feet*

Level: *moderate*

USGS quad map: *Strasburg, VA*

Access: *Follow US-55 to Waterlick, midway between Front Royal and Strasburg, VA. Turn south on Route 678 and continue south about 3.5 miles to an unpaved parking area on the right.*

From the parking area, Signal Knob Trail climbs on a narrow shelf high above a ravine, reaching Sand Spring (reputedly the water supply for Civil War troops stationed high above on Signal Knob) in about 0.3 mile. From Sand Spring, the trail turns northeast and climbs the eastern flank of Green Mountain (the middle of Massanutten's three parallel ridges) through open woods that afford occasional winter views across Passage Creek gorge.

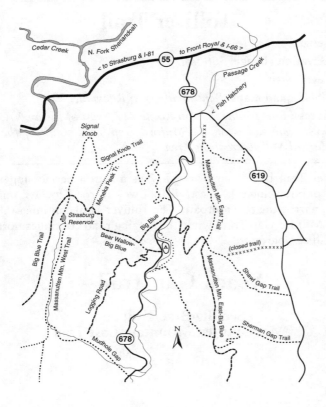

One mile from the spring, reach Buzzard Rock Overlook, which has an excellent open view of the eastern Massanutten, Shenandoah Valley, and Blue Ridge. Directly to the north of the overlook is Richardson Knob, an odd cone-shaped outlier.

Beyond Buzzard Rock Overlook, the Signal Knob Trail makes a sharp switchback, climbing to the south for 0.6 mile to Fort Valley Overlook. Another switchback beyond the overlook returns the trail to its northeasterly course. A moderate 1-mile climb leads to a fork on the northern flank of Green Mountain. Turn right for a short side trip to the Shenandoah Valley Overlook, or left to continue on the main trail. From the fork, an easy, mostly level 1.75-mile hike leads to the viewpoint on Signal Knob (2,106 feet). Situated on a ledge at the northern terminus of Massanutten's middle ridge, Signal Knob was an important Confederate relay station, serving as a link in a primitive system that flashed signals down the crest of Massanutten, across the Blue Ridge, and then on to Richmond. Today, the knob is marred by a telecommunications tower, but the view remains exceptional.

Tolliver Trail

Length: *2.3 miles*

Elevation change: *300 feet*

Level: *easy*

USGS quad maps: *Bentonville, VA; Rileyville, VA*

Access: *East trailhead is on Route 717, west of Luray, VA. West trailhead is on the Milford Gap Trail south of the Hazard Mill Recreation Area.*

The Tolliver Trail begins on Route 717 as a Forest Service logging road (closed to public vehicles). The trail follows the road for 1.7 miles, then veers west, narrowing to a footpath. The Tolliver Trail continues 0.8 mile to end at the Milford Gap Trail, while the logging road continues north to the Hazard Mill campground.

Veach Gap Trail—

See Big Blue Trail and Massanutten Mountain East Trail

Part Four

THE VALLEY-AND-RIDGE PROVINCE

North Fork Mountain, WV — Mill Creek Mountain from North Fork River

The Valley-and-Ridge Province

L ying between the Shenandoah Valley to the east and the Allegheny Front to the west, the valley-and-ridge province is a region of steep,
parallel, northeasterly trending ridges separated by stream and river valleys.
Although the valley-and-ridge province lacks a big-name national park or
similar attraction, it offers a fine array of smaller, lesser-known natural areas.

The George Washington and Monongahela National Forests hold large
tracts in the valley-and-ridge province. Both national forests offer outstanding backcountry camping, and permits are not needed. Forest Service car
campgrounds are widely scattered; all are semi-primitive, and many can be
reached only on rough access roads. Unless posted otherwise, you may also
camp in pull-outs along the Forest Service roads, provided that you don't
block the road.

Trail conditions vary widely in this area, but in general you can expect
trails to be rougher and less well signed than in Shenandoah National Park.
Motorized vehicles are legal on some trails and are used illegally on others.
Hunting and fishing are allowed in the national forests, subject to some restrictions, with proper licenses. Streams tend to be shallow, well suited to
casual canoeing or tubing during normal flow, but springtime run-off can
provide some challenging whitewater. Many of the streams in this region are
prone to flash-flooding after a heavy storm.

North Fork Mountain, WV — View west to Allegheny Front

127

History

Thomas Jefferson noted that Virginia's Indian population had declined by two-thirds between 1607 and 1669, the result of "spirituous liquors, the smallpox, and an abridgment of territory. ..." Departure of the native tribes in the early eighteenth century was hastened by construction of a chain of frontier forts throughout the valley-and-ridge area.

Settlers began to stake their claims to the fertile stream valleys late in the eighteenth century as new transportation routes across the Blue Ridge and down the Shenandoah Valley opened what had been a forbidding wilderness. Easily mined ore, abundant water power, and a seemingly endless forest formed the basis for mining, iron, and timber industries throughout the region. But by the turn of the century, an all-too-familiar pattern was seen. Wealthy absentee landowners, having taken their spoils, left their depleted holdings to burn and erode. Industries in the valley-and-ridge province were small and scattered, limited by steep terrain and difficult access to markets. As production and jobs shifted to larger urban centers, the small valley-and-ridge towns slid into economic depression.

Early in this century, the National Forest Service began to acquire much of what was then deemed worthless land. Today, the forest has regenerated, although there are fresh scars from present-day mining, lumbering, and commercial development.

Natural Features

Tuscarora sandstone caps many of the highest ridges in the valley-and-ridge province. The metamorphosed remains of beaches and sea floors that covered this area 350–400 million years ago, the rock is rich in Devonian marine fossils. Weathering and freeze-fracturing produced the extensive talus slopes below the ridge crests. Lower slopes expose softer sandstones, slates, and shales and are also rich in fossil remains. These softer rocks are easily eroded, forming the steep slopes and deep gorges that characterize the valley-and-ridge province. Limestone underlies many of the wider stream valleys and tends to favor cavern formation.

The valley-and-ridge province exhibits a trellis-like drainage pattern. Larger rivers flow to the north, fed by smaller streams draining down the eastern and western slopes. The several forks of the South Branch of the Potomac—the South Branch, South Fork, and North Fork—rise in high mountains near the Virginia–West Virginia border, eventually meeting the North Branch—the "true" Potomac—near Oldtown, MD.

North-facing slopes tend to be cool, moist, and heavily forested with hemlock and hardwoods, and rocks are often covered by ferns and lichen. In contrast, south- and west-facing slopes are often dry from exposure to the prevailing westerly winds and have a fairly open covering of oak, pine, blueberry, huckleberry, and mountain laurel. Ridge crests are dominated by slightly stunted oak, chestnut oak, mountain laurel, and several types of pine. Among the wildflowers you'll find here are lady slipper, wild iris, columbine, and yellow star grass. Lowbush blueberries and black huckleberries are ready to eat in late summer.

The Virginia white-tailed deer and black bear, two species hunted nearly to extinction here, have made a comeback, and their success draws hordes of hunters to the area in late autumn. The valley-and-ridge province has also been the site of an ambitious program to reintroduce the peregrine falcon. The western ridges are choice spots to watch the autumn hawk migration. Copperheads and eastern timber rattlers, as well as several nonpoisonous species of snake, are common in the area.

Wolf Gap, VA/WV — Tibbet Knob (state border)

Chapter 8

WOLF GAP RECREATION AREA
(VIRGINIA/WEST VIRGINIA)

The Wolf Gap Recreation Area is a rugged, heavily forested region straddling the Virginia–West Virginia border along the crest of Great North Mountain. If you hike any of the highest trails, you'll cross and re-cross the unmarked state line many times. Steep ridges, capped by cliffs and outcroppings that provide panoramic views, tower above remote stream valleys. The recreation area, administered by the Forest Service, is popular with hikers and backpackers and remains undeveloped except for a small semi-primitive campground, several roads, and an excellent trail system. Nearby Trout Pond Recreation Area is more heavily developed and better suited to RVs.

History

Once known as Devils Backbone, Great North Mountain presented a formidable barrier to westward travel in pioneer times. Although Wolf Gap was an important pass across the mountain, its higher elevations were never heavily settled. Early German settlers likened the prominent outcropping on Mill Mountain to a *schloss,* or castle. In the last century, this was an important iron-producing region, and the remains of Crack Whip and Van Buren furnaces still stand. Other furnaces have long since vanished, but they are commemorated by the names of small settlements scattered throughout the area.

Much of the forest around Wolf Gap had been clear-cut by the turn of the century, and the land was in poor condition by the time it was acquired by the Forest Service in the 1920s and 1930s. A mature hardwood forest has since returned, although the Forest Service continues isolated clear-cutting operations.

Natural Features

Wolf Gap Recreation Area straddles the Virginia–West Virginia border along the crest of Great North Mountain. Also known as Mill Mountain north of the gap, Great North marks the western edge of the Shenandoah Valley and the beginning of the valley-and-ridge province, a region of narrow, parallel, northeasterly tending ridges. Steep-sided stream valleys parallel the ridges, and streams here flow generally northeast into the Potomac.

An eastern hardwood forest—predominantly oak with an understory of mountain laurel at the higher elevations—blankets the ridges. Look for dwarf iris in dry sandy soil, especially along trails and roadsides. Trillium and lady slipper flourish in the deeper woods, and wild blueberries—ready to eat in late summer—are common in open woods and clearings.

Devil's Hole Mountain along FS-691 provides a good look at a recovering forest fire area. The high ridge was severely burned in the early 1980s, leaving a ghostly forest of dead timber that still stands. The area is recovering slowly and is now carpeted with a nearly impenetrable thicket of chestnut oak, lowbush blueberries, and mountain laurel.

Nearby Towns and Attractions

WARDENSVILLE, WV—

Wardensville, approximately 12 miles north of Wolf Gap, offers a limited but reliable array of restaurants, grocery and convenience stores, and gas stations.

PERRY, WV—

This small settlement approximately 4 miles north of Wolf Gap on Trout Run Road (County Road 23-10) has a general store offering basic groceries, supplies, and (at last visit) a not-so-wild wildlife exhibit.

WOODSTOCK, VA—

Approximately 13 miles east of Wolf Gap, on US-11 just east of I-81, Woodstock is a good place to fill the gas tank and pick up supplies if you're approaching Wolf Gap from I-81. Gas, food, and lodging are available immediately off the interstate, but I recommend a short side-trip into this picturesque old Shenandoah Valley town. You'll find an assortment of shops and restaurants catering to locals and tourists alike strung along old US-11, ancestor of present-day I-81.

HAWK RECREATION AREA (WV)—

A small, primitive campground near the crest of Great North Mountain with Big Blue Trail access (see the Other Natural Areas chapter).

Access

From the east, take I-66 west to its junction with I-81, merge onto southbound I-81, and continue a short distance to the Route 55 exit. Follow Route 55 southwest into Strasburg, VA. In Strasburg, Route 55 turns west toward Wardensville, WV. Continue through Wardensville on Route 55 and make a left turn onto Trout Run Road just beyond the town. Follow Trout Run Road through a scenic valley for approximately 12 miles to Wolf Gap Recreation Area. Alternatively, you could continue down I-81 to the Woodstock exit and follow directions in the next paragraph.

From the north or south, follow I-81 to the Woodstock, VA, exit. Turn west and follow Route 42 for 6 miles to the small settlement of Columbia Furnace, VA. Make a sharp right turn, follow the road a short distance over a low bridge, then immediately make a sharp left onto County Road 675, which follows the stream at first, then climbs to Wolf Gap. The road narrows and becomes steep and winding as it approaches the gap.

Camping

The Wolf Gap area offers outstanding opportunities for backcountry camping. Permits are not needed, and backcountry camping is allowed throughout the area except in the Little Stony Creek watershed above Woodstock Reservoir. In Virginia, open fires are permitted only between 4:00 P.M. and midnight from March 1 through May 15. Be aware that private inholdings are scattered throughout George Washington National Forest, mostly at the lower elevations; don't camp on posted land. Although you will find water along many trails, springs and streams are not protected, and all drinking water should be boiled or treated.

The Forest Service campground at Wolf Gap offers a limited number of car-camping sites with tent pads and picnic tables. Pit toilets and a pump are usually out of service during the winter months. The Forest Service collects a small fee, usually on the honor system during the off-season. You'll probably find all sites filled by mid-morning on weekends and holidays in good weather. You can also camp free of charge in the undeveloped clearing across the road from the main campground. So far, the Forest Service hasn't restricted use of this area, but that's always subject to change. You may also camp at informal pull-outs on Forest Service land along Trout Run Road north of the gap, along FS-92 east of the gap, and along County Road 691 west of the gap. These are undeveloped sites and may be used free of charge.

Trail Guide:
WOLF GAP AREA

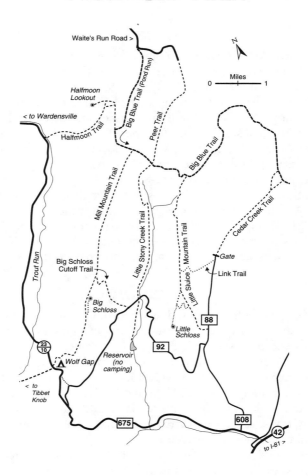

Big Blue Trail

The Big Blue is a 144-mile trail beginning at the C&O Canal near Hancock, MD, and ending at the Appalachian Trail in the Matthews Arm area of Shenandoah National Park, VA. An especially scenic portion of the trail runs through the Wolf Gap Recreation Area. See the Big Blue Trail chapter for more information.

Big Schloss Cutoff Trail (#415)[1]

Length: *1.3 miles (1.8 miles to Big Schloss)*
Elevation change: *1,355 feet*
Level: *moderate*
USGS quad map: *Wolf Gap, WV*
Access: *To reach the east trailhead, take Route 675 west from Columbia Furnace and watch for a wide turn-out at Forest Service Road 92 as you approach the gap. Turn right on FS-92 and drive approximately 3 miles to an inconspicuous trailhead on your left. There is ample parking nearby. The west trailhead is on the Mill Mountain Trail north of Big Schloss.*

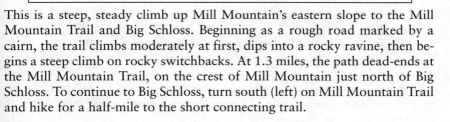

This is a steep, steady climb up Mill Mountain's eastern slope to the Mill Mountain Trail and Big Schloss. Beginning as a rough road marked by a cairn, the trail climbs moderately at first, dips into a rocky ravine, then begins a steep climb on rocky switchbacks. At 1.3 miles, the path dead-ends at the Mill Mountain Trail, on the crest of Mill Mountain just north of Big Schloss. To continue to Big Schloss, turn south (left) on Mill Mountain Trail and hike for a half-mile to the short connecting trail.

Big Schloss Trail—

See Mill Mountain Trail

Cedar Creek Trail

Length: *3.2 miles*
Elevation change: *700 feet*
Level: *easy to moderate (wet/muddy in spots)*
USGS quad map: *Woodstock, VA–WV*
Access: *To reach the south trailhead, take County Road 675 west from Columbia Furnace and drive for a half-mile to a right turn on County Road 608, which becomes FS-88. Stay on FS-88 until you reach the gate, and park. The north trailhead is on the Big Blue Trail approximately a half-mile south of Route 713.*

From the gate on FS-88, hike a half-mile to the north, cross a clearing, and look for the unblazed footpath. Cedar Creek Trail follows the stream throughout

---

1 Trail numbers in parentheses refer to Forest Service trail number designations.

most of its length, passing through woods and scattered clearings with some minor ups and downs. At its northern end, Cedar Creek Trail meets the Big Blue Trail, which it shares briefly before Big Blue veers off to the east. Except in the driest weather, hiking the Cedar Creek Trail can be a soggy experience. Waterproof boots are recommended.

Cut-Off Trail

Length: *0.5 mile*
Elevation change: *330 feet*
Level: *easy*
USGS quad map: *Wolf Gap, WV–VA (not marked)*
Access: *From County Route 675, turn onto FS-92, drive about a half-mile, and park. Search for an obscure unmarked trail leading uphill to your left. The trailhead is difficult to locate. This trail is not blazed or maintained. The name has been used unofficially for many years.*

The remains of an old wagon road across Wolf Gap, this trail is no longer maintained and serves no particular purpose. It's worth a visit if you're interested in seeing an early wagon road (which now looks like a jeep road). The roadbed is deeply cut and climbs steeply to end along County Route 675 just below Wolf Gap Campground.

Falls Ridge Trail—
See North Mountain Trail

Halfmoon Trail (#1003)

Length: *2.5 miles*
Elevation change: *1,530 feet*
Level: *moderate (strenuous)*
USGS quad maps: *Wolf Gap, WV–VA; Woodstock, VA–WV*
Access: *Trailhead is on Trout Run Road approximately 6.0 miles north of Wolf Gap Campground or 7.5 miles south of Wardensville, WV. Park near the power line on the east side of the road.*

From the parking area, follow a dirt road downhill to Trout Run and cross the stream. In high water, you may need to wade. Beyond the stream crossing, the road passes under a power line and then begins a moderate climb, crossing several small side-streams. Just short of a mile, the road crosses Halfmoon Run. Turn right onto a steep footpath just beyond the crossing (the road you've been on to this point continues downhill to private property) and begin a steady climb that will take you high above the stream.

At 1.8 miles, the trail forks in a rocky ravine. Both forks eventually meet the Halfmoon Lookout Trail, so take your pick. The branch straight ahead is a steep, rocky climb up the ravine; the main trail branches right and is not quite as rough, although it is less direct. To visit Halfmoon Lookout from either branch, turn left on Halfmoon Lookout Trail (#1003-A) and hike for less than a mile to its end, where the trail makes a short, steep climb to a viewpoint near the remains of an old cabin. Return the way you came.

From its junction with the lookout trail, the Halfmoon Trail turns right, meeting the Pond Run section of the Big Blue Trail, which enters from the north at 2.5 miles. The Halfmoon Trail continues, but it is designated as the Big Blue Trail from this point.

Laurel Run Trail (#568)—
See North Mountain Trail

Link Trail

Length: *1 mile*
Elevation change: *680 feet*
Level: *moderate*
USGS quad map: *Woodstock, VA–WV (not shown)*
Access: *Take County Road 675 west from Columbia Furnace and drive for a half-mile to a right turn on County Road 608, which becomes FS-88. Stay on FS-88 until you reach the chain, and park. This trail is not numbered or blazed. The name has been used unofficially for many years.*

This trail provides a little-used alternate route to Little Schloss and the crest of Little Sluice Mountain. The trail begins as a dirt road on the west side of FS-88. Look for a fork a short distance from the trailhead and bear left. The trail passes through several overgrown clearings, becoming steeper and rougher as it approaches the top of the ridge. At the junction with Little Sluice Mountain Trail, turn left to reach Little Schloss (see Little Sluice Mountain Trail), or turn right to continue north to the Big Blue Trail.

Little Schloss Bushwhack—
See Little Sluice Mountain Trail

Little Sluice Mountain Trail

Length: *4.5 miles*

Elevation change: *1,130 feet*

Level: *moderate (first mile is strenuous)*

USGS quad maps: *Wolf Gap, WV–VA; Woodstock, VA–WV*

Access: *To reach the south trailhead, take County Road 675 west from Columbia Furnace for a half-mile and turn right on County Road 608, which becomes FS-88. The trailhead is on the west side of FS-88, with limited parking along both sides of the road. The north trailhead is on the Big Blue Trail.*

Precautions: Although the trail is open to vehicles, leave your vehicle at the trailhead! The road is in fair condition at its lower end, but it soon becomes impassable except to four-wheel-drive vehicles with extreme ground clearance. As it approaches the ridge top, the road becomes a deeply cut and severely rutted single lane with little or no space to pass, maneuver, or turn around. The clearing at the ridge crest attracts large and sometimes rowdy camping parties and is best avoided on weekends, holidays, and during hunting season. Some vandalism and theft from autos have been reported in the vicinity.

Hiking the lower end of Little Sluice Mountain Trail isn't a very rewarding experience. The trail is actually a rough jeep road, and you may find yourself occasionally dodging off-road vehicles, especially during hunting season. The trail's beginning is marred by illegal dumping. That aside, it's the most direct route to Little Schloss.

The jeep road climbs steeply for the first mile before reaching a fork. From the fork, either branch will take you to a large, level clearing at the crest of the ridge. The left-hand fork is badly eroded, so it receives less use from off-road vehicles. From the clearing, you can make an easy bushwhack to Little Schloss, a prominent outcropping with a panoramic view. There is no trail, but you can find your way easily. From the clearing, turn south (left), and continue along the ridge through open woods. After passing over a small rise, you'll see a high sandstone outcropping directly ahead. Work your way up the talus slope on the formation's west side for a spectacular view, then return the way you came.

From the clearing, Little Sluice Mountain Trail continues north along the ridge top, with minor ups and downs and occasional views of Big Schloss to the west. At about 3 miles, pass an old hunting cabin, then descend to cross a small stream before beginning a moderate climb to a junction with the Big Blue Trail.

Little Stony Creek Trail (#571)

Length: *4.8 miles*

Elevation change: *1,700 feet*

Level: *easy to moderate*

USGS quad maps: *Wolf Gap, WV–VA; Woodstock, VA–WV*

Access: *The lower (southern) portion of Little Stony Creek Trail is bisected by FS-92, from which you can hike in either direction. The north trailhead is on the Big Blue Trail, opposite the end of Peer Trail.*

This is a fairly easy hike through a secluded ravine. From the trailhead on FS-92, the southern portion of Stony Creek Trail descends 1.5 miles to end at the Woodstock Reservoir and private property. The property is posted, and camping is prohibited in the watershed area. Don't continue south of the lake.

From the same trailhead on FS-92, the northern extension of Little Stony Creek Trail climbs along the west bank of a stream, then passes through a scrubby, overgrown area that was thinned by the Forest Service more than a decade ago. Beyond this area, the trail climbs steadily by switchbacks, passing several reliable but unprotected springs before reaching its junction with the Big Blue Trail.

Mill Mountain Trail (#1004)

Length: *2 miles (to Big Schloss); 5.9 miles (to Big Blue Trail)*

Elevation change: *1,040 feet*

Level: *moderate*

USGS quad maps: *Wolf Gap, WV–VA; Woodstock, VA–WV*

Access: *The south trailhead is near campsite #9 at the northern end of Wolf Gap Campground. If you aren't a registered camper, park in the adjacent day-use lot. The north trailhead is on the Big Blue Trail east of Halfmoon Lookout.*

One of the most scenic trails in the Wolf Gap area, the Mill Mountain Trail begins as a wide orange-blazed jeep road (closed to public vehicles), then narrows to a footpath and climbs steadily, affording occasional views north toward Big Schloss. The trail reaches the crest of Mill Mountain (the local name for this section of Great North Mountain) in about a mile. If you feel like exploring, turn right and follow an obscure path a short distance uphill to the wooded southern summit of Mill Mountain. An easy scramble up the outcropping at the summit will reward you with a good, if slightly overgrown, view across Wolf Gap to the southern extension of Great North Mountain.

If you decide to skip the bushwhack, bear left and continue for the next mile along mostly level trail on the ridge top. You'll cross and recross the unmarked Virginia–West Virginia border, which follows the ridge. Low outcroppings along this section offer good views to the east. At approximately 2 miles from the trailhead you'll reach Big Schloss Trail, a conspicuous spur leading uphill to Big Schloss, a prominent sandstone outcropping on Mill Mountain that offers a 360-degree view. To the west, across Trout Run Valley, is Long Mountain; to the east, the large outcropping on the nearest ridge is Little Schloss, with the Stony Run Valley beyond and the long ridge of Massanutten Mountain visible on the horizon. Big Schloss is a fine spot to relax or practice your rock scrambling, but expect plenty of company on weekends and holidays.

If Big Schloss was your destination, return the way you came. Otherwise, return to the main trail and turn north (right). The Mill Mountain Trail continues to follow the ridge line, then at 4 miles begins a steady climb to Sandstone Spring, a small spring in a deeply shaded hemlock grove. The spring is a popular camping site that shows signs of overuse. Beyond Sandstone Spring, Mill Mountain Trail climbs moderately, skirts a knob (the trail's high point, at 3,293 feet, unfortunately marred by a radio tower), then merges with a rough jeep service road and descends to end at the Big Blue Trail.

North Mountain Trail (#1009)

Length: *6.5 miles*

Elevation change: *500 feet*

Level: *moderate*

USGS quad maps: *Wolf Gap, WV–VA; Lost City, WV*

Access: *North trailhead is on the south side of County Road 57/691 on Devil's Hole Mountain, near the state boundary sign. There is ample parking nearby. This is a shared trailhead; Laurel Run Trail also begins here, heading downhill. Private property and a very rough road make access to the south trailhead uncertain; inquire locally.*

This trail follows the crest of Great North Mountain southward for 6.5 miles, passing occasional views across the Shenandoah Valley from scattered outcroppings. The Laurel Run Trail, which also begins at this trailhead, descends steeply to the left into a narrow valley along the eastern flank of Great North Mountain, passing some imposing rock formations along the way. At 2.2 miles from the North Mountain trailhead is a junction with the Table Rock Trail, a spur trail leading to a low outcropping with a mediocre, overgrown view. Falls Ridge Trail, just a short distance beyond, descends steeply to the east. From there, the Great North Mountain Trail continues along the ridge, passes an abandoned homesite at 6 miles, then continues an additional half-mile to its southern terminus at a gate on private property.

Peer Trail (#1002)

Length: *3 miles*

Elevation change: *1,300 feet*

Level: *moderate to easy*

USGS quad map: *Woodstock, VA–WV*

Access: *To reach the north trailhead, take Route 55 into Wardensville, WV, turn south on Carpenter Avenue, and drive 1 mile to Waites Run Road. Turn right on Waites Run Road and continue south for approximately 6 miles. Look for a small parking area near a gate marking the beginning of private land. The south trailhead is on Big Blue Trail, opposite the Little Stony Creek Trail. The lower portion of this trail, along Waites Run, crosses private property. Although the land is posted, the owner so far has permitted hikers to cross. Stay on the trail, pass quietly, and don't camp, hunt, or fish in this area. As is so often the case with trail access across private land, conditions can change suddenly.*

The Peer Trail is a fairly easy hike along Waites Run. From the parking area, hike up the dirt road and pass through a farm gate, being sure to close it behind you. After crossing a small bridge near a group of farm buildings, the road climbs through woods and meadows. At approximately a half-mile from the trailhead, the Peer Trail veers from the road into the woods as a blazed footpath, skirts another meadow, and then enters Forest Service land. From there, the trail makes a steady climb through open forest high above Waites Run to a junction with the Big Blue Trail. The trail continues southward, as Little Stony Creek Trail (see entry), for 3.5 miles downhill to a junction with FS-92.

Pond Run Trail

This trail is now a part of the Big Blue Trail. See the Big Blue chapter (Sugar Knob section) for details.

Table Rock Trail—

See North Mountain Trail

Tibbet Knob Trail (#578)

Length: *3 miles*

Elevation change: *700 feet*

Level: *moderately difficult (County Road 675 to Tibbet Knob); moderate (Tibbet Knob to County Road 691)*

USGS quad map: *Wolf Gap, WV–VA*

Access: *North trailhead is in a clearing opposite the entrance to Wolf Gap Campground. South trailhead is at a large parking pull-out on unpaved County Road 691 several miles from its junction with County Road 675.*

One of the lesser-known trails in the Wolf Gap area (it is inexplicably omitted from some maps and guides), Tibbet Knob Trail is also one of the most scenic and challenging.

To hike from the campground, cross County Road 675 to a clearing opposite the campground entrance and follow the wide dirt road southwest, passing the foundation of an old cabin. The road is gated to public vehicles beyond the clearing and soon narrows to a rocky, moss-covered footpath climbing through open woods. The trail is obscure in spots but is fairly well blazed. At about a half-mile from the trailhead, cross a narrow rocky ridge with good views across Wolf Gap from the outcroppings on your left. The trail then skirts a ravine in a gradual curving descent through dense scrub.

After crossing a low rocky area, the trail begins an uphill climb that becomes progressively steeper and requires some rock scrambling as you near the Knob. Just below the summit, you will pass a clearing made several years ago as part of the peregrine falcon reintroduction program; please keep your distance if the area is still posted. Immediately below the summit, the trail becomes obscure as it turns right along the base of a low cliff. Continue for a short distance along the foot of the cliff until you see a rocky and inconspicuously blazed chute leading upward. Scramble up the chute and continue along the top of the cliff for spectacular views. To your far left is Devil's Hole Mountain, with its conspicuous burned area. Trout Run Valley, directly below you, is flanked by Long Mountain on your left and Great North (Mill) Mountain on your right. The prominent sandstone outcropping on Mill Mountain is Big Schloss.

To continue, follow the Tibbet Knob Trail downhill, away from the cliff, and begin a steady 1-mile descent to County Road 691. Otherwise, return as you came.

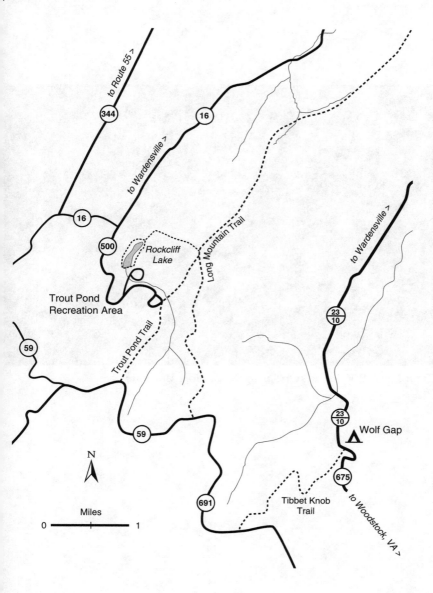

Trout Pond, WV — Forest fire area, Devil's Hole Mountain

Chapter 9

TROUT POND RECREATION AREA
(WEST VIRGINIA)

Lying just to the west of Wolf Gap, Trout Pond is a popular Forest Service recreation area surrounding West Virginia's only natural lake. Adjacent Rock Cliff Lake, a 16-acre man-made reservoir, allows swimming and nonmotorized boating. With a developed campground, modern bath houses, picnic areas, and groomed nature trails, Trout Pond Recreation Area caters primarily to day users and the RV crowd. Luckily, these folks tend not to venture far from their vehicles, and if you can overlook the development, you'll find excellent hiking nearby. Two trails, Long Mountain/Crack Whip Furnace and Trout Pond, extend into the Wolf Gap area, offering fine medium-distance hikes.

Camping

Trout Pond is the site of a large developed campground, open April 1 through December 1, that's often noisy and crowded. But good backcountry sites are plentiful throughout the area, including the adjacent Wolf Gap Recreation Area, and backcountry permits are not needed.

Nearby Towns

See the Wolf Gap chapter. Several small towns along Route 259 west of the recreation area (Baker, Lost River, Lost City, and Mathias, WV) also offer limited supplies and services.

Access

Take I-66 west to its junction with I-81, merge onto southbound I-81, and continue a short distance to the Route 55 exit. Follow Route 55 north and then west to Wardensville, WV. Continue through Wardensville on Route 55, then make a left turn onto Trout Run Road just beyond the town. Follow Trout Run Road for 5 miles to a fork and bear right onto County Road 16 (Mill Gap Road). At the junction of County Roads 16 and 500, bear left on 500 and continue to the well-marked Trout Pond Recreation Area.

145

Trail Guide:
TROUT POND RECREATION AREA
(See page 143 for area map.)

Crack Whip Furnace Trail—
See Long Mountain Trail

Long MountainTrail (Crack Whip Furnace) (#1007)

Length: *7.8 miles*

Elevation change: *1,400 feet*

Level: *moderate*

USGS quad map: *Wolf Gap, WV (shown as Crack Whip Furnace Trail)*

Access: *North trailhead is on County Road 23-10 approximately 6 miles south of Wardensville, WV. South trailhead is on unpaved County Road 691 west of Wolf Gap, near the crest of Devil's Hole Mountain.*

To hike from the north trailhead, look for the trail entrance next to a privately owned cabin opposite the Crack Whip Furnace ruins. The southbound trail is narrow and wet at first, but within a mile it joins an old jeep road that passes through open woods with scattered clearings. At approximately 3.5 miles, the trail passes the first of two spurs that lead west to Trout Pond Trail and the Trout Pond Recreation Area; the second spur lies a short distance beyond.

Trout Pond, WV — Forest fire area, Devil's Hole Mtn.

From the second spur, the Long Mountain Trail turns due south and climbs steadily to its south trailhead on County Road 691, becoming steeper as it approaches the ridge top. The last half-mile follows another old jeep road before ending on County Road 691 on Devil's Hole Mountain.

Rock Cliff Trail (#1010)/
Chimney Rock Trail (#1010-B)

Length: *1 mile (#1010); 0.8 mile (#1010-B)*

Elevation change: *insignificant*

Level: *easy*

USGS quad map: *Wolf Gap, WV (not shown)*

Access: *Trailhead is at the fishermen's parking area on Rock Cliff Lake.*

Follow the well-marked and nearly level Rock Cliff Trail around the shoreline of Rock Cliff Lake. At 0.4 mile, the trail crosses the dam crest. Beyond the dam, you have the choice of continuing straight ahead on the Rock Cliff Trail or turning right onto the short Chimney Rock Trail. From the dam, Rock Cliff Trail continues around the lake for about a half-mile before returning to the parking area.

Chimney Rock Trail makes a moderate descent, passes a large outcropping of Oriskany sandstone, then continues across Trout Run to make an easy climb to the Trout Pond Trail. Explore at will, then backtrack to Rock Cliff Trail.

Trout Pond Trail (#1008)

Length: *1.5 miles (campground to CR-59); 2.7 miles (total)*

Elevation change: *710 feet (campground to CR-59); 1,140 feet (total)*

Level: *moderate*

USGS quad map: *Wolf Gap, WV*

Access: *From the Trout Pond Recreation Area campground.*

Trout Pond Trail is a jeep road that begins at Route 500 north of the Trout Pond Recreation Area. The lower half is open to vehicles using the primitive campground on Trout Pond Run. South of the primitive campground, it continues to the main Trout Pond Recreation Area campground, passing two short spurs that link it to the Long Mountain/Crack Whip Furnace Trail.

From the main campground, the Trout Pond Trail continues on the old jeep road, climbing steadily for 1.5 miles to a junction with County Road 59 (the continuation of County Road 691) near the crest of Devil's Hole Mountain.

Smoke Hole, WV — Eagle Rock

Chapter 10

SMOKE HOLE (WEST VIRGINIA)

A t Smoke Hole, the South Branch of the Potomac breaches the mountains to enter an otherworldly region often shrouded in shadow and fog. The river carves its way past cliffs and outcroppings in a narrow gorge between North Fork and Cave Mountains to finally break free of the canyon and join the North Fork near Hopeville. The South Branch is fickle here: a sluggish ankle-deep trickle at times, a torrent devouring everything in its path at others.

Compared to other areas in the Monongahela National Forest, Smoke Hole is barely developed. Flash floods, nearly vertical terrain, and private inholdings have discouraged any but the most primitive Forest Service "improvements." The roads are rough, the few trails obscure. Aside from a couple of small general stores and the Forest Service campground at Big Bend, there are no public facilities in the gorge.

For the whitewater enthusiast, the South Branch provides some exciting riffles along miles of unspoiled river. For the experienced hiker, Smoke Hole holds a wealth of unmarked paths and old road traces to explore. There are opportunities for some serious bushwhacking, although good backcountry campsites are scarce. USGS topo maps, a compass, and the skill to use them are essential.

History

Depending on which source you choose to believe, Smoke Hole got its name from (1) smoke from fires used by Indians and early settlers to cure meat; (2) steam from moonshiners' stills; or (3) the valley's tendency to produce heavy early-morning fog. Take your pick; they're all based on fact.

Native tribes occupied this isolated valley until they were forced from the area during the French and Indian Wars. Settlement began before 1760, and English and Hessian deserters found their way into Smoke Hole after the Revolution. Swiss, German, and Scots-Irish immigrants managed to eke out a marginal existence here, and if you look carefully you'll see scattered remains of their descendants' cabins and farms as you drive along FS-74 in the north end of Smoke Hole.

When Work Project Administration (WPA) writers ventured into Smoke Hole in 1935, they found conditions similar to those in the poorest hollows of the Blue Ridge. According to the WPA guide, the inhabitants had "little or no contact or commerce outside their valley. The typical Smoke Holer leads a simple life hunting, fishing, and farming just enough to provide him and his family with food. ... Their speech is quaint, containing many archaic forms handed down from the first settlers of the eighteenth century. Most Smoke Hole families ... live in tiny one- and two-bedroom log houses. A few families have phonographs, with hillbilly records, but many have never heard a radio. Two or three of the most prosperous families drive automobiles."

*Smoke Hole, WV —
Morning fog from
North Fork Mountain*

Far more populous than it is today, Smoke Hole at the turn of the century was a necessarily self-sufficient community, boasting schools, churches, its own peculiar forms of commerce, and more than a few illegal stills. Until the late 1930s, the only entrance to Smoke Hole was from the south, on a road that was higher up the mountain than the present-day riverside route. Little more than a set of cliff-hanging ruts, it discouraged passage into and out of the gorge. Beyond its end at Ketterman lay "an unbroken wilderness of mountains and forest, for 20 miles impassable except on horse or on foot," according to the WPA guide.

Conditions began to change in Smoke Hole in the mid-1930s. The road was improved and extended north to Highway 28 near Hopeville, bringing traffic and outside influences to the valley for the first time. Demand for moonshine tapered off with the repeal of Prohibition, and many Smoke Holers left to work at nearby Civilian Conservation Corps camps. With the outbreak of World War II, men were drafted, and many settled elsewhere after the war. As had happened in the Blue Ridge, some families were squatters on land they never owned and eventually were displaced.

With the Forest Service acquisition of acreage in Smoke Hole, buildings were left to crumble as the forest reclaimed abandoned fields. Today, Smoke Hole retains much of its rural character, but with development escalating nearby, this may not be the case much longer.

Camping

Except for scattered sites on the crest of Cave Mountain, most of the Smoke Hole region is poorly suited to backcountry camping. Level land is rare except along the river, where sites are often damp or in danger of flooding. The valley and lower mountain slopes are a checkerboard of private inholdings; take the "No Trespassing" signs seriously.

Big Bend Recreation Area, at the north end of County Road 2 in Smoke Hole, is a 45-site semi-primitive campground on a scenic bend of the South Branch. Smoke Hole Campground, shown on older maps and still mentioned in several guides, washed away in the 1985 flood and will not be rebuilt. Roadside camping along the southern end of Route 2 (Smoke Hole Road) is no longer permitted.

Access (via County and Forest Service Roads)

Private residences are located throughout Smoke Hole; consequently, the back roads carry more traffic than you might expect. The locals sometimes drive faster than common sense would seem to dictate, especially on Friday and Saturday nights.

SMOKE HOLE ROAD (COUNTY ROAD 2)—

This is a scenic, roughly paved riverside route in the southern end of Smoke Hole. From its junction with US-220 north of Upper Tract, Smoke Hole Road follows the South Branch northward below sheer cliffs, passing Eagle Rock and Smoke Hole Cave (not the commercially developed caverns). Both features are marked by plaques but are on private land. A junction with Forest Service Road 79 lies midway up the canyon. Beyond that point, County Road 2 continues north along the river to dead-end at Big Bend Recreation Area. The road's northern end is narrow and winding and is not suited for long trailers.

FS-74 (COUNTY ROAD 28-11)—

Use this route to enter Smoke Hole if you're coming from Petersburg. From its northern junction with Route 28/55 west of Petersburg, FS-74 climbs steeply to a switchback at 1.5 miles, affording a surprisingly close-up view of New Creek Mountain across an open meadow. From there, the road winds southward through fields and forest with many ups and downs, passing the Landes and Redman Run trailheads and eventually ending at an intersection with FS-79 (see next entry). At the junction, turn right on FS-79 to climb to the old fire tower site on the crest of North Fork Mountain (but see the cautionary note below) or left to descend steeply to Smoke Hole Road. FS-74 is a narrow, unpaved route. It is passable to passenger cars in good weather, but a four-wheel-drive vehicle is recommended in rain or snow.

FS-79—

A former fire tower service road, the lower end of FS-79 provides a connecting link between FS-74 and Smoke Hole Road. At higher elevations, the road is poorly maintained and requires a four-wheel-drive vehicle (see the North Fork Mountain chapter).

Trail Guide:
SMOKE HOLE REGION

Note: Smoke Hole is subject to frequent flooding. Conditions change following every flood, so what you read here may not be correct by the time you arrive. Inquire locally. See map on page 157.

Big Bend Trail

Length: *1.5 miles*
Elevation change: *insignificant*
Level: *easy*
USGS quad map: *Petersburg, WV (not shown)*
Access: *From the Big Bend Campground service road at site #12.*

This is an easy loop trail around Big Bend Campground. From the service road, Big Bend Trail follows the South Branch for a short distance. In late summer look for pawpaws (one of the few edible fruits native to this region) along the riverbank. The trail then climbs a low knob for a good view across the river bend before descending past some interesting outcroppings. From the rocks, the trail skirts the edge of a meadow, then returns to its starting point on the service road.

Smoke Hole Cave Trail

Length: *0.5 mile*
Elevation change: *480 feet*
Level: *difficult*
USGS quad map: *Upper Tract, WV*
Access: *The unmarked trailhead is on Smoke Hole Road, near a historical marker approximately a half-mile south of the Smoke Hole picnic area. There is another, less difficult, route to the cave, which I will not describe here because of reports of overuse and vandalism.*

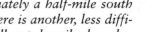

Note: This is not the commercially developed cavern (see the Seneca Rocks chapter). Smoke Hole Cave is a high, narrow chamber on the hillside to the west of County Road 2. The cave is on private land, and public access is no longer certain. Inquire locally.

The trail begins as a difficult, nearly vertical climb up an intermittent stream bed. This climb shouldn't be attempted when the rocks are wet, icy, or snow-covered. As it nears the hilltop, the trail levels out slightly and approaches a north-facing cliff in which there are several openings that lead to the main room, a dome-shaped chamber approximately 14 feet in diameter and 35 feet high. The main room is surrounded by a maze of side passages, many of which were blocked years ago after visitors were lost or injured in them. The cave was used by Indians and early settlers alike for shelter and for preserving meat by smoking.

South Branch Trail (#539)

Length: *3.5 miles*

Elevation change: *approximately 600 feet*

Level: *moderate*

USGS quad map: *Upper Tract, WV (not marked)*

Access: *Trailhead at Smoke Hole picnic area on Smoke Hole Road (County Road 2) south of its junction with FS-79.*

Also known as the Cave Mountain Trail, this scenic loop begins as a moderate climb through hardwood forest along the western slope of Cave Mountain. The trail crosses an old wagon road at approximately a half-mile from the trailhead, then crosses several intermittent streams before turning north. At 1.2 miles, South Branch Trail crosses a gas-line swath, then passes under a power line a short distance beyond. Both openings provide good views. At 2 miles, the trail crosses an abandoned pasture before descending on an old jeep road. At 2.5 miles, the trail veers left from the jeep road to continue as a foot-path through rhododendron and mountain laurel thickets. Where the trail reaches the river, turn south (up-stream) and return to the picnic area.

*Smoke Hole, WV —
Eagle Rock*

North Fork Mountain, WV — View south from Chimney Top

Chapter 11

NORTH FORK MOUNTAIN
(WEST VIRGINIA)

A narrow hogback ridge towering nearly 2,000 feet above the North Fork of the South Branch of the Potomac, North Fork Mountain offers sweeping views from its high sandstone cliffs. Despite its proximity to Seneca Rocks, Dolly Sods, and other heavily used areas, North Fork Mountain offers outstanding hiking and camping without the crowds. Limited access, a scarcity of level campsites, and lack of water along the ridge top discourage many visitors.

Geology

North Fork Mountain marks the western edge of the valley-and-ridge province. The ridge lies on the Wills Mountain anticline, a major geologic formation that includes New Creek and Wills Mountains to the north.

North Fork Mountain is capped by a layer of erosion-resistant Tuscarora sandstone, the remains of an ancient seabed. Devonian marine fossils, approximately 350–400 million years old, can be found in some sandstone layers. In the collision between the North American and African land masses that occurred 250 million years ago during the Allegheny Orogeny, the sandstone was forced to a nearly vertical position. Weathering along the previously horizontal layers produced the sheer cliffs and high blades of sandstone that characterize the area today.

North Fork's hard sandstone cap overlies softer shale and red sandstone of the Juniata formation, which have eroded deeply on the mountain's western face. The result is a classic hogback formation, characterized by a moderate, terraced eastern slope, a narrow crest capped by high westward-facing cliffs with extensive talus slopes below, and a steep, deeply eroded western face.

155

Camping

There are no developed campgrounds on or near North Fork Mountain. The former fire tower site, gas-line swaths, and other clearings along the upper end of FS-79 are popular primitive camping areas, but they offer no facilities of any kind. Car-campers will probably want to stay at the Big Bend Campground (see the Smoke Hole chapter) or seek out a commercial campground in the nearby valleys.

The crest of North Fork Mountain is narrow and rocky, but some small backcountry sites can be found if you explore off the trail. Level areas occur at widely spaced intervals along the mountain's southern half but are scarce north of FS-79. Parts of the North Fork Mountain Trail south of FS-79 cross private land and may be posted against camping. If the weather cooperates and you don't need to pitch a tent, you'll find terrific sites with spectacular views on solid rock at the cliff's edge.

There is no reliable water along the ridge or upper slopes; you'll need to carry an ample supply.

Nearby Towns and Attractions

FRANKLIN, WV—

Limited services, supplies, and lodging at the junction of US-33 and US-220 south of the Smoke Hole area (see the Spruce Knob chapter).

PETERSBURG, WV—

A good array of restaurants, motels, stores, and services north of the Smoke Hole area at the junction of Routes 28/55 and US-220 (see the Dolly Sods chapter).

SENECA CAVERNS AND SMOKE HOLE CAVERNS—

Two commercially developed caverns offer guided tours daily (see the Seneca Rocks chapter).

Access

To reach the north end of North Fork Mountain from Petersburg, follow combined Routes 28/55 south for approximately 7 miles. Turn left across the North Fork at unpaved FS-74 (well marked with a sign pointing to Big Bend Recreation Area). The north trailhead of the North Fork Mountain Trail is a short distance uphill on FS-74, and well-marked trailheads for other access routes are farther south along the same road.

US-33 crosses the crest of North Fork Mountain west of Franklin, passing the unmarked south entrance to the North Fork Mountain Trail (see North Fork Mountain Trail section in the trail guide below).

You can also drive to the crest of North Fork Mountain on FS-79, an old service road that climbs from Smoke Hole Road to a large clearing and popular primitive camping area at a former fire tower site. Maintenance is minimal, and the road is not suited for low-slung passenger cars, trailers, or oversized RVs. A four-wheel-drive vehicle is recommended in good weather and is essential in bad. For hikers, FS-79 road provides a good emergency exit from the ridge and is the only access route that leads to something resembling civilization.

Trail Guide:
NORTH FORK MOUNTAIN

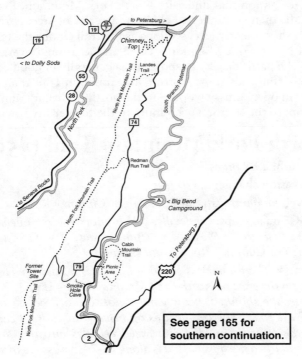

See page 165 for southern continuation.

Kimble Trail

Although this trail is still mentioned in some guides and shown on USGS quad maps, it has been abandoned for some time, and there is no longer access across private property.

Landes Trail (#502)

Length: *1.4 miles*

Elevation change: *1,000 feet*

Level: *moderate (strenuous)*

USGS quad map: *Hopeville, WV (shown incorrectly as north end of North Fork Mountain Trail)*

Access: *East trailhead is on the west side of FS-74, approximately 2 miles from its junction with Route 28/55. Parking is limited; don't block the road. West trailhead is on the North Fork Mountain Trail.*

Landes Trail climbs steeply at first, crossing the red sandstone and shale of the Juniata formation that underlies North Fork Mountain. Eventually the trail levels off, then continues to climb in a series of steep stretches interspersed with short, nearly level sections as the trail climbs the terraced eastern flank of North Fork Mountain. There are occasional overgrown views to the east. The path is rocky in spots but is generally in good condition.

The Landes Trail ends at the North Fork Mountain Trail at an inconspicuous junction in open, grassy woods. To the north (right), it's another mile to Chimney Top; to the south, it's 9.3 miles to the former fire tower site.

North Fork Mountain Trail (#501)

Length: *23.8 miles*

Elevation change: *2,570 feet*

Level: *moderate (strenuous north of Chimney Rock)*

USGS quad maps: *Circleville, WV; Franklin, WV; Hopeville, WV; Petersburg West, WV; Upper Tract, WV. (The trail north of Chimney Rock is not shown.)*

Access: *The unmarked south trailhead is across the clearing on the crest of North Fork Mountain along US-33. Park along the shoulder, being careful not to block access to a private road. The trailhead is on private land; don't camp in the clearing or take motorized vehicles into this area. The marked north trailhead is along FS-74, across the bridge and just a short distance uphill from its intersection with Route 28/55. Park in the pull-out or along the shoulder.*

Most of this trail is routed slightly to the east and behind the cliffs on North Fork Mountain. Consequently, many of the best views are blocked. For a much more scenic and challenging alternative, leave the trail and bushwhack along the edge of the open cliffs wherever possible. This requires a little rock scrambling, good non-slip hiking boots, simple common sense, and occasional detours into the woods, but the open views are well worth the extra effort. If the going gets rough, just bushwhack downhill (east) to the trail, which parallels the ridge along all but the northernmost mile.

The south trailhead is at the far edge of a clearing off of US-33. Skirt the edge of the woods until you find a wide, grassy forest road (closed to public vehicles); this is the unmarked start of the North Fork Trail. Avoid the old footpath on the southwest side of the clearing, which leads downhill and quickly becomes overgrown.

A short distance from the trailhead, the road narrows to a rocky footpath. At a half-mile from the trailhead, bushwhack west to an outcropping for outstanding views of Germany Valley immediately below and the Spruce Knob region of the Allegheny Front directly to the west. You can follow the rocks for a short distance, then bushwhack back to the trail. Trillium, lady slipper, and wild blueberries grow here.

At 1.7 miles, the trail enters private land, and at 2 miles it widens to a dirt road, passing through overgrown woods. At 3.3 miles, pass under a power line and along a timber cutting area. Stay on the main trail, avoiding two old roads ahead. The trail reaches a junction with an old dirt road over North Fork Mountain at 4.3 miles. To the west, this road descends 2 miles to Harpers Gap and County Road 9 in Germany Valley. To the east, it descends 2.3 miles to a junction with County Road 8 in Reeds Gap. Just beyond the road, the trail reenters Forest Service land.

At 5.5 miles are good views to the west, and a level backcountry camping area comes at 6.7 miles. A short distance beyond the campsite, the trail passes private land to the west. Survey markers along this section have been in place for some time, an ominous sign of possible impending development. The trail ascends steeply behind the cliffs, which block some of the most spectacular views in the area. For a scenic and challenging alternative to the trail, bushwhack west to the cliffs after reaching the high point on the trail. Follow the rocks as far as you can, making occasional detours into the woods.

The trail widens to a rough jeep road at 9.5 miles, and this section is sometimes used by four-wheel-drive vehicles coming from the former fire tower site ahead. At 10.3 miles, the trail leaves the woods and enters a large open clearing, bearing right along the jeep road; the left fork goes to a microwave tower in a clearing at the edge of the mountain, affording a good view to the west. The open meadow is a good camping area, a little more secluded than the main clearing ahead. Continue to the north through open meadows, passing a pipeline swath at 10.7 miles; it makes a steep descent west to Seneca Rocks (see the Seneca Rocks chapter). The main trail bears right on a wide jeep road through an extensive, level clearing that was once the site of a fire tower. The tower is long gone, but there are sweeping views from the clearing's western edge. This is a popular primitive camping area for vehicles coming from Smoke Hole on FS-79. Just ahead, the highest point on the

North Fork Mountain Trail (3,795 feet) is marred by the presence of a radio tower. The trail joins FS-79 at this point, following it downhill for the next 1.3 miles. Watch for vehicles.

At 12.2 miles, the trail veers away from FS-79 at a parking pull-out along a switchback. From here, FS-79 descends 3.5 miles to Smoke Hole Road (see the Smoke Hole chapter). The North Fork Mountain Trail continues north as a narrow, rocky footpath. As before, the trail is routed to the east of the cliffs, which block the views. You can bushwhack along the cliffs, but this stretch is rough going through table mountain pine and mountain laurel thickets along a crumbling, sloping cliff. If you enjoy this sort of challenge, the views are worth the effort.

The abandoned and badly overgrown Kimble Trail enters from the east at 14.3, and at 15.7 miles the Redman Run Trail (#507) enters from the right. The trail starts at Smoke Hole Road and climbs steeply to this junction. Just north of the Redman Run Trail junction, a large sandstone formation to the west of the trail offers outstanding views. From there, the trail begins a steady descent to a fascinating area offering spectacular views and a chance for some rock scrambling. From the trail, look uphill for a high, honeycombed sandstone wall. A short, easy walk uphill will bring you to the wall, which hides a towering sandstone monolith to the west and is breached by an impressive wind gap. In a strong wind, you'll find yourself under assault by tiny rock chips and grains of sand blown free from the high sandstone walls.

At 19 miles, the trail begins a moderate descent from the ridge into a saddle. If you prefer, you can bushwhack along the cliffs; the trail eventually rejoins the ridge to the north. Landes Trail (#502) enters from the east at 20 miles, at a poorly marked fork in grassy, open woods. From here, Landes Trail descends steeply to Smoke Hole Road. Keep to the uphill side of the fork if you're continuing on the North Fork Mountain Trail. This is another good point to leave the main trail and bushwhack along the open cliffs to the west. Immediately below the cliffs are the remains of a 1980s plane crash, and just ahead is an outstanding view north along the cliffs to Chimney Top and New Creek Mountain. Directly below you is the Hopeville Gorge Pioneer Zone, a steep, undeveloped, and virtually inaccessible area in which black bear are making a modest comeback. Ahead, the trail skirts a clearing that has been used in a peregrine falcon reintroduction program. The trail was rerouted slightly to avoid the area; if the shelter boxes are still in place, please keep your distance.

At 21 miles, an unmarked and overgrown path branches to the west and uphill, leading along the edge of the cliff to Chimney Top. This is an easy point to overlook if you're coming from the north; if you miss it, backtrack to the high point on the main trail, bushwhack uphill to the cliffs, and turn right (north). Chimney Top is a spectacular sandstone formation towering above an extensive talus slope. This is a favorite roost for buzzards, and if you arrive here in the early morning or after a rain, you'll be treated to the grisly sight of dozens of birds with their wings spread to dry.

From Chimney Top, the view to the east is of Petersburg and receding parallel ridges in the valley-and-ridge province. Immediately to the north is New Creek Mountain, a continuation of the Wills Mountain anticline. Immediately below you is the valley of the North Fork; the high, forested wall of the Allegheny Front, in the vicinity of Dolly Sods, rises to the west.

In returning to the main trail from Chimney Top, avoid an unmarked but obvious path that leads north from the main formation. It goes a short distance before ending abruptly at a cliff in a deep thicket. If you find yourself at this dead end (and many have, judging from the fine condition of this deceptive little spur), backtrack to the south of Chimney Top, then bushwhack directly downhill to rejoin the main trail.

North of Chimney Top, the trail begins a steep descent to Smoke Hole Road. An interesting alternative is to bushwhack west a short distance to the open cliffs below Chimney Top; there are many obvious access points. Follow the open cliffs downhill as far as you can; once you find that you can't continue easily, bushwhack back to the main trail. Theoretically, it's possible to follow the cliffs all the way to the river, but the last stretch is extremely difficult and probably not worth the effort or risk.

Reach the north trailhead on FS-74 at 23.8 miles. (From the parking area, FS-74 climbs steeply to the south before descending into Smoke Hole valley, along the South Fork. To the north, it descends a short distance to combined Routes 28/55. Turn right on 28/55 to reach Petersburg or left to reach Seneca Rocks.)

Redman Run Trail (#507)

Length: *1.6 miles*

Elevation change: *900 feet*

Level: *moderate*

USGS quad map: *Hopeville, WV*

Access: *East trailhead is on the west side of FS-74, approximately 5 miles south of its junction with Route 28/55. Parking is limited; don't block the road or access to private lanes. West trailhead is on the North Fork Mountain Trail.*

Redman Run Trail (marked as Redman Trail on some maps) begins as a steep and rocky footpath, then levels off before climbing more moderately through a series of switchbacks, alternating steep climbs with several relatively level stretches on the eastern flank of North Fork Mountain. The upper end is very narrow and rocky. From the junction with North Fork Mountain Trail, it is 5.3 miles north to Chimney Top or 5.0 miles south to the former fire tower site on the North Fork Mountain Trail.

Seneca Rocks, WV — From Seneca Creek

Chapter 12

SENECA ROCKS (WEST VIRGINIA)

Generally acknowledged as one of the best technical climbing sites east of Colorado, Seneca Rocks is a 960-foot-high blade of Tuscarora sandstone looming above the North Fork.

If you haven't visited Seneca Rocks since the late 1980s, be prepared for some changes. Roy Gap Road, once a popular informal camping area, is now closed to public use. Access to the Rocks is now from the visitor center via a new steel structure that replaced the old suspension bridge above Roy Gap. A new graded trail to the summit has replaced the old, nearly vertical scramble up the Rocks' southwestern slope. Stop by the visitor center for the latest updates.

History

Any connection between Seneca Rocks and the Seneca tribe is dubious. The Seneca were Iroquoian-speaking natives of present-day western New York state, and although isolated trading parties may have journeyed this far, archeologists have found no conclusive evidence of Seneca settlement or presence here. Early European settlers reportedly applied the term "Seneca" (or some variant) indiscriminately to any number of unrelated tribes along the eastern seaboard. Archaeological evidence points instead to habitation during the Late Woodland Period (A.D. 900–C. 1600) by a group of loosely allied Algonquin-speaking tribes. Romantic local legends involving Princess Snow Bird, Chief Bald Eagle, and others probably sprang from the Victorian imagination and should be taken with a healthy dose of skepticism.

During the Depression years, a Civilian Conservation Corps camp operated near the present-day visitor center, and the Rocks drew the attention of Arnold Wexler and Paul Brandt, two pioneering technical climbers who first mapped climbing routes here in the 1930s. Army climbers trained on the Rocks during World War II.

At 3:27 on the afternoon of October 22, 1987, the face of Seneca Rocks was changed forever as the Gendarme, a 20-ton free-standing slab of Tuscarora sandstone, crashed to the ground. Perched in the gap between Seneca Rocks' northern and southern peaks, the Gendarme took on an oddly human appearance from the ground. The rock had been the victim of a dynamite attack by vandals during the 1930s and probably was further weakened by excessive hardware placement and overuse by climbers. Forest Service officials estimate that more than a thousand climbers scaled the 5.4 technical climbing route annually.

Natural Features

Seneca Rocks is an outlying fragment of the Wills Mountain anticline, the major geologic structure that forms North Fork Mountain immediately to the east as well as New Creek Mountain (in West Virginia) and Wills Mountain (in Maryland) to the north. Erosion along a fault has isolated this 960-foot sandstone blade from the main formation and is responsible for similar formations at nearby Champe and Yellow Rocks (neither open to public use).

Seneca Rocks, WV — Seneca Rocks before the Gendarme fell

Tuscarora sandstone, a highly erosion-resistant quartz sandstone, is the primary ridge-maker in the valley-and-ridge province. The remains of a 400-million-year-old ocean floor, tilted nearly vertical 250 million years ago, much of the stone contains Devonian marine fossils.

The North Fork flood plain is dominated by sycamore, while an eastern hardwood forest covers the higher slopes. Table mountain pine, various ferns and grasses, mountain laurel, and blueberry survive on the thin, sandy soils that cover the Rocks' higher slopes. This is one of several areas to report growths of silvery whitlowwort, a very rare plant found only on outcroppings of Tuscarora sandstone.

Environmental Concerns

Seneca Rocks and the surrounding area are seriously threatened by possible development of Corridor H, a proposed interstate highway that would bisect Monongahela National Forest nearby. Virginia has already rejected the road, thus severing its link to heavily traveled I-81. Unless West Virginia takes similar action, completion of the new interstate will almost certainly accelerate commercial exploitation of the Seneca Rocks area. A coalition of environmental organizations has proposed development of alternate routes or improvement of existing roads.

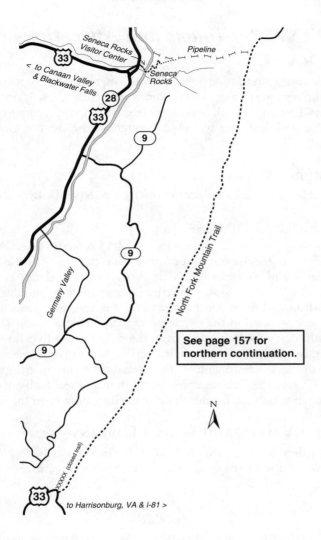

Floods have played an important role in controlling riverside development along the North Fork. A major flood in the autumn of 1985 did an efficient housecleaning, sweeping away many nondescript riverside shacks and house trailers and opening striking new river vistas along Route 28/55. Unfortunately, growth in nearby Petersburg is increasing demand for land in the North Fork Valley, and development is again under way, often in the flood plain. As in the past, the taxpayers will bear the burden of insurance payouts following the next (and inevitable) flood.

Nearby Towns and Attractions

SENECA ROCKS, WV—

This small village straddling Seneca Creek offers limited supplies and services, including a post office, and is home to the commercially operated Seneca Rocks Climbing School. Several motels, commercial campgrounds, and rental cabin complexes are scattered throughout the vicinity, along Routes 33 and 28/55.

PETERSBURG, WV—

The nearest large town, 22 miles north on Route 28 (see Dolly Sods chapter).

SMOKE HOLE CAVERNS—

A commercially developed cave on Route 28/55 south of Petersburg. Don't be put off by its tourist-trap appearance. The cave is rich in natural and human history and is well worth a visit. Native tribes used the cave to smoke meat over slow-burning fires, a practice later adopted by the European settlers who displaced them. During the Civil War, the cave was used for ammunition storage, and in the twentieth century it hid a moonshiner's corn whiskey still that relied on water from the clear stream that flows through the cavern. Geologically, the cave is interesting because it was literally turned on its side during the continental collision that thrust up the Allegheny Front 250 million years ago. The result is a main room 274 feet high but only a few yards wide, in which the former floor and ceiling now form the side walls.

GERMANY VALLEY AND SENECA CAVERNS—

Germany Valley is a high, isolated valley at the foot of North Fork Mountain, and site of the commercially developed Seneca Caverns. See the Spruce Knob chapter for details.

Access

From the north, drive through Petersburg, WV, and continue south on combined Route 28/55 for approximately 22 miles to the well-marked visitor center entrance just north of the Seneca Creek bridge. From the south, follow Route 33 west from Franklin, WV, and drive 14 miles to a junction with Route 28 at Judy Gap. Turn right on combined Route 28/33 and continue north to the town of Seneca Rocks. Turn right into the visitor center just beyond the Seneca Creek bridge. From the Canaan Valley–Blackwater Falls area, follow Route 32 through Canaan Valley and make a steady descent to the junction with Route 55 at Harman. Turn left (east) on Route 55 and descend into North Fork Valley. As you approach the valley, Seneca Rocks is directly ahead. Follow the signs to the visitor center.

Camping

Car-camping near Seneca Rocks Visitor Center is limited to scattered commercial campgrounds and the Forest Service's Seneca Shadows Campground. Camping and overnight stays are not allowed at the visitor center or on the Rocks. Roy Gap, once a popular unofficial car-camping area upstream from the visitor center, was closed to public use several years ago.

Opportunities for backcountry camping are also scarce in this area. Most of the land surrounding Seneca Rocks is private, and the public land is generally too steep and rocky to provide good campsites. There are much better opportunities for backcountry camping on National Forest lands in the nearby Dolly Sods, Spruce Knob, or North Fork Mountain areas.

Technical Climbing

Despite the loss of the Gendarme, Seneca Rocks remains a popular and often overused climbing area. For climbing information, contact Seneca Rocks Visitor Center or the privately owned Seneca Rocks Climbing School (see Appendix I).

Trail Guide:
SENECA ROCKS

Note: Only general-purpose hiking trails are listed. Other trails on and around Seneca Rocks are primarily for climber access. Inquire at the visitor center for details.

North Fork Mountain Access

Length: *3.5 miles (from visitor center); 2 miles (from observation deck)*

Elevation change: *2,180 feet (from visitor center); 1,980 feet (from observation deck)*

Level: *moderately difficult (strenuous)*

USGS quad map: *Upper Tract, WV (shown as pipeline)*

Access: *From Seneca Rocks Trail.*

The only connecting link between Seneca Rocks and the North Fork Mountain Trail, this is a long, hard climb along an exposed gas-line swath. This is not an official trail, and the gas line crosses private land; stay on the main clearing and don't camp. To find the gas line, follow Seneca Rocks Trail to the observation platform. Bushwack uphill and to the east from the observation platform; you should come out on a high, narrow ridge to the northeast of the main formation. Continue to bushwack to the east through open woods and along an indistinct path until you see a wide, grassy swath that leads up North Fork Mountain; that is your route. The gas-line swath makes a direct and steep assault on North Fork Mountain's western flank, ending near the old tower clearing north of High Knob (see the North Fork Mountain chapter) and affording sweeping views along the way. This is an exhausting climb, especially in warm weather. Carry ample water; there is none along the route or on the crest of North Fork Mountain.

Old Railroad Grade

Length: *less than 1 mile*
Elevation change: *none*
Level: *easy*
USGS quad map: *Upper Tract, WV (not shown)*
Access: *From Seneca Rocks Visitor Center or picnic area, walk across the open field to the woods along the river. Along the riverbank, you should find an old rock-strewn trail, the remains of an abandoned railroad grade. Turn left or right and explore at will.*

This is not a formal trail; it is neither signed nor maintained and may be overgrown during the summer. But the old rail bed is generally so obvious that you should have little trouble following it, although repeated flooding has left piles of rock in the trail. There's no risk of getting lost, and the old rail grade provides a pleasant, shaded walk along the banks of the North Fork. Upstream, the trail ends at the confluence of Seneca Creek and the North Fork in Roy Gap. Downstream, the trail eventually enters private property.

Seneca Nature Trail

Length: *less than 1 mile*
Elevation change: *none*
Level: *easy (wheelchair-accessible)*
USGS quad map: *Upper Tract, WV (not shown)*
Access: *From the southern end of the Seneca Rocks Visitor Center parking area.*

This level loop trail passes through open woods along the floodplain of the North Fork. This is a good area to look for wildflowers; crimson bee balm (Oswego tea) and jimson weed are two common varieties.

Seneca Rocks Trail

Length: *1.5 miles*
Elevation change: *900 feet (to observation deck)*
Level: *moderate*
USGS quad map: *Upper Tract, WV (not shown)*
Access: *From Seneca Rocks Visitor Center, follow the signs to a footbridge crossing the North Fork.*

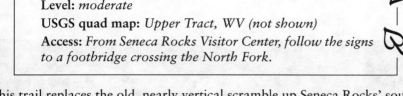

This trail replaces the old, nearly vertical scramble up Seneca Rocks' southeastern slope, which had become severely eroded and is now closed to public use. Although nicely graded, the new trail—whatever its merits from an administrative viewpoint—lacks the character and challenge of the old.

Follow the trail from the visitor center to a crossing on a new steel bridge that replaces the old Roy Gap suspension bridge, which washed away in the 1985 flood. Beyond the bridge, follow a well-graded trail northward along the base of Seneca Rocks. At first the trail climbs gently through open woods at the foot of Seneca Rocks; it then becomes steeper as it ascends the Rocks' northern slope on a series of switchbacks. The trail ends at an observation deck below Seneca Rocks' northern peak. From the deck you'll have a dramatic view down the North Fork Valley, with the high wall of the Allegheny Front looming straight ahead.

From the observation deck, experienced hikers can scramble onto the knife-edged north summit of Seneca Rocks. Wear sturdy non-slip hiking or climbing boots and be careful not to loosen or throw rocks; there may be climbers below you. This is not an undertaking for pets, small children, inexperienced hikers, or those who fear heights. From the deck, the Rocks rise to a narrow ridge with sheer drops of several hundred feet on both sides.

North Fork Mountain, WV — Mountain laurel in bloom

Chapter 13

Other Natural Areas in the Valley-and-Ridge Province

The valley-and-ridge province holds a wealth of natural areas, far too many to report in detail in a single guide. What follows is a brief sampling of the most interesting spots, running the gamut from primitive wildlife management areas to heavily developed resort parks. See Appendix I for a list of organizations to contact for further information.

Cacapon Resort State Park (WV)

This is a heavily developed resort on Cacapon Mountain south of Berkeley Springs, WV. Follow US-522 through Berkeley Springs and continue to the well-marked park entrance. Amenities include a lodge, economy and deluxe cabins, restaurant and snack bar, picnic area, swimming beach, boat rentals, gift shop, arts and crafts center, and horse and hiking trails. There is no campground. The scenic Cacapon River, which flows to the west of the park at the foot of picturesque high ridges and cliffs, is a perennial favorite for fishing, tubing, and canoeing.

Nearby is Berkeley Springs, WV. Founded in 1776 as the town of Bath, this is the site of a natural warm spring once frequented by Indian tribes. The springs were celebrated as a resort for the well-to-do during the Revolutionary era, and George Washington was an occasional visitor. Francis Asbury, a circuit-riding Methodist minister, disapproved of what he saw in Bath in the early 1800s: "My spirit is grieved at so much vanity as is seen here. ... The living is expensive, four dollars per week." The springs, housed in a historic structure along Washington Street, fell from favor with the elite long ago and are now maintained as a state park. Immediately west of town on Route 9 is Berkeley Castle, a pseudo-Norman structure built by Colonel Samuel Taylor Suit in 1885–1886. It is furnished with period pieces and is open to the public for a small fee.

George Washington National Forest (VA/WV)

Approximately 1.3 million acres of this national forest lie primarily in the valley-and-ridge province along the Virginia–West Virginia border. Two of the most popular sections—Massanutten Mountain and Wolf Gap—are described in detail elsewhere in this guide.

Elevations in the national forest range from 600 feet along the Shenandoah River to 4,472 feet at Elliott Knob, VA. This was one of the first national forests to be established in the East. Much of the land was acquired by the Forest Service early in the century, after timbering, mining, and overgrazing rendered it essentially worthless. Photographs taken in the 1930s in what is now the national forest show deeply eroded land stripped of all vegetation. A mature forest is now returning, although the Forest Service continues clearcutting operations on a limited scale.

Contrary to its appearance on road maps, George Washington National Forest is not one contiguous wilderness. A closer look reveals that the Forest Service holdings are punctuated by private inholdings (primarily at lower elevations) and crossed by numerous state, local, and private roads. Nevertheless, you'll find large tracts of virtually unbroken wilderness. With over 400 miles of trails, the forest offers tremendous opportunities for backcountry exploration.

The Deerfield Ranger District, west of Staunton, VA, includes Elliott Knob, the highest peak in the National Forest, as well as the 31-mile Shenandoah Mountain Trail, 10-mile North Mountain Trail, and an excellent network of shorter routes through the Shenandoah Mountains. This is high, rugged, and isolated country, a fine place to escape crowds.

Contact George Washington National Forest headquarters (see Appendix I) for maps and information.

Greenland Gap (WV)

The gap is a steep, mile-long break where Patterson Creek breaches New Creek Mountain—the northern continuation of North Fork Mountain—north of Hopeville Gap. Greenland is one of several prominent east-west gaps in New Creek Mountain clearly visible from the north end of Dolly Sods and a good example of the trellis-like drainage pattern that characterizes the valley-and-ridge province.

To reach the gap, drive to the intersection of Routes 93 and 42 at the small settlement of Scherr. Just north of the intersection, turn east onto Greenland Gap Road and bear left at a fork, cross a small bridge, and continue for a mile to the right turn into Greenland Gap. There are several parking pull-offs along the road near the Greenland Gap Nature Preserve sign

The preserve itself is administered by the Nature Conservancy and is not open to the general public, but you may use a steep trail to the crest of New Creek Mountain along the preserve's boundary. The trail is not marked or maintained, is steep and very rough, and is recommended for experienced hikers only.

Green Ridge
State Forest (MD)

Green Ridge State Forest comprises 38,811 acres of state-managed land on Town Hill, Polish Mountain, and Green Ridge Mountain between Hancock and Cumberland, MD (see Little Orleans to Paw Paw Tunnel in the C&O Canal chapter). The forest offers miles of primitive roads, and camping, hunting, and fishing are allowed with proper permits. Contact the Green Ridge State Forest headquarters for further information (see Appendix I).

Hawk
Recreation Area (WV)

This is an isolated primitive camping area on the crest of Great North Mountain approximately 15 miles west of Strasburg, VA. The Big Blue Trail passes through this rugged and remote area on the western edge of the Shenandoah Valley, leading to the Wolf Gap Recreation Area to the south and the C&O Canal towpath at Hancock, MD, to the north.

Indian Springs
Wildlife Management Area (MD)

Three miles north of the Clear Spring exit on I-70, on Blairs Valley Road near the Maryland-Pennsylvania border, Indian Springs is typical of the many small wildlife management areas scattered throughout the valley-and-ridge province. It is the site of the Indian Springs Wildlife Trail. Hunting and fishing are allowed with proper licenses.

Lost River
State Park (WV)

This scenic mountain park is situated on a land grant originally awarded to General "Light-Horse" Harry Lee for his service during the Revolutionary War. Lee built a cabin here in 1800, later developing the property to become Lee's

White Sulphur Springs, a once-famous resort. Today, the park is a popular day-use area (no camping or overnight stays) offering a good network of short hiking trails.

Nathaniel Mountain and Short Mountain Public Hunting and Fishing Areas (WV)

These two areas lie on thickly forested ridges punctuated by occasional game clearings. Primitive campsites are scattered throughout both areas. Except during hunting seasons (generally from mid-October through early January), these areas are underused. Although scenic value isn't high compared with other areas in this guide, Nathaniel and Short Mountain offer good opportunities for backcountry camping and exploring away from crowds and development.

To reach Nathaniel Mountain, follow US-50 to a point approximately 2 miles east of Romney, WV, turn south on Route 10, and continue to a marked entrance on the right. To reach Short Mountain, take US-50 to Augusta, WV, turn south on Route 7, and continue to a marked entrance on the left.

Part Five

THE
ALLEGHENY FRONT

Dolly Sods, WV — Flagged spruce

The high crest of the Allegheny Front marks the eastern edge of the Allegheny Plateau from southern Virginia into north-central Pennsylvania. Capped by a layer of erosion-resistant Pottsville conglomerate through much of West Virginia, the front reaches a series of high points between Spruce Knob (4,863 feet) and Dolly Sods (4,200 feet). Once blanketed by a virgin spruce and hemlock forest, most of the front in West Virginia was clear-cut early in the century. Unlike other areas in the central Appalachians, however, the forest did not return to all of the front. Between Spruce Knob and Dolly Sods are remarkable open areas that resemble Canadian tundra more than West Virginia mountains.

Algonquin-speaking tribes once inhabited the North Fork Valley, at the foot of the Allegheny Front, although there is no evidence of permanent settlements at the higher elevations. This was the American frontier when George Washington surveyed the region for Lord Fairfax. Washington wasn't fond of the rugged and nearly impassable terrain, although he later returned to inspect the chain of frontier forts—built to protect early settlers from attack during the French and Indian Wars— that stretched along the Allegheny Front. The forts are long gone, their approximate sites now commemorated by roadside historical markers.

English, Scottish, and German settlers arrived at the foot of the Allegheny Front late in the eighteenth century. The newcomers farmed the valleys at first, but as more bottomland was claimed, farmers drove their livestock to the sods—grassy openings high in the spruce forests—for summer grazing. The Dahle family lent its name (later anglicized as "Dolly") to one of the larger sods, but until late in the last century there was little interest in this rugged land overlooking the North Fork.

Dolly Sods, WV — Allegheny Front north of Bell Knob

As demand for lumber, coal, and iron decimated much of the Blue Ridge and valley-and-ridge provinces to the east, timber and mining operations moved westward toward the Allegheny Plateau. Narrow-gauge railroads opened routes into the rugged terrain late in the last century, and lumber and mining camps sprang up in the deep woods. A forest of virgin spruce and hemlock, some measuring nine feet in diameter, grew in the thick, peaty soil that once covered the Allegheny Front and Plateau. Eventually, hundreds of thousands of acres were clear-cut, the camps were abandoned, and wildfires swept the brush and stubble left behind. Stripped of vegetation and burned repeatedly, much of Allegheny Front in West Virginia had eroded to bare rock by the 1920s. In time, much of this ruined land was acquired by the Forest Service, and a slow healing process began.

Dolly Sods, WV — Boulder field west of Bear Rocks

Today, the Allegheny Front in West Virginia is again threatened, this time by the very institutions that once saved it. Construction of a proposed interstate highway that would bisect Monongahela National Forest near Seneca Rocks would undoubtedly lead to the sort of overuse and commercial exploitation seen in and around the Shenandoah and Great Smoky Mountains National Parks. This obvious pork-barrel project, which has been rejected by neighboring Virginia, aroused little interest when first proposed in 1965 but has been revived through the efforts of Senator Robert Byrd (Democrat–WV). It is opposed by a strong coalition of environmental organizations, which advocates development of alternate routes or improvement of existing roads.

The Allegheny Front is rich in natural resources. The Forest Service continues large clear-cutting operations along the front and owns mineral rights to five major commercial-grade coal seams underlying the Dolly Sods area, not a comforting thought given the Forest Service's record in awarding mining rights in other regions. Mineral rights in adjacent areas remain in private hands. The front also lies atop a rich natural gas reservoir, and gas exploration is increasing in an area that is already heavily scarred by gas-line swaths and service roads.

A major flood in late 1985 slowed development in the North Fork and Red Creek Valleys, but the area once again faces pressure from commercial and residential developers. The Allegheny Front's apparent isolation is now largely illusory, particularly in the Dolly Sods area. Just west of Dolly Sods, sheltered from view by an intervening ridge, Canaan Valley ski resort development is sprawling toward the western flank of Cabin Mountain. Land surrounding Dolly Sods' western and northern borders is privately owned, and it is possible that development will eventually spread to within sight of the Dolly Sods Scenic Area. The small town of Laneville, straddling Red Creek at the southern edge of the wilderness area, is also ripe for a boom in vacation-housing construction.

A less obvious but equally serious threat to the Allegheny Front comes from a public that is loving the area to death. As early as the mid-1970s, experts warned that Dolly Sods was being overused. At that time, rough access roads still discouraged many visitors, and permits were required to enter the Dolly Sods Wilderness Area. But the permit requirement was dropped in the 1980s, the popularity of four-wheel-drive vehicles has made the area more accessible, and Forest Service patrols have been reduced in the wake of federal deficit-cutting. More private land owners are closing trail access across their property. In at least one case, access to a major scenic attraction on private land—Seneca Creek Falls—is now denied, and several trails in the Spruce Knob area now dead-end at private property. Increased traffic and vandalism are degrading this area. Clearly, access must be restricted if the Allegheny Front is to retain its unique wilderness quality.

Dolly Sods, WV — Near Bear Rocks

Chapter 14

DOLLY SODS (WEST VIRGINIA)

Dolly Sods' miles of high, open plateau stand in stark contrast to the East's heavily forested mountains. Spread along the high scarp of the Allegheny Front, the sods offer a hiking experience unlike any other in West Virginia.

Dolly Sods consists of two adjoining units—the Dolly Sods Wilderness Area and Dolly Sods Scenic Area—within the Monongahela National Forest. The 2,400-acre Dolly Sods Scenic Area parallels Forest Service Road 75 along the crest of the Allegheny Front from Bear Rocks to slightly south of the Red Creek Campground and includes minor man-made features that disqualify it for Wilderness Area status. Off-road vehicle use is prohibited, hunting is subject to restrictions, and car-camping is limited to the Red Creek Campground. The area is often overused on weekends and holidays in good weather, although few visitors venture far from the road. On weekdays, you'll often find it virtually deserted.

The adjacent 10,215-acre Dolly Sods Wilderness Area includes Red Creek and its tributaries. Except for its trail network, the wilderness area is undeveloped. In contrast to the Dolly Sods Scenic Area, with its sweeping views across the open tundra-like plateau, the wilderness area is heavily forested and cut by deep, narrow gorges. Backcountry camping is allowed, as are hunting and fishing with proper licenses (see Appendix I). Vehicles, including mountain bikes, are prohibited except on established Forest Service roads.

Land west and north of Dolly Sods, including large tracts on Cabin Mountain, the upper end of Red Creek, and the Allegheny Front north of Bear Rocks, is privately owned. In 1993, the Nature Conservancy acquired a large tract north of the wilderness area, running from Bear Rocks (in the scenic area) to the northwestern tip of the wilderness area on Cabin Mountain. The Nature Conservancy is in the process of turning this parcel over to the Forest Service, which as we go to press has yet to establish a permanent access and management policy. Most of Cabin Mountain north of the wilderness area remains in private hands, and entry requires purchase of a permit from CSK Resources (see Appendix I; permits may also be purchased from the volunteer fire departments at Davis and Thomas, WV). Permits must be obtained in advance, and fees are based on applicants' place of residence. Out-of-staters pay the most.

History

Like the balds of North Carolina, Dolly Sods' origin is shrouded in mystery. The earliest settlers found isolated grassy clearings along the Allegheny Front, but the original sods were far smaller than the vast open area now bearing the Dolly family name. The tundra-like landscape seen today is the result of an environmental catastrophe.

Loggers invaded the virgin red spruce forests along the Allegheny Front late in the nineteenth century. Lumber operations peaked in 1909, and by 1913 most of the Dolly Sods area had been clear-cut. Stubble and brush left behind became tinder in an area prone to frequent lightning strikes. More than 10 percent of the surface of West Virginia burned during this period, and at one point a wall of fire swept across Cabin Mountain and up Canaan Valley to the outskirts of Davis, northwest of the present-day Dolly Sods Wilderness Area. By the 1920s, repeated burning and uncontrolled erosion had stripped much of the land to bare rock. The great boulder fields at the northern end of Dolly Sods and Cabin Mountain were once covered by a thick forest of red spruce and hemlock averaging 60 to 90 feet in height, with the largest specimens found along the headwaters of Red Creek. Amazingly, a few charred and weathered stumps still cling to the rocks, mute reminders of what was once here. The final devastation came during World War II, when the Army conducted military exercises on Dolly Sods. You'll see signs warning you to watch for unexploded shells, which contain highly volatile nitroglycerin, although few shells have been reported in recent years.

The Army eventually abandoned Dolly Sods, a portion of which was declared a National Wilderness Area in 1966. As the land recovered, what evolved was strikingly different from what had been. The most heavily damaged area, north of Bear Rocks, remains a barren stretch of shattered sandstone. Alder, lowbush blueberries, huckleberries, bracken fern, and grasses are reclaiming much of the northern plateau, and red spruce is surviving (thriving is not the word) at higher elevations. Abandoned railroad grades, their hardware long since removed, now serve as hiking trails.

Natural Features

As you stand on the cliffs at Dolly Sods, you are at the far eastern edge of the Allegheny Plateau, a high, deeply eroded plain stretching westward to the Ohio River Valley. Although the plateau appears mountainous, its features are the result of eons of erosion rather than the more dynamic mountain-building processes that went on to the east. Three thousand feet below you, North Fork Valley marks the western end of the valley-and-ridge province, a region of narrow, northeast-trending parallel ridges that stretches eastward to the Shenandoah Valley in Virginia. The cliffs and outcroppings common to this section of the Allegheny Front are formed from a hard cap of Pottsville conglomerate, remnant of prehistoric beaches and river deltas now thrust to an average altitude of 3,500 to 4,000 feet above sea level. Where this erosion-resistant cap is absent, softer underlying sandstones and shales have eroded to produce the steep gorges and flat-topped ridges typical of the Allegheny Plateau.

During the last Ice Age, the glaciers stopped short of the Dolly Sods area, but its climate was affected by the advance of the Wisconsin Glacier to the north, and tundra-like vegetation remained as the ice retreated. Sphagnum moss bogs, reindeer lichen, lowbush blueberry, bearberry, and stunted red spruce (the latter "flagged" to the east from constant exposure to prevailing west winds) give the area its distinctive northern appearance. On lower slopes, a typical eastern hardwood forest is again reaching maturity, with many trees now more than sixty years old. Rhododendron, alder, yellow birch, beech, maple, hemlock, and hawthorn are common in lower, sheltered locations, and mountain cranberries and insectivorous pitcher plants survive in the small wetlands that dot the area. Several useful herbs occur here: Wintergreen is a native, but pineapple weed (a variety of chamomile) and catnip probably were introduced by early settlers.

Dolly Sods, WV — Approaching storm near Bear Rocks

The area is rich in wildlife. Virginia whitetailed deer are common, and the black bear is making a comeback. Beaver have returned, too. You'll pass their work along Red Creek and in marshy meadows and sphagnum bogs at higher elevations, but don't count on seeing these wary and largely nocturnal animals. Another elusive resident is the snowshoe hare, which adopts a snow-white coat for winter. Several nonpoisonous snakes are common among the rocks, as are skinks and other small lizards.

A former fire tower on Bell Knob now serves as a bird-counting and banding station. The Allegheny Front is a major flyway on autumn bird migrations. Although the ridge is noted for its hawk and eagle migrations, prevailing west winds often prevent formation of the thermal currents that these large birds seek. Under favorable conditions, several hundred hawks may be spotted in a single day, but that's the exception. Not as well known, but sometimes equally spectacular, is the monarch butterfly migration, which reaches its peak here in early September. In a good year, swarms of monarchs pass along the cliffs on their marathon flight to Mexico.

Nearby Towns and Attractions

PETERSBURG, WV—

Just east of Hopeville Gorge, this friendly small town of 2,400 is a good spot to pick up last-minute supplies and top off the gas tank. Petersburg offers several reliable motels and restaurants as well as the usual array of fast-food places, convenience stores, and service stations. The Potomac District Ranger Station is located on Route 55 several miles east of town. If you have time, or if the weather turns nasty, a visit to Smoke Hole Caverns on Route 28 south of town is worthwhile.

LANEVILLE, WV—

Once the site of Parsons Pulp & Lumber Company, Laneville at the turn of the century was a rough-and-tumble lumber camp along Red Creek. Today, with all traces of the sawmills gone, it is a secluded hodgepodge of vacation homes, cabins, and house trailers clustered at the southern foot of Dolly Sods. There is no commercial development in Laneville, and the locals value their privacy.

SENECA ROCKS, WV—

Nearby are several motels, restaurants, and general stores, as well as a post office and technical climbing outfitter (see the Seneca Rocks chapter).

CANAAN VALLEY RESORT STATE PARK—

At 3,200 feet above sea level, Canaan is among the highest valleys in the East. It is the site of a popular and heavily developed 6,500-acre park adjoining the Canaan Valley ski area. The park offers a 250-room lodge, tent and trailer sites with RV hookups, restaurant and snack bar, swimming pool, tennis courts, 18-hole golf course, bike rentals, fishing, and hiking trails. The ski area boasts 21 trails, with up to 850 feet of vertical drop, and 18 miles of cross-country trails. One lift operates during off-season, from late May through early October, providing easy access to short, scenic trails on Weiss and Bald Knobs. Commercial and residential development is booming along Route 32 north of the park, and you'll have no trouble finding convenience stores, gas stations, and tacky souvenirs. Several motels and commercial campgrounds are nearby, and reasonably priced ski-condo rentals are available off-season. Because of the area's proximity to Blackwater Falls and other popular tourist attractions, lodge and campground reservations are recommended.

BLACKWATER FALLS STATE PARK—

This is a popular and often crowded attraction 3 miles southwest of Davis, off of Route 32. The park is famous for a high falls on the Blackwater River, but hiking to the base of the falls is discouraged, so you'll have to settle for the view from an observation platform midway down the gorge. The heavily developed park offers a lodge and gift shop, deluxe cabins, tent and trailer sites with electric hookups, a swimming beach with bathhouse, and short hiking trails.

WHITE GRASS TOURING CENTER—

Just north of Canaan Valley Resort State Park on Freeland Road, this cross-country ski area boasts 36 miles of backcountry trails, telemark slopes, and guided tours from late November through March.

Camping

Backcountry camping is permitted throughout the Dolly Sods Wilderness Area. Contrary to what older guidebooks say, permits are no longer needed to enter or camp in the wilderness area. Good sites are plentiful on the relatively level plateau west of Red Creek, but avoid camping within a quarter-mile of any road or within 1,000 feet of a trail or stream. Streams and springs are unprotected, and many drain beaver ponds or sheep grazing areas; boil or purify your drinking water.

Car-camping is difficult on Dolly Sods. Red Creek Campground, the only legal drive-in campground in the area, offers only a limited number of semi-primitive sites (tent pad, picnic table, pit toilets). Camping is on a first-come, first-served basis, and spaces are usually filled by mid-morning on weekends and holidays in good weather. Illegal car-camping in the scenic area along FS-75 has become more prevalent recently, bringing increased vandalism and environmental damage. FS-75, between Bear Rocks and FS-19, is clearly posted against roadside camping, and enforcement efforts are being stepped up. Unless you're willing to be roused from a warm sleeping bag at 2 A.M., don't car-camp along the posted stretch of FS-75.

In the likely event that you arrive at Dolly Sods only to find all legal car-camping spots taken, there a several possible solutions: (1) Beyond the north section, you may find space available on the levels halfway down FS-75 between Bear Rocks and Jordan Run Road (Route 4). This is not a campground, and it has no facilities, but so far the area has not been posted against camping. Pay close attention to trespassing warnings (some of the adjacent land is private), and avoid blocking access to private property beyond the right-of-way. (2) Settle for a commercial or state park campground in nearby North Fork or Canaan Valleys. (3) Strap on a backpack, and get to know this unique area by sleeping under the stars. I recommend the latter.

There is no permanent ranger station or commercial development near Dolly Sods. Stock up in advance on supplies, including drinking water and a full tank of gas, and be prepared for sudden changes in weather at any time of year.

If there is even a remote possibility of snow, be prepared to make a fast exit from the plateau. The Forest Service roads are not plowed and can quickly become impassable even to four-wheel-drive vehicles.

Access

Depending upon your point of view and the condition of your vehicle, simply getting to Dolly Sods can be half the fun. Be prepared for steep, unpaved Forest Service roads that are not always passable to ordinary passenger cars.

From the east, drive through Petersburg, WV, and continue south on Route 28. Turn right on Route 4 (Jordan Run Road) approximately 9 miles from Petersburg, a short distance south of Smoke Hole Caverns. The road climbs steeply, then levels off at a fork. To your left is unpaved FS-19, which climbs to the central section of the wilderness area near the picnic and overlook areas. To your right, paved Route 4 continues north, intersecting FS-75 (access to the Sods' northern edge) at approximately 7 miles.

From the west, pass through the small towns of Thomas and Davis, then continue south on Route 32 through Canaan Valley. South of the state park, Route 32 begins a steep descent; watch for a wide turnoff to Route 45 (Laneville Road) on your left. Continue along Route 45 to its end at Laneville. The road is narrow and winding, passing through picturesque hill country that is marred at one point by a roadside dump in the worst West Virginia tradition. At Laneville, pick up unpaved FS-19 and make a steady climb to Dolly Sods.

Forest Service Roads

Unpaved Forest Service roads in the Dolly Sods are steep, narrow, and rocky. Although most are passable to ordinary passenger cars in good weather, a four-wheel-drive vehicle is recommended. The roads are not suitable for oversized RVs, towed trailers, or cars with low ground clearance, worn tires, or bad brakes. Two vehicles cannot pass along some stretches; local custom gives right-of-way to the descending vehicle, but common sense sometimes dictates otherwise. Stay alert and be prepared to maneuver. The Forest Service does not plow these roads in the winter, and the upper elevations are often icy, snow-packed, or deeply drifted. Don't attempt these roads in icy conditions without a reliable four-wheel-drive vehicle, tire chains, an experienced driver, and adequate survival gear. Winter patrols are rare, and in an emergency you'll be on your own.

FS-19—This road leaves Jordan Run Road and climbs steadily through a series of switchbacks up the eastern flank of Allegheny Front Mountain, at one point crossing a privately owned meadow with a fine view of North Fork Mountain. After a steep climb to the ridge line, the road intersects FS-75, which leads north to an overlook, Red Creek Campground, Bear Rocks, and other points of interest. From this intersection, FS-19 turns south to make a steady descent to Laneville, providing a connecting link to the Canaan Valley and Seneca Rocks areas. FS-19 is the most heavily traveled route to Dolly Sods and is in fairly good condition in dry weather.

FS-70—This road intersects FS-19 at a half-mile south of the Dolly Sods Picnic Area and usually is gated to public vehicles. The road is sometimes opened to vehicles during hunting season; inquire at the ranger station east of Petersburg. The road makes a moderate climb to the south-southwest, providing hiker access to Flatrock and Roaring Plains.

FS-75—Intersecting Route 4 (Jordan Run Road) approximately 7 miles north of the Route 4/FS-19 fork (a church on the northwest corner makes a reliable landmark) this road is steep, rocky, and rough at first. It levels off briefly along the Fore Knobs, then resumes a steep climb along switchbacks to the ridge-top parking area at Bear Rocks. FS-75 then turns south to parallel the edge of the ridge, affording outstanding views along the way to Red Creek Campground and an eventual junction with FS-19. Roadside camping is prohibited along FS-75.

FS-80—A road that begins as Route 37 and is shown as such on some maps, FS-80 leaves Route 32 in Canaan Valley, climbing steeply up the western flank of Cabin Mountain to the Big Stonecoal and Breathed Mountain trailheads and the western edge of Dolly Sods. The road is rough, narrow, and badly eroded; a four-wheel-drive vehicle is required.

Trail Guide:

DOLLY SODS WILDERNESS AND SCENIC AREAS

Allegheny Front Bushwhack

Length: *1–12 miles*

Elevation change: *100–500 feet*

Level: *easy to difficult*

USGS quad maps: *Blackbird Knob, WV; Hopeville, WV (not shown)*

Access: *Park at Bear Rocks and hike north or south along cliff's edge.*

I hesitate to include this hike for fear of bringing still more people into a fragile area. But the route is so obvious that visitors usually discover it for themselves, so I will include it here with the hope that you will take these precautions to heart: Rock-hop or follow existing game trails to avoid trampling fragile vegetation. Don't camp or take pets, small children, or large groups into this environmentally sensitive area.

Dolly Sods, WV —
Wintergreen and reindeer lichen

Mountain bikes and motorized vehicles are prohibited. The open cliffs are vulnerable to high winds and lightning strikes, and they are very slippery when wet. Several deaths and numerous injuries have occurred here recently. Land north of Bear Rocks is private but not posted; enter at your own risk. So far, the Forest Service has not restricted hiker access to the cliffs, but that is always subject to change.

This isn't a trail but an impromptu scramble along the cliffs and outcroppings at the eastern edge of the Allegheny Front. You can hike parts of the 12-mile length from Bear Rocks south to FS-19 on or near cliffs' edge, although you'll need to detour into the brush more frequently the farther south you go. You can't really get lost; your route will be obvious in the open country. The views are spectacular, and you can feast on wild blueberries and huckleberries in late summer.

North of Bear Rocks, the cliffs of the Allegheny Front begin a gradual descent toward Maryland. A moderately difficult 1.5-mile bushwhack to the north will bring you to Stack Rock, the high box-like outcropping visible from Bear Rocks. Hikers have used this private (but unposted) area freely for at least three decades. Nevertheless, inclusion in this guide does not confer permission to cross the property.

South of Bear Rocks, the cliffs rise steadily to a barren, rock-strewn plateau 4,080 feet above sea level, offering sweeping 360-degree views. The high stack to the northwest is the PEPCO power plant at Mount Storm, WV. To the northeast are the parallel ranges in the valley-and-ridge province. Hopeville Gorge and the high cliffs of North Fork Mountain face you to the southeast, with Petersburg visible beyond. The high point to the south is Bell Knob with its former fire tower (now a bird-banding station), and to the west the ridge line of Cabin Mountain mercifully blocks your view of Canaan Valley ski resort development. The first few miles south of Bear Rocks are open and easy to navigate, but as you near Red Creek Campground, gaps in the cliff will test your ingenuity and rock-scrambling skill. The going gets still rougher south of the campground, forcing frequent detours into the woods along many stretches. In the vicinity of Bell Knob, you'll have to return to the road, which is never more than a half-mile from cliff's edge. South of the knob, you can eventually make your way back to the cliff's edge near the Dolly Sods overlook area.

Big Stonecoal Trail (#513)

Length: *4.5 miles*

Elevation change: *900 feet*

Level: *moderate (trail); difficult (access)*

USGS quad maps: *Blackwater Falls, WV; Hopeville, WV*

Access: *Access to this trail is difficult. The south trailhead, 1.5 miles north of Laneville opposite the Red Creek Trail, requires crossing Red Creek, a feat for experienced hikers only. The crossing is not possible during above-normal flow. The footbridge that once provided access to this trailhead washed out years ago and will not be rebuilt, in keeping with wilderness area regulations. The north trailhead is located near the upper end of FS-80 (accessible from Route 32 in Canaan Valley), which is badly eroded and passable only to four-wheel-drive vehicles with good ground clearance.*

Big Stonecoal Trail is a steady, scenic ascent through varied terrain from Red Creek to Cabin Mountain. From its south trailhead on the west bank of Red Creek, Big Stonecoal Trail climbs steadily along Big Stonecoal Run on an abandoned railroad grade, passing several falls and cascades. Rocky Point Trail enters from the east at approximately 1.4 miles. The trail then passes

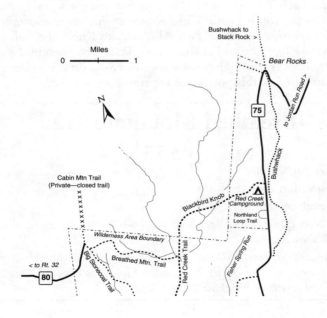

the site of an old logging camp on an abandoned railroad grade, crosses Big Stonecoal Run, and skirts several beaver ponds in an open meadow. The trail continues an additional 1.5 miles, with several more stream crossings, to its north trailhead (shared with Breathed Mountain Trail) at FS-80.

Blackbird Knob Trail (#511)

Length: *2 miles*

Elevation change: *1,200 feet*

Level: *moderate (fairly difficult at stream crossings)*

USGS quad map: *Blackbird Knob, WV*

Access: *The east trailhead is on FS-75 immediately north of Red Creek Campground, with ample parking nearby. The west trailhead is at a junction with Red Creek Trail on private land, approximately 6 miles north of Laneville.*

The Blackbird Knob Trail is a scenic link to Red Creek Trail, with two potentially difficult stream crossings. From its east trailhead, Blackbird Knob Trail skirts to the north of Red Creek Campground, passing an excellent viewpoint on a low sandstone outcropping before turning west through open meadows. Within a half-mile, the trail enters private land (no camping) and descends to the first, and easier, of two stream crossings. The second crossing comes in another half-mile and may require shin-deep wading in a swift current; turn back if the water level is high. Beyond the second crossing, the trail skirts to the south of Blackbird Knob, an inconspicuous and heavily wooded rise offering no views. Beyond Blackbird Knob, the trail continues through mature forest to end at Red Creek Trail. The Blackbird Knob Trail once continued west through private land to FS-80 on the western flank of Cabin Mountain, but this portion of the trail is now closed.

Breathed Mountain Trail (#553)

Length: *2 miles*

Elevation change: *300 feet*

Level: *moderate*

USGS quad map: *Blackbird Knob, WV; Blackwater Falls, WV (not shown)*

Access: *West trailhead is a shared trailhead with Big Stonecoal Trail on FS-80. East trailhead is on Red Creek Trail south of Blackbird Knob Trail.*

From FS-80, Breathed Mountain Trail skirts open meadows and boggy areas, passing several beaver ponds. Parts of the trail are wet and muddy, and there are two easy stream crossings. Two miles east of the trailhead, Breathed Mountain Trail dead-ends at Red Creek Trail just below the forks of Red Creek.

Cabin Mountain Trail

This scenic trail leaves FS-80 along the crest of Cabin Mountain, immediately to the west of Dolly Sods. Most of the trail is on private land, and entry is by paid permit only (see CSK Resources, Inc., in Appendix I).

Dobbin Slashings

Length: *less than 0.5 mile*

Elevation change: *150 feet*

Level: *easy*

USGS quad map: *Blackbird Knob, WV (not shown)*

Access: *From Bear Rocks parking area.*

This short, unmarked path leads to an interesting wetland at the headwaters of Red Creek.

   From the parking area, look for an obvious but unmarked trail leading downhill and to the west through knee-high blueberry bushes. Follow the trail to a low, boggy area. Like other bogs on Dolly Sods, this one is the result of water accumulating above relatively impermeable sandstone. Don't cross the bog; it is easily damaged, and the status of the land beyond—in the process of being transferred to the Forest Service—is currently in limbo. Explore carefully, then return the way you came.

Fisher Spring Run Trail (#510)

Length: *2 miles*

Elevation change: *1,300 feet*

Level: *moderate (strenuous)*

USGS quad maps: *Blackbird Knob, WV; Hopeville, WV*

Access: *East trailhead is on FS-75 approximately 4.5 miles south of Bear Rocks, with ample parking nearby. West trailhead is on Red Creek Trail (#514) in upper Red Creek Canyon, approximately 3 miles northwest of Laneville.*

This is one of the most popular trails in the wilderness area. From FS-75, Fisher Spring Run Trail first makes a moderate descent through overgrown fields and scrub, passing some scattered junk predating Forest Service management. The trail becomes steeper as it enters open hardwood forest on the eastern slope of Red Creek Canyon. At approximately 1.3 miles from the trailhead, Rohrbaugh Plains Trail enters from the south; a half-mile side-trip on that trail will take you to a good viewpoint across Red Creek. Just beyond this junction, the trail crosses Fisher Spring Run, which vanishes underground for a short stretch, and soon comes to the head of a high waterfall in a steep ravine. A short but difficult bushwhack, recommended for experienced hikers only, leads to a pool at the base of the falls. To continue on the main trail, wade the shallow stream at the head of the falls and descend steeply on a rocky bank above the ravine to Red Creek Trail. From this junction, Red Creek Trail leads south 3 miles to Laneville or north 2 miles to its junction with Blackbird Knob Trail on private land.

High Water Route
(#552-A)

Listed in many guides as an alternate route to Little Stonecoal Trail along the north bank of Red Creek, this trail is rough and informal at best. Its southern end has been destroyed repeatedly during recent floods and may be barely passable. Inquire locally.

Northland Loop
Interpretive Trail

Length: *less than 1 mile*
Elevation change: *insignificant*
Level: *easy (wheelchair-accessible)*
USGS quad map: *Blackbird Knob, WV (not shown)*
Access: *From the large parking area on FS-75 south of Red Creek Campground.*

This short loop trail is keyed to an interpretive brochure, rather inconveniently available at Seneca Rocks Visitor Center. From the parking area, it loops through dense spruce, mountain laurel, and rhododendron thicket to a boardwalk extending into Alder Run Bog, one of several large wetlands along this portion of the Allegheny Front.

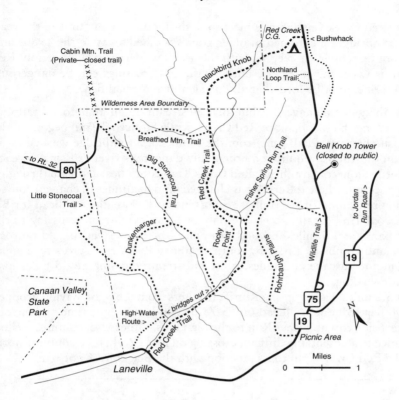

Red Creek Trail
(#514)

Length: *6 miles*
Elevation change: *500 feet*
Level: *moderate*
USGS quad map: *Blackbird Knob, WV*
Access: *South trailhead is at the north end of the parking area at the game warden's cabin in Laneville. If the lot is filled, as it often is on weekends and holidays, park along FS-19 nearby, being careful not to block the road or access to private drives. Parking illegally in Laneville is a very bad idea. North trailhead is on private land at the end of the Blackbird Knob Trail.*

Note: Red Creek Canyon is subject to flash-flooding at any time of the year. The footbridges mentioned in older guides washed away in the 1980s and will not be rebuilt, in keeping with the area's wilderness classification. Red Creek is wide, the current is fairly swift, and crossings can be dangerous. The creek cannot be forded at all during above-normal flow.

From the game manager's cabin, hike upstream on an abandoned railroad grade along the east bank of Red Creek. Little Stonecoal Trail begins on the opposite bank at a half-mile from the trailhead; a footbridge washed away here in the 1980s, requiring a potentially dangerous river crossing to reach the Little Stonecoal trailhead. Red Creek Trail continues upstream through a boggy section where the creek has changed (and continues to change) course, forcing relocation of the trail at regular intervals. Pass the trailhead for Big Stonecoal Trail (again, accessible only by a difficult stream crossing to the west bank) at 1.5 miles. Beyond this point, the trail leaves the old railroad grade and climbs as a narrow footpath above Red Creek, crossing a small stream and cascade at 2 miles. A second stream crossing at 2.5 miles may require wading.

At 3.2 miles, Fisher Spring Run Trail enters from the right, having dropped 1,300 feet from its trailhead on FS-75. If you have ample time and energy, make a side trip up Fisher Run to the high falls. Otherwise, continue a short distance to a potentially difficult crossing on Red Creek, then continue north on the Red Creek Trail to its junction with the Blackbird Knob Trail.

Rocky Point Trail (#554)

Length: *1.8 miles*

Elevation change: *100 feet*

Level: *moderate*

USGS quad maps: *Blackbird Knob, WV; Hopeville, WV (not shown)*

Access: *West trailhead is on Big Stonecoal Trail. East trailhead is on Red Creek Trail north of Fisher Run Trail.*

A short connector linking the Big Stonecoal and Red Creek Trails, the Rocky Point Trail passes an outstanding view from a high outcropping. From its western trailhead on Big Stonecoal Trail, Rocky Point Trail follows an old railroad grade along the western edge of the Red Creek Canyon for approximately a half-mile to high sandstone cliffs and outcroppings. Scramble to the top for a panoramic view across Red Creek Canyon. Beyond the cliffs, the trail remains mostly level for another 1.3 miles to the west bank of Red Creek.

Rohrbaugh Plains Trail (#508)

Length: *3.5 miles*
Elevation change: *150 feet*
Level: *easy to moderate*
USGS quad maps: *Blackbird Knob, WV; Hopeville, WV (not shown)*
Access: *South trailhead is on FS-19 just east of its junction with FS-70, with parking available along the road. North trailhead is at a junction near the midpoint of Fisher Spring Run Trail.*

Rohrbaugh Plains is a rocky trail through thick forest leading to a good overlook on the eastern rim of Red Creek Canyon. From its south end, Rohrbaugh Plains Trail descends through dense hemlock and rhododendron thicket, passes through younger growth in an old clear-cut area, then reenters older forest and follows an abandoned and relatively level railroad grade to its junction with Fisher Spring Run Trail. Be prepared for several stream crossings and wet sections along the trail. At 2.6 miles from the road, the trail makes a short detour west to sandstone cliffs overlooking the Red Creek canyon. North of the overlook area, Wildlife Trail #560 enters from the east and provides easy access to FS-75. From this junction, Rohrbaugh Plains Trail continues north for a half-mile to end at Fisher Spring Run Trail. Turn left (west) to descend to Red Creek Trail via Fisher Spring Run Trail or right (east) to ascend to FS-75.

Wildlife Trail (#560)

Length: 1.3 miles
Elevation change: *200 feet*
Level: *easy*
USGS quad map: *Blackbird Knob, WV*
Access: *From FS-75 south of the Bell Knob Lookout spur, with ample parking in a pullout or along the shoulder.*

This abandoned Forest Service road is a short connector to the Rohrbaugh Plains Trail. From FS-75, the trail makes a moderate ascent through several old game clearings, then descends to a dead end at Rohrbaugh Plains Trail near a good overlook above Red Creek Canyon. This trail is a favorite with hunters and should be avoided during deer season (see Appendix I).

The Allegheny Front near Roaring Plains

Chapter 15

Flatrock and Roaring Plains Area (West Virginia)

The Flatrock and Roaring Plains lie to the south of Dolly Sods, along an undeveloped stretch of the Allegheny Front that receives relatively few visitors. Scenery, elevations, and natural features aren't much different from what you'll encounter on Dolly Sods, although the area is more heavily wooded and lacks Dolly Sods' high cliffs and outcroppings. Trails are generally rougher than those on Dolly Sods, and many are poorly marked and maintained; USGS topographic maps and a compass are recommended. For the experienced hiker, the high plateau surrounding Mt. Porte Crayon offers some outstanding bushwhacking terrain. Good backcountry campsites are plentiful.

Trail Guide:
Flatrock and Roaring Plains Area

Black Trail (#5011)

This old, unmarked trail is mentioned in several guides and shown on the USGS topo maps, but it is not recommended. The trail leads downhill from the South Prong Trail to private land on the Fore Knobs and is badly overgrown.

Boar's Nest Trail (#518)

Length: *3 miles*
Elevation change: *1,300 feet*
Level: *moderate (strenuous)*
USGS quad map: *Laneville, WV*
Access: *North trailhead (shared with the South Prong Trail) is on FS-19 approximately 1 mile east of Laneville, with ample parking nearby. South trailhead is off FS-70 on Flatrock Plains.*

Boar's Nest Trail commemorates a notorious saloon that flourished on the outskirts of Laneville in lumber-camp days. The trail is steep and is hard to follow in spots, and it receives little use except during hunting season (see Appendix I for addresses of state departments of natural resources).

From the trailhead on FS-19, Boar's Nest Trail descends to a game clearing, then follows the South Fork of Red Creek upstream to a fairly easy crossing. It may take some searching to find the trail on the opposite bank, and the pathway becomes still harder to locate as it climbs steeply to Flatrock Plains over a series of switchbacks through an old logging area. This slope is crisscrossed by abandoned railroad grades and logging roads, and you stand a fair chance of getting lost even with a topo map and compass. General direction of travel is south and uphill. The last 1.25-mile stretch is a fairly level hike across Flatrock Plains, with good views from scattered meadows and openings. Beyond the junction with FS-70, a short, somewhat overgrown spur continues south to a wide gas-line swath and spectacular views from the open meadows of Roaring Plains (see South Prong Trail).

Flatrock Run Trail (#519)

Length: *5 miles*
Elevation change: *2,000 feet*
Level: *moderate (strenuous)*
USGS quad map: *Laneville, WV*
Access: *From Laneville, follow Route 45 west 1.5 miles and turn left on an unmarked paved road. Continue 0.8 mile to a parking area at the north trailhead. South trailhead is on the Roaring Plains Trail near its end on Mt. Porte Crayon.*

Flatrock Run is a scenic, isolated trail on the north flank of Mt. Porte Crayon. From the north trailhead, the trail crosses private land. The landowner has granted trail access; stay on the trail, close all gates, and avoid camping in the area. Climb over a farm gate and follow the dirt road through a pasture, dodging livestock as necessary. Pass through two more at about 1.2 miles, marking the end of private land, and enter the woods. Make an easy stream crossing at 3 miles and begin a steep climb a short distance beyond, cutting across an abandoned railroad switchback. After a mile of steady climbing, the trail rejoins the relatively level railroad grade, on which it remains to its end at Roaring Plains Trail.

The old railroad grade continues to the right (west) for another mile to 4,770-foot Mt. Porte Crayon. The peak was named in honor of David Hunter Strother, a noted artist, author, and outdoorsman better known by the pseudonym Porte Crayon, who explored this area in the nineteenth century. Unfortunately, heavy ATV use has reduced much of the trail to a muddy rut.

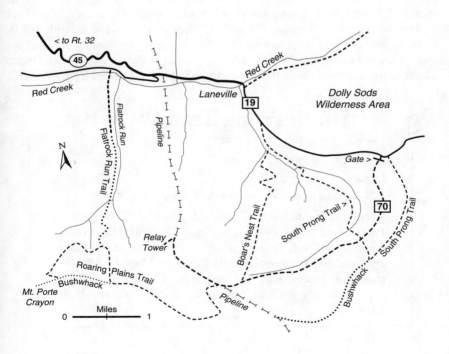

Roaring Plains Trail (#548)

Length: *3 miles*

Elevation change: *600 feet*

Level: *moderate*

USGS quad map: *Laneville, WV*

Access: *East trailhead is along FS-70 approximately 3.5 miles from its junction with FS-19. FS-70 is normally gated to public vehicles; park at the gate and hike steadily uphill. A more scenic, but fairly strenuous, alternative is to take the Boar's Head Trail to its junction with Roaring Plains Trail, thus avoiding the monotonous road walk.*

Roaring Plains Trail bears southwest as it leaves FS-70, burrowing through heavy thickets and a small clearing. After a short ascent, the trail reaches a boggy, level area and turns west (right) along an old railroad grade. The trail remains on the old grade for the next 2.8 miles, offering occasional overgrown views from the edge of Roaring Plains. To your right, at approximately 2.5 miles, is the junction with Flatrock Run Trail, a steady 2,000-foot descent to Laneville. Roaring Plains Trail ends on the northern flank of Mt. Porte Crayon, where there are plentiful backcountry campsites. Beyond the end of the official trail, the old railroad grade continues west to Mt. Porte Crayon, but the area tends to be wet and has been degraded by ATV use.

South Prong Trail (#517)

Length: *5 miles*

Elevation change: *1,950 feet*

Level: *easy to moderate*

USGS quad maps: *Hopeville, WV; Laneville, WV*

Access: *East trailhead is a half-mile south of the Dolly Sods Picnic Area on FS-19, with parking for several vehicles on a rough pull-off. If the pull-off is full, park at the picnic area and hike back to the trailhead; don't block FS-19. West trailhead (shared with the Boar's Nest Trail) is on FS-19 approximately midway between Laneville and the Dolly Sods Scenic Area.*

From FS-19, South Prong Trail bears east through a dark, boggy area. Primitive boardwalks are in place at several spots, but they have deteriorated and much of the first mile is muddy. Hikers and mountain bikers have turned this section into a quagmire by detouring around the wet areas. The mostly level trail tunnels through dense thickets, dark spruce forest, and marshy areas, occasionally crossing small clearings. Scramble up scattered conglomerate outcroppings for views to the north and east. The clearings provide good backcountry campsites, and in late summer huckleberries and blueberries are plentiful.

At approximately 2.5 miles, South Prong Trail turns north to cross FS-70. From this point, it's possible to bushwhack southwest for about 1.5 miles, along traces of an abandoned footpath and through the open woods, to a wide meadow on the Allegheny Front. If you're feeling less adventurous, turn left on FS-70 and walk uphill for another 2 miles to a wide gas-line swath, turn left, and walk uphill to the meadow. Although this area lacks Dolly Sods' distinctive cliffs and outcroppings, the views are equally dramatic and far-reaching. This is wide-open country offering ample opportunities for backcountry camping without enduring the ever-growing crowds at Dolly Sods.

To continue on the South Prong Trail, cross FS-70 and begin a steep descent to FS-19. The trail becomes obscure as it enters a patch of dead trees, girdled to prevent the spread of disease. Cross the old railroad grade (which leads slightly uphill) and continue to descend to the west, meeting the Boar's Nest Trail shortly before reaching the west trailhead on FS-19.

Spruce Knob, WV — Rime on spruce at summit

Chapter 16

SPRUCE KNOB (WEST VIRGINIA)

Wind-blasted and boulder-strewn, Spruce Knob at 4,863 feet is the highest point in West Virginia. The summit, with its flagged spruce and sparkling conglomerate outcroppings, resembles the open plateau on Dolly Sods, while the surrounding slopes are heavily forested and cut by deep ravines. An observation deck and loop trail at the summit offer unbroken views across the surrounding ranges, and an extensive trail network crosses National Forest Service land to the north and west. While a few attractions—the lake, observation tower, and Seneca Creek—attract crowds, the more remote parts of Spruce Knob's backcountry are often virtually deserted.

Natural Features

Spruce Knob is not a true knob but a narrow spur rising above the main crest of the Allegheny Front, which is known here as Spruce Mountain. The summit is capped by an erosion-resistant layer of 300-million-year-old Pottsville sandstone, the same conglomerate that forms the cliffs and outcroppings at Dolly Sods to the north. Land to the west of the knob is typical of the deeply eroded, heavily forested Allegheny Plateau. The crest of Middle Mountain, the next major ridge west of Spruce Knob, marks the eastern Continental Divide (and, incidentally, the western boundary of this guide). Streams on its eastern slope flow to the Atlantic; those on the west flow to the Gulf of Mexico.

From the Spruce Knob observation deck, Middle Mountain lies directly to the west, across the Gandy Creek Valley. To the north is the long scarp of the Allegheny Front leading to the Flatrock Plains and Dolly Sods areas. From here, the front loses elevation steadily as it curves to the northeast to end as little more than a hill in north-central Pennsylvania. The North Fork Valley, flanked by the peculiar undulating ridge line of the River Knobs, lies to the east. Separating the River Knobs from the higher ridge of North Fork Mountain is Germany Valley, an isolated farming area and site of Seneca Caverns. Beyond North Fork Mountain, on a clear day, you may catch glimpses of ranges in the valley-and-ridge province rolling eastward toward the Shenandoah Valley.

Red spruce, remnants of a forest that flourished here during the last Ice Age, blanket the higher ridges. In the harsh environment at the summit of Spruce Knob, where trees are "flagged" by prevailing west winds, a spruce may struggle for fifty years to reach a height of only twenty feet. Isolated heath barrens, characterized by low growths of black huckleberry, lowbush blueberry, mountain cranberry, minniebush, bracken fern, and club mosses, are scattered throughout the forest along the ridge. Wildflowers, including deptford pink, birdsfoot-trefoil, trillium, lady slipper, and bittersweet nightshade, flourish in more protected areas.

Camping

Good backcountry campsites are plentiful throughout the Spruce Knob Recreation Area, and permits are not needed. However, most of the eastern portion of the recreation area—including Seneca Creek and the western slope and ridge line of Spruce Mountain—lies in the Seneca Creek Pioneer Zone, which restricts backcountry camping to designated areas. Judy Springs Campground, a popular hike-in site in the pioneer zone, provides gravel tent pads, pump, and pit toilets. Sites at Judy Springs occupy a mixture of meadow and woods and are open to hikers on a first-come, first-served basis.

Spruce Knob Lake Campground, along FS-112 west of Spruce Knob, has 45 semi-primitive sites for cars or small trailers. The campground perches on a steep hillside, and RVs will need to use levelers at many sites. The campground is open from March through December and provides picnic tables, fireplaces, drinking water, and pit toilets. Registered campers can launch non-motorized boats at nearby Spruce Knob Lake. Unless posted otherwise, roadside camping is allowed in pull-outs scattered along the forest service roads. Seneca Creek Recreation Area, a popular campground still mentioned in some guides, was destroyed in the 1985 flood and will not be rebuilt.

Nearby Towns and Attractions

FRANKLIN, WV—

Seventeen miles south of Riverton at the crossroads of Routes 220 and 33, this town of approximately 1,000 is home to the Treasure Mountain Festival, highlighting mountain culture and crafts, during the third weekend of each September. Franklin offers a modest array of stores, restaurants, and motels.

GERMANY VALLEY AND SENECA CAVERNS—

Germany Valley is a high, narrow valley sheltered between the River Knobs and North Fork Mountain. The valley was the site of Fort Hinkle, built in 1761–1762 after Shawnees destroyed nearby Fort Upper Tract and Fort Seybert. Sparsely settled by German immigrants in the late eighteenth century, the valley retains its rural character. Most of the land is private. Explore the back roads at will, but be sure to respect property rights.

Seneca Caverns, a commercially developed cave in Germany Valley, lies at the foot of North Fork Mountain. Blackened walls supposedly show use by Indians, but early settlers and latter-day explorers used the cave as well. You'll have to endure quaint Indian tales of dubious historical accuracy, but if you can overlook that sort of tourist hokum, the cave is well worth a visit for its array of flowstone, rimstone, soda straw stalactites, stalagmites, and columns.

To visit Germany Valley and Seneca Caverns, turn east on Route 9 from its junction with Route 33 at Riverton and drive 3 miles to the caverns.

GERMANY VALLEY OVERLOOK—

You'll find this overlook at a wide parking pull-out along Route 33 on the western flank of North Fork Mountain. From here, you look north directly up Germany Valley, separating the high ridge of North Fork Mountain (on your right) from the lower River Knobs (on your left). To the left of the River Knobs is the deeply cut North Fork Valley, marking the western edge of the valley-and-ridge province, with the crest of the Allegheny Front towering above.

Access (via Forest Service Roads)

Coming from the east, main access to the Spruce Knob area is from combined Route 33/28 near Riverton, between Franklin and Seneca Rocks. The well-marked turn is approximately 2 miles north of Judy Gap or 9 miles south of Seneca Rocks. From the turn-off on Route 33/28, paved County Road 13 climbs steeply to a fork at the head of a hollow. Bear left at the fork, regardless of what the sign may say (sign turning seems to be a favorite prank here), onto unpaved FS-112. FS-112 climbs to Spruce Knob, then descends to Spruce Knob Lake.

To reach the Spruce Knob area from the west, follow US-33 east of Wymer and turn south on Route 29 (Whitmer Road). Continue south on Route 29 for approximately 16 miles, then bear left onto Forest Service Road 1 at the well-marked entrance to the recreation area. FS-1 connects to FS-112 near Spruce Knob Lake.

Forest Service roads in the Spruce Knob area are steep and unpaved, but they generally aren't as rough or narrow as those on Dolly Sods. The roads aren't plowed in winter and are treacherous when wet, icy, or snow-packed. In dry weather, all roads are passable to ordinary passenger cars with sturdy tires and good ground clearance, but a four-wheel-drive vehicle is recommended in poor weather. The roads are especially rough during spring thaw, usually from late March through early May.

FS-1—

Main access to the Spruce Knob area from the west. The road begins on Route 29 (Whitmer Road) approximately 16 miles south of US-33 and joins FS-112 near Spruce Knob Lake.

FS-104—

A short spur road leading northeast from FS-112 at the summit of the Allegheny Front. The road makes a dramatic approach to the Spruce Knob observation tower across open, rocky terrain.

FS-112—

Shown on some older maps as FS-103, this is the main route through the Spruce Knob area. From Route 13 (off of combined Route 28/33 north of Judy Gap), FS-112 climbs the eastern flank of the Allegheny Front on a series of long switchbacks, passes FS-104 at the summit, then descends the western slope of Spruce Mountain to Spruce Knob Lake and an intersection with FS-1. Beyond the lake, FS-112 continues south to the Sinks of Gandy but is recommended only for four-wheel-drive vehicles.

FS-131—

A short spur leading west from FS-112 to the Gatewood Lookout Tower site. It is usually gated to public vehicles but is open to hikers.

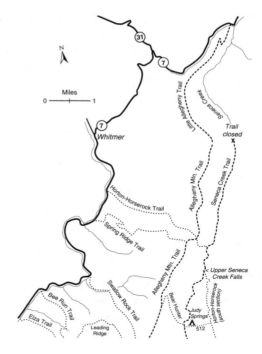

Trail Guide:
SPRUCE KNOB AREA

Note: Trails marked with an asterisk lie within the Seneca Creek Pioneer Zone and are subject to the following restrictions: All vehicles, including mountain bikes, are prohibited. Saddle and pack animals are prohibited on all trails except 530, 532, 534, and 535. Backcountry camping is permitted only at designated sites, and open fires are permitted only in USFS fireplaces. The Pioneer Zone designation is similar to Wilderness Area status, which mandates elimination of man-made structures from the zone. Consequently, many footbridges that have washed away in recent floods will not be rebuilt. Expect to make frequent, and sometimes difficult, stream crossings.

---

*Allegheny Mountain Trail (#532)

Length: *8.1 miles*
Elevation change: *355 feet*
Level: *moderate*
USGS quad maps: *Onego, WV; Spruce Knob, WV; Whitmer, WV*
Access: *From FS-112, 1.5 miles northeast of Spruce Knob Lake. This is a shared trailhead; bear right (the spur to the left leads to Big Run Trail).*

The first 6 miles of this trail follow a gated wildlife access road northward. Trail intersections are Tom Lick Run Trail (at 2.1 miles), North Prong Trail (2.3 miles), Leading Ridge Trail (3.1 miles), and Swallow Rock Run Trail (3.3 miles). Bear Hunter Trail, at 4.7 miles, leads east to the Judy Springs hike-in campground.

From its junction with Bear Hunter Trail, the Allegheny Mountain Trail climbs northward, passing a good viewpoint at 5 miles and an open meadow at 5.5 miles. At 6.2 miles, the road you've followed to this point veers to the west in a meadow to become the Spring Ridge Trail. The Allegheny Trail continues north, skirting the meadow before narrowing to a rough path and crossing the Horton-Horserock Trail a short distance beyond. The Allegheny Mountain Trail turns left at 8 miles, intersecting the Little Allegheny Trail, and continues about another half-mile to a dead end on private land. To continue hiking north to White's Run Road, avoid the spur and keep straight ahead on the Little Allegheny Trail (see entry).

Back Ridge Trail (#526)

Length: *5 miles*
Elevation change: *1,450 feet*
Level: *moderately difficult (strenuous)*
USGS quad map: *Spruce Knob, WV*
Access: *South trailhead is on Route 28 at the west end of Big Run bridge, southwest of Circleville. North trailhead is on Sawmill Run Road (County Road 28-10) south of its junction with FS-112 near Spruce Knob Lake.*

From its south trailhead on Route 28, Back Ridge Trail climbs steadily along Big Run, crossing the stream several times. At 1.5 miles the trail reaches an abandoned railroad grade, crosses Big Run one more time, then begins a steep, rocky climb. The climb eventually becomes easier as the trail follows old logging roads high above Big Run Falls. At 3.6 miles, the trail reaches the ridge line, from which there are overgrown views to the east, then continues for another mile to end on Sawmill Run Road.

Bee Run Trail (#555)

Length: *1.8 miles*
Elevation change: *895 feet*
Level: *moderate*

USGS quad maps: *Spruce Knob, WV; Whitmer, WV*
Access: *West trailhead is on Route 29 approximately 0.75 mile north of the Elza Trail. East trailhead is at a junction with the Elza and Leading Ridge Trails.*

Cross Gandy Creek to the trailhead; a footbridge may or may not be in place. The trail climbs steadily through mostly open woods, skirting the head of a hollow just before reaching a junction with the Elza and Leading Ridge Trails.

Big Run Trail (#527)

Length: *3.1 miles*
Elevation change: *695 feet*
Level: *easy to moderate*
USGS quad map: *Spruce Knob, WV*
Access: *West trailhead is on Route 29 (Whitmer Road) at Gandy Creek. East trailhead is on FS-112, 1.5 miles*

northeast of Spruce Knob Lake. The east trailhead is a shared one; bear left (the Allegheny Mountain Trail is to the right).

From its eastern trailhead, Big Run Trail descends steadily for 1.5 miles to a grassy meadow and abandoned apple orchard, where the North Prong Trail enters from the east. Continue downstream on the Big Run Trail, occasionally following an abandoned railroad grade and making several stream crossings. Just before reaching its western trailhead, Big Run Trail crosses a pasture to Gandy Run, where a footbridge may or may not be in place. Wade if necessary to reach the parking area along Whitmer Road.

Elza Trail (#556)

Length: *2 miles*
Elevation change: *720 feet*
Level: *moderate*
USGS quad maps: *Spruce Knob, WV; Whitmer, WV*
Access: *West trailhead is on Whitmer Road (Route 29) at Elza Run. East trailhead is on the North Prong Trail.*

To reach the west trailhead, wade across the Gandy River near its confluence with Elza Run. Elza Trail begins in a grassy field, then crosses a stream in a small wooded ravine. At 1.5 miles, the Bee Run Trail enters from the north, and just beyond is a junction with Leading Ridge Trail. Continue straight ahead for another half-mile to the trail's eastern terminus on North Prong Trail.

Gatewood Resource Management Trail

Length: *2.3 miles*
Elevation change: *insignificant*
Level: *easy*
USGS quad map: *Spruce Knob, WV (not shown)*
Access: *Trailhead is on FS-112 approximately 0.4 mile south of its intersection with FS-1.*

An interpretive trail keyed to an educational brochure, the Gatewood Trail is an easy-to-follow loop through a Department of Natural Resources demonstration area. Pick up a brochure at the trailhead and follow the well-marked path through varied environments, including an old farmstead that is being slowly reclaimed by the forest, a grazing area still in use, an abandoned railroad grade, a red pine plantation, and a former clear-cut area.

*Horton-Horserock Trail (#530)

Length: *8 miles*
Elevation change: *1,700 feet*
Level: *moderate (strenuous)*
USGS quad maps: *Spruce Knob, WV; Whitmer, WV (formerly Horton-Riverton Trail)*
Access: *North trailhead is on Whitmer Road (Route 29) 1 mile south of Whitmer. Park at the Potomac Cooperative Wildlife Management Area sign; the trailhead is marked. South trailhead is at the northern terminus of the Huckleberry Trail.*

Once an important route across the Allegheny Front, the Horton-Horserock Trail still begins near the community of Horton but now ends at Horse Rock, far short of its original terminus at Riverton. From the parking area near Horton, the trail begins as an old wagon road; keep to the right of Lower Two Spring Run. There are two easy stream crossings at 1 and 1.1 miles. Continue to follow the stream (which vanishes underground twice) for another mile beyond the crossings, reaching a level backcountry camping area at 2 miles. From this point, the trail makes a steep, rocky climb up the western slope of Allegheny Mountain to cross the Allegheny Trail at 2.4 miles.

From the crest of Allegheny Mountain, the trail descends steeply, losing 800 feet in elevation, to intersect Seneca Creek at 3.5 miles. Rock-hop or wade across the creek; the footbridge mentioned in some guides washed away in 1985. Turn right to follow Seneca Creek Trail south for a short distance before veering left (east) at Upper Seneca Creek Falls, where the Horton-Horserock Trail leaves the creek to climb the western slope of Spruce Mountain. At 4 miles, turn right and follow the rock cairns through an open pasture, where you'll find a tremendous variety of wildflowers during the summer. Reenter the forest on a rocky footpath and intersect the Judy Springs Trail (providing access to the Judy Springs hike-in campground) at 4.9 miles. A junction with the Lumberjack Trail is a short distance beyond. The Horton-Horserock Trail then continues its climb up Spruce Mountain, ending at an intersection with the Huckleberry Trail. Many years ago, the trail continued down the mountain to end near the town of Riverton, on the North Fork. A faint trace of the old trail remains, but it eventually leads to private land.

*Huckleberry Trail (#533)

Length: *3.3 miles*

Elevation change: *840 feet*

Level: *moderate to easy*

USGS quad map: *Spruce Knob, WV*

Access: *South trailhead is at the north end of the Spruce Knob observation tower parking area (FS-104). North trailhead is on the Horton-Horserock Trail at the crest of Spruce Mountain.*

Although the Huckleberry Trail follows the crest of the Allegheny Front (known here as Spruce Mountain), many of the views mentioned in older guides are becoming overgrown as the forest matures. The trail begins as a rocky footpath through spruce forest and mountain laurel thickets. At 1 mile, the trail emerges from the woods briefly to cross a heath meadow with a good view to the west, then passes the remains of an old plane crash at 2 miles. From here, the trail reenters deep forest, passing scattered outcroppings.

The Huckleberry Trail dead-ends at the Horton-Horserock Trail, where an open area provides a popular backcountry campsite. An unmarked and abandoned spur of the Huckleberry Trail continues northward from the junction. Parts of it have been replanted, but if you can locate the old trace, it makes for an interesting bushwhack northward into a secluded and rarely visited area on the eastern flank of the Allegheny Front.

*Judy Springs Trail (#512)

Length: *1.2 miles*

Elevation change: *670 feet*

Level: *moderate*

USGS quad maps: *Spruce Knob, WV; Whitmer, WV (not shown)*

Access: *East trailhead is on the Horton-Horserock Trail near the north end of the Lumberjack Trail. West trailhead is on the Seneca Creek Trail at Judy Springs hike-in campground, approximately 3 miles north of FS-112.*

From the campground, cross the stream and look for two trails. The path to the right leads a short distance to Judy Springs, a reliable but unprotected water source. The path to the left is the Judy Springs Trail, which enters the woods and then crosses an old stile at the edge of a pasture. Follow the rock cairns across the pasture, a good wildflower area in the summer. The trail climbs steadily eastward to end at a junction with the Horton Horserock Trail.

Leading Ridge Trail (#557)

Length: *4.5 miles*

Elevation change: *640 feet*

Level: *moderate*

USGS quad maps: *Spruce Knob, WV; Whitmer, WV (marked as jeep trail)*

Access: *West trailhead is on Whitmer Road (Route 29). East trailhead is on the Allegheny Mountain Trail 3.1 miles north of its FS-112 trailhead.*

Wade across Gandy Creek to a Forest Service wildlife road that is gated to public vehicles. The Leading Ridge Trail makes an easy climb through open forest and crosses Elza Trail at about 3 miles. From that intersection, the Leading Ridge Trail continues to the northeast, making a steady climb to its western terminus on the Allegheny Mountain Trail.

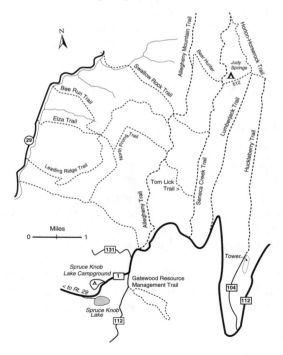